P9-DOG-733

TO FORGIVE *IS* HUMAN

HOW TO PUT YOUR *PAST IN* THE PAST

MICHAEL E. McCULLOUGH, PH.D.
STEVEN J. SANDAGE, PH.D.
EVERETT L. WORTHINGTON JR., PH.D.

IVP Books

An imprint of InterVarsity Press
Downers Grove, Illinois

InterVarsity Press
P.O. Box 1400, Downers Grove, IL 60515-1426
World Wide Web: www.ivpress.com
E-mail: email@ivpress.com

©1997 by Michael E. McCullough, Steven J. Sandage and Everett L. Worthington Jr.

All rights reserved. No part of this book may be reproduced in any form without written permission from InterVarsity Press.

InterVarsity Press®is the book-publishing division of InterVarsity Christian Fellowship®, a movement of students and faculty active on campus at hundreds of universities, colleges and schools of nursing in the United States of America, and a member movement of the International Fellowship of Evangelical Students. For information about local and regional activities, write Public Relations Dept., InterVarsity Christian Fellowship, 6400 Schroeder Rd., P.O. Box 7895, Madison, WI 53707-7895, or visit the IVCF website at <www.intervarsity.org>.

All Scripture quotations, unless otherwise indicated, are taken from the Holy Bible, New International Version®. NIV®. *Copyright ©1973, 1978, 1984 by International Bible Society. Used by permission of Zondervan Publishing House. All rights reserved.*

ISBN 978-0-8308-1683-5

Printed in the United States of America ∞

Library of Congress Cataloging-in-Publication Data

McCullough, Michael E.
 To forgive is human: how to put your past in the past/Michael
E. McCullough, Steven J. Sandage, Everett L. Worthington, Jr.
  p. cm.
 Includes bibliographical references (p.).
 ISBN 0-8308-1683-6 (alk. paper)
 1. Forgiveness. 2. Interpersonal relations. I. Sandage, Steven
J. II. Worthington, Everett L., 1946- . III. Title.
BF637.F67M33 1997
158.2—dc21
                         96-46371
                            CIP

P	26	25	24	23	22	21	20	19	18	17	16	15	14	13	12	11	10	9	8	7
Y	27	26	25	24	23	22	21	20	19	18	17	16	15	14	13	12	11	10	09		

To my Aunt Francis,
who learned how to forgive (MEM)
To Danielle (SJS)
To Larry Christenson (ELW)

Acknowledgments

This book is the product of friendship. This book and our friendships grew out of our conversations about the meaning of forgiveness and its relevance for psychology. In the course of our academic work and informal conversations, Everett suggested that we consolidate those ideas under one cover so that others might, hopefully, benefit from them. This book is that consolidation of ideas.

I would like to thank my college mentor, J. Patout Burns, for encouraging me and for teaching me how to learn. I would also like to thank the John M. Templeton Foundation and King Pharmaceuticals for their generosity.

Michael E. McCullough

Forgiveness is primarily learned through relationships. I now realize that forgiveness would not have become a scholarly or professional interest for me were it not for those people who graciously modeled forgiveness in my own personal journey.

I am grateful to my wife, Danielle, for offering her encouragement for this project and for forgiving me so many times. My parents have fostered a family story where forgiveness is an implicit theme. I have enjoyed the benefits of forgiveness with each of my family members, and I am thankful for the profound influence of such supportive relationships.

My mentors during my seminary years in Chicago, Dr. Gary R. Collins and Dr. Robert G. Tuttle Jr., are unique men whose living examples of forgiveness continue to shape both my mind and my heart. Finally I am deeply indebted to Mike and Ev for the "conversation of friendship." It has been a privilege to share in the creative ideas of Mike and Ev and to know the authentic commitment to forgiveness of both men.

Steven J. Sandage

In 1970 Pastor Larry Christenson wrote *The Christian Family* (Minneapolis: Bethany). In that book, and in an audiotape in the series by the same name, he suggested a concept called "empathetic repentance." Whenever a person found himself or herself judging another person, said Christenson, the person should look within to see whether the same problem was lurking there. I have repeatedly found that concept to make me squirm at its uncomfortable truth. I don't like to admit it, but usually when I feel really bothered about being hurt it tells more about me than about the person who hurt me. As Christenson said, "We rarely lose our peace over someone else's sin." That concept has affected me deeply, helping me deal with my responses to many hurts over the last quarter of a century.

When I began to do marital counseling in 1975, I could not escape the observation that troubled couples continually hurt each other and that most had little inclination to forgive. It was natural for me to attempt to help couples by using the truth that Larry Christenson had taught. I began to experiment with helping partners look within themselves before they condemned each other. Remarkable things happened.

In 1978 I took a faculty position at Virginia Commonwealth University and began to teach graduate students. The joy of teaching graduate students is that we professors often learn more than we teach, and that has often been my experience. Don Danser, my good friend and former graduate student, not only helped me personally many times but also helped develop a standard intervention with couples to promote mutual forgiveness. Fred DiBlasio, a faculty colleague at VCU, worked with me to publish an article describing the technique. That article caught Mike McCullough's, and later Steve Sandage's, attention.

Since they became interested in studying forgiveness, I have simply held on to their coattails for an exciting, wild ride in discovery and growth. I have been enriched in my heart and in my understanding by their research and creative thinking about forgiveness. The fruit of that collaboration is this book. I hope you will be excited about their ideas, as I have been. And I hope you will benefit as much as I have from applying these ideas to your life.

Everett L. Worthington Jr.

Introduction

You can use this book to live better. Perhaps after reading an inspiring book or watching a motivating television program, you have risen with a determination to make significant changes in your life. But too often resolutions evaporate quickly. Ideas excite, but if you do not apply your learning, the excitement rapidly fades. In this book, we attempt to excite you and show you how to translate your excitement into lasting change.

When we wrote this book, about seventy other books on the topic were available, and we are familiar with many of those. They include books on forgiveness written by philosophers, political scientists, theologians, pastors and counselors. Many are well-written, encouraging and full of good advice and wisdom, but we could not find a book that examined what psychology has to say about how people forgive, how forgiveness can be encouraged and what the effects of forgiveness can be on people's lives.

Little wonder. Only in the last ten years or so has psychological theory and its scientific research had anything to say about forgiveness. Despite the importance of forgiveness to many people, it has apparently been ignored by most psychologists—maybe because forgiveness has mistakenly been thought of as something that "religious people do." Perhaps because of mutual suspicion between religion and psychology, forgiveness has been consigned to the realm of religious thought, where it could be preached and encouraged by pastors, theologians and pastoral counselors but conveniently ignored by psychologists.

Psychology has opened its doors much wider to religion and spirituality in the last twenty years than they have been in a long time—wide enough, in fact, to encourage professional psychologists to think about the psychology of forgiveness. In this book, we distill what psychological theory and research have to teach us about forgiveness and how we might become better at forgiving. In the following chapters we describe what forgiveness is, how it fits into our moral and interpersonal lives, how forgiveness might be encouraged and what forgiveness might mean for our lives as individuals, members of families and participants in communities or cultural groups.

This book is intended to be informative, but it is also intended to be *helpful*. We want you to *think* stimulating thoughts about forgiveness and apply those insights to your life. We offer practical advice, grounded in relevant psychological theory and research, hopefully without making it sound like a textbook. If you don't enjoy reading this book, we will have failed at one of our important goals. We have included exercises that will help you apply the insights. The use of psychological theory and research and the inclusion of exercises for applying these insights are the qualities that make this book unique.

The three of us are Christians. Our commitment to the Christian worldview undoubtedly shapes our presuppositions about what forgiveness is, how forgiveness occurs and why forgiveness is important. However, we have chosen to avoid excessive reliance on explicitly Christian language and on theological constructs as we discuss forgiveness. Instead, we have chosen to write about forgiveness by using the language of psychology. Nevertheless, we find that psychological research on forgiveness is easily harmonized with traditional Christian theology. If theology is of interest to you, we challenge you to identify the ways in which our findings are consistent with Christian understandings of forgiveness.

A Guide to Reading and Application

The book can be divided into four themes: forgiveness involves the entire person; empathy is at the heart of forgiveness; forgiveness is for relationships; forgiveness requires commitment. As you read, look for those four themes. As you find material that relates to them, perhaps you can make a note to that effect in the margins.

Use the exercises that we have presented throughout the book. By using them, you can make the changes that will help you to forgive. As you apply the exercises, also reflect on how the exercises relate to the main themes of the book.

One

Forgiveness
& You

U NFORGIVEN HURTS ARE LIKE ROCKS TOSSED INTO A PEACE-
ful sea, creating ripples and turbulence that disturb the
placid surface. If many hurts occur at nearly the same
time, the previously calm water of our lives is churned
into whitecaps of distress.

Recall a time when you have been hurt. If you bitterly held onto
the hurt, it disturbed your peace. If you allowed anger and hurt
feelings to creep into your soul, you might have disturbed the peace
of your family, friends or coworkers. If you passed along your irritation
to others, you may have seen the negative effects of your own pain
ripple throughout your family, community or workplace.

Forgiveness calms turbulence, dampens the need to lash out at
others, keeps families together and maintains harmony in relationships. Forgiveness is a place of calm in an angry sea. Forgiveness is
often sought but less often found.

A Civilization Founded on Forgiveness

People in Western civilization have been trying to learn how to forgive for at least thirty-five hundred years.[1] According to Jewish tradition, God obligated himself to a covenant with Israel because of which he would forgive and sustain Israel as a nation, despite the nation's periodic transgressions and unfaithfulness. In response the Israelites resolved to honor God by forgiving *one another.*

According to Christian tradition Jesus took the Hebrew vision of forgiveness a step further. He proposed a radical new culture that would not be limited by ethnic, religious, political or economic boundaries, a culture in which our relationships with others would be defined and regulated by our continual recognition of God's forgiving love for each of us and for the entire world.[2] In this radical culture our relationships with others—family, friends, strangers and even enemies—would be guided by our attempts to live out our forgiven-ness.

Based on these initial Judeo-Christian roots, good and wise people wrote theology, philosophy and political theory that would shape Western civilization and insure that forgiveness would be an ideal for how we led our lives.

Their efforts paid off. Thousands of years later, forgiveness is still highly prized. Research by the Gallup Organization found that 94 percent of Americans have prayed for forgiveness at some time.[3] If what we pray for points to what is important to us, then forgiveness appears to be important to nearly all of us. In another study, 45 percent of a random sample of Americans indicated that they regularly tried to forgive as a response to being hurt by the actions of others.[4] Concerns about forgiveness are not limited to the United States, for around the world people want to forgive and to be forgiven.

But although forgiveness may be an ideal for many, we must ask practical questions about forgiveness. Can forgiveness heal the wounds that we encounter? Can it heal broken relationships? Does a life of forgiveness have the potential to transform our culture? If forgiveness really does have promise as a resource for healing, how do we actually forgive? Most people at times want to forgive someone who hurt them, but they don't know how. Even many therapists and counselors—people who should know something about human behavior—are not sure how to help their clients forgive.[5]

Solid, practical guidance about forgiveness is scarce. None of us receives much instruction about forgiveness. We learn about forgiveness from watching and imitating our parents or from paying attention to church sermons or religious education. Maybe we watch a talk show or read a book. We are not required to take a course in forgiveness before making friends, establishing a romantic relationship, getting a marriage license or having children. Acquiring practical skills about forgiving is not like going to driving school. Most training about forgiveness takes place in the school of hard knocks.

This book is for people who want to go beyond what the school of hard knocks has taught them. It is for people who want to forgive but are struggling to free themselves from the shackles of bitterness and unforgiveness.

Since the early 1980s, a small, quiet movement has been taking place in psychological science. Scientists have been studying the practical side of forgiving by asking probing questions:

What happens in people's hearts and minds when they forgive?

What can people do to increase their ability to forgive?

Are psychological treatments helpful in encouraging people to forgive?

Who seeks forgiveness when they hurt others?

Is the willingness to seek forgiveness helpful in relationships?

What are the effects of forgiveness on mental and physical health? On the health of our relationships? On the health of our communities and society?

Psychological research has discovered important insights about how to become better at forgiving, and how to use forgiveness to promote healing for yourself, your relationships and the world around you. We will share these findings with you. Our approach is based on science and is immensely practical. Reading this book should add to the skills and knowledge about forgiving that you already possess.

We have tried to rely on scientific research by ourselves and others as our basis for what we tell you. Many people have written books about forgiveness based on opinion, personal experience, clinical experience and theology. Although we draw on each of these important sources of knowledge occasionally throughout the book, we have focused on scientific research because its methods and conclusions are open to public scrutiny.

What Does Forgiveness Mean?

The facts. Empirical research reveals some surprising and important findings about forgiveness:

☐ You can forgive *without* compromising your moral integrity.

☐ Your painful memories of being hurt by others can be changed more easily than you might think.

☐ You can improve your ability to forgive by improving your ability to empathize with others.

☐ You can increase the likelihood of being forgiven by someone *you have hurt* by providing an adequate and sincere apology.

☐ Caring *too much* about what others think of you will inhibit you from seeking forgiveness when you hurt others.

☐ You can improve your ability to forgive others in as little as one hour.

☐ Resentment and hostility can affect your physical health.

☐ You can improve your physical health, mental health and relationships by maintaining a forgiving lifestyle.

Before we embark on our exploration of the psychology of forgiveness, we need to describe what forgiveness means and how we use this term throughout the book. As a backdrop, let's look at the situations in which forgiveness takes place.

The context. Forgiveness takes place in relationships with other people who expect us to act in certain ways toward them and vice versa. We trust that those with whom we are in relationships will fulfill those expectations. At any given time, we are in relationships of trust with many people: romantic partners, family members, close friends, more distant friends, extended family, acquaintances and coworkers. We have relationships with people who wait on us in restaurants, banks and grocery stores. You might even say that we are in relationships of trust, more or less, with the people we pass on the freeway: we trust them and they trust us to drive safely and with concern for the welfare of those with whom they share the road.

Forgiveness becomes an issue any time the actions of one person hurt another person and, consequently, damage their relationship. Many actions fall into this category. Obviously relationships can be damaged by actions such as violence or abuse, but they can also be hurt by a careless word, a betrayal, a backhanded compliment, a racist remark, dishonest behavior, sexual infidelity, and even reckless and aggressive driving.

Over the years we have surveyed many people about events that they have a difficult time forgiving. Here is a list of the most common:
☐ betrayal of trust by a friend
☐ infidelity in a romantic relationship
☐ mistreatment or dishonesty by an employer or coworker
☐ termination of a romantic relationship or marriage
☐ neglect or insult by a parent
☐ rejection by a friend[6]

Exercise 1-1
Prepare to Apply Your Knowledge

Get a notebook and pen, and keep them with your book as you read. In each chapter you'll be given exercises that show how to build forgiveness.

The first exercise helps you think about forgiveness in your life. Forgiveness consists of two parts: granting forgiveness to people who have hurt you, and seeking forgiveness for things you have done to hurt others. Most people find it easier to think of people who have hurt them than to think of people they have hurt.

Write "People Who Have Hurt Me." Make two columns under that heading. Over one column write "Person Who Hurt Me." Over the

other column write "Circumstances." As illustrated below, list people
who have hurt you and describe the circumstances. These people will
provide examples for you to work with as you read the book. Add to
your list as you recall incidents that call for your forgiveness.

Person Who Hurt Me	*Circumstances*
Gloria	Didn't come to my dad's funeral.
Richard	Stopped returning my letters and phone calls after Dad died. Finally told me to stop calling him because he "couldn't handle it."
guy at tennis courts	Yelled at us because he thought we were on a court that he reserved. He never apologized.

On a separate page write "People I Hurt." Make two similar columns under that heading labeled "Person I Hurt" and "Circumstances." Describe times when you have hurt someone else, as in the
following examples:

Person I Hurt	*Circumstances*
Paul (a coworker)	Gossiped about him at work. He got in trouble for it.
Mia	Said something insulting about people from her ethnic background (Japanese). It was a joke that backfired, but it really hurt her.

When we (and our relationships) are hurt by other people's actions, we have many choices about how to respond. In most cases our
actions are primarily motivated by the desire to protect our own
integrity and safety. We might take outward actions, such as retaliating, avoiding or ignoring, gossiping about the other person or ending
the relationship. We might seek justice by calling the police or

contacting a counselor. We might try to protect our integrity and safety by inward actions as well, such as replaying hurtful memories, telling ourselves how bad the person who hurt us really is and dreaming up plots of how we could get revenge.

Being concerned with our own integrity and safety is good. We should not allow the hurtful behavior of others to inflict continued damage on us or other people. However, the motivation to protect the self is so powerful that it tends to overshadow any motivation to heal or restore the damaged relationship, and that prevents us from doing our part to make things right again.

Exercise 1-2
What Do You Think Forgiveness Is?
  In your notebook write a complete definition of forgiveness.
  The definition. An increase in our motivation to restore a relationship of goodwill and trust with the person who hurt us is bound to lead to changes in our actions. When we forgive we are no longer motivated solely by the desire to protect ourselves. We also become motivated to heal our relationship. Thus forgiveness might motivate us to try to talk things over with the other person, speak well of the other person, help or cooperate with the other person. We might also inhibit the desire to retaliate, think good thoughts about the other person and rehearse positive, rather than negative, memories of the other person.

  Some people are concerned that when we forgive we must compromise our motivation to protect our integrity and safety. Not true! We might still protect ourselves from further hurts. We might still seek justice and rehabilitation for the person who hurt us. We might still refuse to restore a relationship with someone who does not demonstrate sincere regret and willingness to refrain from hurting us again. But forgiving means that we have a new motivation to rebuild a relationship of goodwill and trust with someone who hurt us. When we forgive, we hope and work for a day when we might experience the healing of the relationship.

Exercise 1-3

Our Definition of Forgiveness

After you complete this chapter, compare your definition with the one we suggest:

Forgiveness is an increase in our internal motivation to repair and maintain a relationship after the relationship has been damaged by the hurtful actions of the other person.

Becoming a Forgiving Person: A Question of Character

The main point of this book is that *forgiveness involves the whole person.* Forgiveness is difficult precisely because it requires that we make comprehensive changes in who we are and how we relate to others. Forgiveness requires that *we develop a forgiving character.* Character cannot be achieved simply through learning information, hearing inspiring stories or completing paper-and-pencil exercises. Instead, we offer instruction to people who want to integrate the virtue of forgiveness into their character. That requires a multifaceted approach.

To address the complexities of forgiveness, we encourage you to examine your philosophy of life and your understandings of morality. We will encourage you to develop your reasoning about forgiveness. We will challenge your notions of how "change" really happens. We will examine how the brain and the memory work. We will encourage you to increase your empathy for others. We will ask you to examine many of the stories you tell yourself about who you are and who you want to be in relation to others. We will underscore the importance of seeking and receiving forgiveness for the times when you hurt others. Finally, we will invite you to think about the benefits that forgiveness will have for yourself, your relationships and your community.

Summing Up

Our civilization has been founded on forgiveness. In this book we will explore what psychology can tell us about how to develop into people whose lives are also founded on forgiveness and who forgive in order to heal and preserve our relationships and ourselves. Throughout our exploration we will rely heavily on empirical research as one trustworthy source of guidance for how we can build forgiveness.

T w o

Forgiveness &
the Moral Sense

FORGIVENESS INVOLVES THE MORAL REALITIES OF HUMAN
relationships. A recent television documentary focused on
families in which one parent had suddenly left for another lover. In one family the father, Greg, came home and
announced that he was no longer in love with Diane, his wife of
eighteen years, and that he had fallen in love with another woman.
After leaving to be with the other woman, Greg had sought to
continue a relationship with his three children for four years, but his
eldest son, Rick, had not been able to adjust to the divorce.

Rick, now seventeen, spoke with harsh confusion: "I just can't
accept what Dad did. I *won't* accept it! He can find another family."

The sixteen-year-old daughter, Lisa, failed to sympathize with her
brother, explaining defensively, "I talked to my therapist about my
feelings. [Rick] needs to just learn to deal with it. After all, he is our
father."

How does this story affect you? Can you sense the many moral dilemmas that are intertwined in this family's relationships? How should Rick view his father's actions? How should Lisa respond to her brother's bitterness?

In this chapter we are going to argue that people have a *moral sense:* they need to act responsibly, fairly and justly, and at the same time they need to act empathically, compassionately and mercifully. Those two sets of moral imperatives often conflict with each other, as they did in the story of this family. People try to resolve the tension in several ways, most of which are not very satisfactory because the solutions offend one side of the moral equation. Forgiveness, however, satisfies our needs for both justice and mercy.

Moral Sense

Humans have a moral sense. We regularly praise or criticize people on the basis of moral standards that may be unconscious. "He is so rude" and "She is incredibly kind" are not just comments about the contours of a personality. They are statements about vices and virtues.

James Q. Wilson, a psychologist at the University of California— Berkeley, suggests that the reason we do this is that human beings have a moral sense.[1] Almost everyone starts making moral judgments about right and wrong at an early age. These judgments may differ in complexity, but they usually develop into social habits that we use to evaluate ourselves and others. Wilson points out that our everyday conversations are filled with the "language of morality" cloaked in psychological terminology. Our discussions of what is bad and what is good in relationships reflect our assumptions of how relationships ought to be: sincere, fair, loyal and the like. That does not mean that humans are innately morally good or that the moral sense is the only sense that influences behavior. It simply means that most people around the world—and in virtually *every* culture—sense a moral oughtness and distinguish good from bad.

Our moral sense stimulates our moral judgments. In Western culture, the moral sense has traditionally been cultivated and informed by religious institutions and the family. This is still true to some degree, but television talk shows now provide our contemporary culture with a public forum for exercising the moral sense and considering various moral judgments. Even the attitude of tolerance for diverse lifestyles represents a moral judgment informed by respect for human freedom.

Morality is universal. All cultures express some common morals.[2] Few would argue against the notion that justice, responsibility, empathy, compassion and mercy are all expressions of the moral sense needed in some degree in every culture.

Wilson suggests evidence that there are some moral universals. For example, murder without justification is prohibited in every known culture. The very fact that a justification is always required for killing suggests a universal moral sense about the value of life. Incest is universally condemned. Infanticide, the killing of newborn infants, is extremely rare after infants are more than one month old and, where it does occur, almost always subsides when economic stresses are under control.

When we say that certain morals are "universal," we do not mean that every culture, without exception, embraces those morals. When Susan Smith murdered her young children in 1995 by driving into a lake, it did not invalidate the universal moral that infanticide is wrong. When a psychopathic killer murders without compunction, it does not mean that people do not have a moral sense. One exception, or even a few exceptions, does not disprove the universality of human moral sense (in the way we are using "universal"). In the same way, one culture that takes a nonmoral stance on one issue does not invalidate the universality of the morals.

Wilson acknowledges that many moral *rules* vary across cultures, but he argues that *the need for moral standards* is sensed cross-culturally and that a few common moral sentiments—empathy, fairness, duty and self-control, for example—are valued around the globe. The need for moral standards arises wherever relationships exist.

Relationships embody morality. Relationships are a moral enterprise. Our moral sense is most deeply tested in the crucible of human interactions. Person-to-person interactions constantly engage the underlying moral issue of the intrinsic value of persons. Acts of wrongdoing question the status of persons as having equal value. Philosopher Margaret Holmgren suggests that an interpersonal offense involves a wrongdoer who is morally confused about the victim's status as a person.[3]

Relationships rest on a foundation of mutual respect and trust. Interpersonal offenses attack this sense of respect and destroy trust. J. Arthur Martin describes relationships as governed by moral norms (or a "moral law") that serves to protect respect and trust. We may not articulate the moral norms that guide our relationships, but we usually sense when they have been violated. Most of us would expect a friend to replace a borrowed item that he ruined or to refrain from slandering us publicly. Forgiveness, argues Martin, presupposes the violation of moral norms.[4]

Forgiveness, then, emerges within the moral dynamics of relationships. Philosopher J. Kellenberger suggests that forgiveness is morally possible because of the inherent value of all persons. Kellenberger notes that the *moral status* of an offender may be troublesome, but that does not diminish his or her inherent worth as a person. Forgiveness is a relational stance of *accepting* the inherent worth of another person even after judging the wrong action.[5]

Relationships need virtues. Forgiveness is a moral *virtue* embodied in the context of relationships. The topic of virtue has been revived in recent years by political leaders within both parties in an effort to speak to the widespread sense of moral decline in the United States.[6] A *virtue* is an internal quality of character that is morally good. Aristotle, an early advocate of virtue, suggested that there were four classic virtues—fortitude, temperance, prudence and justice.[7]

As in Medieval Europe, where the seven virtues were placed in opposition to the seven deadly sins, our list of virtues could go well beyond Aristotle's classic four. Some modern philosophers have suggested that recovery of the virtues is essential to ethical living in today's society. Modern approaches to ethics focus on dilemmas and the question "What shall I do?" Virtues, on the other hand, start with the question "Who shall I be?"[8]

There is a vital need for virtue ethics in contemporary discussion of morality and relationships. But virtue ethics also involves moral dilemmas. How is a person like Rick, full of pain and resentment at his father for leaving the family, to reconcile the virtues of justice and mercy?

How Do We Balance Competing Moral Imperatives?

We can often feel torn between two sets of moral imperatives when we attempt to address offenses that violate our moral sense. We could think of the dilemma of warring virtues as involving a moral balance with responsibility, justice and fairness on one side of the scale and empathy, compassion and mercy on the other side (see figure 2-1). All these moral imperatives could be considered virtuous to some degree and in some situations. Yet the conflict between them can create dilemmas that are hard for people to resolve.

Demands of	Demands of
Responsibility	Empathy
Justice	Compassion
Fairness	Mercy

Λ

Figure   2-1.

Rick represents the side of the scale committed to responsibility, justice and fairness. He believes that his father was unfair in leaving his mother and temporarily abandoning the family, and he cannot simply "let go" of his sense of injustice.

Lisa is committed to the other side of the scale. She feels mercy and compassion for Greg because, after all, he is her father. The two sides of the moral balance have actually pitted these two siblings against each other, which further adds to the conflict within this family.

Conflict between the two sides of the moral balance can divide friends, families, organizations, political parties and even nations. Yet the same conflict can also rage within ourselves. We may try to resolve the dilemma of the moral balance in several ways, all of which involve some form of denial: by denying responsibility for our response to the offense; by denying mercy; by denying moral absolutes; by denying moral consequences; by denying that anything is wrong.

By denying responsibility for our response to the offense. During the late 1980s cultural critics began to lament the rise of "victimology" in the United States. These critics contended that massive numbers of people were claiming to be victims of various factors outside their control. The "blame game" became the popular phrase for explaining away one's moral failures by blaming other people or circumstances.

Almost twenty years before the "outbreak" of victimology, psychiatrist Karl Menninger warned of the decline of moral responsibility in Western culture. In his book *Whatever Became of Sin?* Menninger raised concerns about the disappearance of the word *sin* from modern vocabulary. Menninger suggested that terms such as *crime* and *sickness* had taken the place of sin, thereby reducing our awareness of moral responsibility. As a major figure in the field of mental health, Menninger did not deny the importance of understanding and treating mental illness, but he did foresee the dangers of discarding the concept of sin altogether.[9] Some of Menninger's prophecies came to fruition in the victimology mentality.

In our story, Rick could become tempted to deny that he is responsible for his anger toward his father. He could blame his father for all his future problems. Rick's pain and anger are legitimate, but a pattern of blaming his father could harden into a victim identity that is harmful to himself and others. Those who have worked with troubled adolescents know that such responses frequently become realities.

The cost of denying personal responsibility is perhaps most evident in troubled marriages, where entrenched patterns of blaming the other person can lead to the courtroom. Social psychologists have called this tendency the fundamental attribution error.[10] People tend to attribute their own negative behavior to circumstances beyond their control (for example, finishing a project late because the boss gave him or her too much work) but attribute the negative behavior of others to something wrong with *them* (for example, he finished the project late because he is lazy). The fundamental attribution error suggests that we are more willing to deny our own personal responsibility than we are to allow others to deny their responsibility.

Some critics of victimology seem to overlook the social, psychological and physical dimensions that restrict human choice. Abuse, disease, poverty and many other factors can certainly contribute to behavior. Compassion requires that we admit that many people *are* victims. But respect for human dignity requires us to admit that people are also agents who make choices.

By denying mercy. A second way people attempt to balance competing moral imperatives is to deny mercy. There is the adage "We must forgive our enemies, but not until they have been hanged." This adage is not addressing the ethics of capital punishment but speaks to the human desire to demand revenge. Perhaps the most common form of "relational hanging" is the use of gossip and slander to "even the score" with those who have offended us. In most cases, assaulting the reputation of our offender to friends or coworkers probably feels like a just action.

By focusing solely on justice and fairness it is possible to avoid empathy and mercy. The offender can be viewed as completely evil, which is one way to achieve psychological distance to deaden some of the pain. Anger can also be empowering, at least temporarily. Some counselors encourage clients to channel their anger into energy to accomplish personal goals.

Rick's anger toward his father runs the risk, however, of turning into bitterness. Condemning his father's behavior may be appropriate. But his fervent condemnation of his father as a person keeps the door of reconciliation tightly locked. Further, hostility is hard to keep focused and has a way of spilling into other relationships. Rick has the potential to become a cold, angry man.

By denying moral absolutes. A third way to approach the moral balance is to deny that there are moral absolutes. Many critics have argued that our culture is characterized by moral relativism. People commonly assume that right and wrong are matters of individual opinion rather than absolute moral standards. Good and evil, therefore, are subjectively defined by each person relative to his or her values. Tolerance of diverse lifestyles, rather than forgiveness, is prescribed by the worldview that sees evil and sin as relative or nonexistent.

Many moral issues are complicated and confusing. But without any moral absolutes our confusion is intensified, and we are left to deal with moral failures by condoning rather than forgiving the offenses. Philosopher Robert Roberts has pointed out that condoning is double-minded: when we condone, we admit that an action is morally wrong but then deny the seriousness of the action.[11] Condoning moral offenses does not lead to character development *or* mental health. A society that condones everything may soon find that it cannot control anything.

Woody Allen's movie *Crimes and Misdemeanors* raises the issue of whether there are consequences to moral actions.[12] The lead character is Judah Rosenthal, a mild-mannered ophthalmologist who "just happens" to have engaged in an extramarital affair. Soon Rosenthal decides that he is tired of his emotionally demanding mistress, but his efforts to break off the relationship are met with threats to expose his unethical business deals.

Rosenthal's gangster brother offers to "get rid" of the mistress, which sends him into an existential crisis. Should he simply tell his wife, seek forgiveness and accept the consequences or let his brother kill his mistress? Are there any consequences for such decisions? Is there a moral order? He confides in one of his patients, a rabbi, about the affair. The rabbi votes for seeking forgiveness, of course, but the rabbi is going blind. Rosenthal finds it hard to believe that a blind rabbi's ethical beliefs could actually be working for him.

Rosenthal gives in to the dark side, has the mistress killed, wrestles with a short-term case of guilt and then life goes on. His marriage actually improves and there is no more inconvenient mistress. So much for the moral order, Allen seems to conclude in this antimorality work of fiction.

Few of us wrestle with the temptation to have someone killed, but most of us can identify with the dilemma Allen raises in his movie. Is there a moral order that corresponds to justice? If so, how will we balance the moral scale?

Lisa seems to be condoning her father's actions and condemning her brother's judgment. She may enjoy the benefits of her relationship with her father and deny the nagging tension of the moral questions. But in condoning her father's actions she may compromise her moral discernment. Condoning may weaken her own conscience.

By denying moral consequences. A fourth way people try to resolve competing moral imperatives is to deny that actions have moral consequences. Psychiatrist Ivan Boszormenyi-Nagy was a pioneer in the field of family therapy. Boszormenyi-Nagy sees people as having a strong need for justice and fairness in relationships. Because of this he suggested the existence of a moral ledger in which families keep a record of moral credits and debits. Parents can pass on credits to their children through loving and caring actions. Debits to the account come in the form of neglect, abuse or (more common) moral failures. When the moral ledger is positive, the children will be likely to have the resources they need to be loyal to their parents and grandparents and pass on moral credits to their children. When the debits are greater than the credits, children will experience moral injustice in the form of pain and resentment toward their parents. Whether people's actions create credits or debits in their families, their actions often produce consequences to those around them— even when they don't intend them to—and those consequences may have moral implications.

What does a person do whose parents may have given him or her a debit balance in the moral ledger? Deny the moral consequences, according to Boszormenyi-Nagy. He suggested that people should *exonerate* their parents from their moral guilt. Exoneration involves recognizing the moral debt owed by one's parents (or by others) but deciding to "let them off the hook." To *condone* another person's behavior is to declare it unobjectionable. To *exonerate* the behavior of another is to lessen that person's responsibility and culpability through insight and understanding.

Exoneration entails an understanding that a person has sufficient justification to be entitled to certain behaviors. Rick could decide to exonerate his father from his moral debt. He could try to put the problem in the past and move on. Perhaps that is what his sister has in mind in suggesting that he "deal" with his resentment.[13]

We disagree with Boszormenyi-Nagy. We see exoneration as inconsistent with the moral sense of our human nature. Exoneration—merely relieving blame—offends our sense of justice and fairness. Rick's gnawing sense of injustice will make it difficult for him to somehow see his father as entitled to the course of action he chose.

Forgiveness, though, is consistent with our moral sense of justice, and it affirms our sense of love, compassion, empathy and altruism. Forgiveness acknowledges that moral violations in relationships are wrong. But forgiveness cancels a debt that a person legitimately owes rather than simply lets the person off the hook. Forgiveness does not wink at the moral violation (condoning) or deny the offender's responsibility (exoneration). Forgiveness chooses to cancel a debt that is serious and real. Through canceling the debt, one has the power to balance the moral ledger and break the pattern of passing on pain and anger to others.

By denying that anything is wrong. Some people will simply deny the dilemma created by competing moral imperatives. In some families, this is encouraged by an unspoken rule that interpersonal conflict is to be ignored and forgotten. The moral balance is never resolved, which leads to passing on the moral debit to the next generation. Philip Yancey tells the following story:

> I have a friend whose marriage has gone through rough times. One night George passed a breaking point and emotionally exploded. He pounded the table and floor. "I hate you!" he screamed at his wife. "I won't take it anymore! I've had enough! I won't go on! I

won't let it happen! No! No! No!"

Several months later my friend woke up in the middle of the night and heard strange sounds coming from the room where his two-year-old son slept. He went down the hall, stood outside his son's door, and shivers ran through his flesh. In a soft voice the two year-old was repeating word for word with precise inflection the climactic argument between his mother and father. "I hate you. . . . I won't take it anymore. . . . No! No! No!"

George realized that in some awful way he had just passed on his pain and anger to the next generation.[14]

Yancey's story of the husband's tantrum and the son's mimicking provides a vivid example of how, due to a father's moral debit toward his wife, pain and resentment were passed on to a child. More often, the moral consequences remain less noticeable for those who fail to resolve the moral balance. Yet the pattern is passed on in some form.

Rick's future relationships could be negatively affected by a failure to resolve his moral dilemma of how to respond to his father. Perhaps he will find it difficult to trust people in romantic relationships, constantly feeling suspicious that they will desert him. Or he may feel ambivalent about having children himself out of a fear of causing similar pain to them. Rick may find it tempting to deny the reality of the moral conflict, but a resolution to the moral dilemma that is consistent with both justice and mercy is his only hope.

Exercise 2-1

Consider the Balance

Pick one of the times you have been hurt when you had difficulty forgiving the one who hurt you. Making two columns on your paper, consider the balance. In one column list the actions that considerations of responsibility, justice and fairness would demand of you and of the person who hurt you. In the other column list the actions that considerations of empathy, compassion and mercy would demand of you and the person who hurt you.

Demands of Responsibility, Justice and Fairness	Demands of Empathy, Compassion and Mercy

If you have had difficulty forgiving the person, you probably have a longer list under "Responsibility, Justice and Fairness." You might think that the other person should say that he or she is sorry, should express remorse, should promise not to hurt you again. If that is the case, consider whether you experience a tug at your conscience to empathically understand the person. Could you imagine that you might do something to hurt someone else—something equally (or more) harsh? Consider the desire you might have to extend compassion and mercy to the person who hurt you. Even though you might firmly believe that the person does not deserve mercy but rather justice and punishment, do you have any desire to extend the tender virtues?

Forgiveness Weds Justice and Mercy

Justice and mercy are difficult to reconcile. Yet we make decisions in relationships every day that force us to wrestle with the ethics of justice and the compassion of mercy. Am I being treated fairly by my boss? What should I do about the friend who never returns the books I loan? How should I feel about my ex-boyfriend who is getting married?

Justice and mercy are necessary for healing. The Civil War offers numerous memorable battle stories, but it ended with a dramatic story of justice and mercy. In the spring of 1865 General Robert E. Lee's army was hungry, exhausted and badly outnumbered by General Ulysses S. Grant's men near Petersburg, Virginia.[15] Though Lee said he would rather "die a thousand deaths" than surrender, he realized that he had no choice but to meet with Grant before the South suffered annihilation.

Grant and Lee met for a respectful, albeit awkward, conversation at the Appomattox Court House to negotiate the terms of surrender. Lee showed commendable dignity. Grant offered to send rations to Lee's starving soldiers. News of the surrender led to the exhilarated firing of cannons in the Union camp, which Grant quickly stifled. Three days later Lee's Confederate troops marched into Appomattox village to turn over their arms in submission to the Union.

The next act of healing in this story was initiated by Colonel Joshua L. Chamberlain, who had been a professor of theology and rhetoric at Bowdoin College in Maine prior to enlisting in the Union Army. Chamberlain was an abolitionist who believed in fighting the evil of slavery, a sentiment that was not unanimous among Union soldiers. As Chamberlain watched the ragged Confederate army led by General John B. Gordon coming up the road, he seized the moment with a gesture of healing and honor. With his men standing at attention, he ordered a salute to arms.

Chamberlain recalls in his memoirs, "Gordon, at the head of the column, riding with heavy spirit and downcast face, catches the sound of shifting arms, looks up, and, taking the meaning, wheels superbly, making with himself and his horse one uplifted figure, with profound salutation as he drops the point of his sword to the boot toe; then facing to his own command, gives word to successive brigades to pass with the same position . . . honor answering honor."

Nearly one hundred thousand men passed by Appomattox Court House. Chamberlain led his men in a gesture of forgiveness toward those he tried to kill the previous week. War seeks justice, but Chamberlain understood that his enemies were human and deserved more than justice. They deserved respect. In offering a salute to the humiliated Confederates, Chamberlain communicated that although justice would be served mercy would also be extended. That is forgiveness.

Forgiveness Leads to Moral Honesty

Forgiveness is a virtue that integrates the moral balance of justice and mercy. But forgiveness is also necessary to sustain other virtues, such as honesty and fortitude, that may also conflict at times. For example, theologian Stanley Hauerwas has pointed out that people cannot afford to be honest with one another without forgiveness. Why admit my offense unless there is a way for the debt to be canceled? Perhaps patterns of blame become the organizing rule of some marriages because neither person is willing to risk moral honesty. Forgiveness can offer a relationship the security to handle the honest confession of secrets and the acceptance of blame.[16]

Moral honesty can make relationships feel unstable. People usually avoid discussing topics that are difficult to resolve. Honesty in relationships can be costly, and deep down most of us would admit that we are not always convinced that transparency is worth the cost. What would it have been like for Greg to have admitted to Diane his dissatisfaction with their marriage some time earlier? It is difficult to speculate, but it is not difficult to think of numerous relationships where secrets have temporarily maintained a false harmony because the hope of forgiveness did not seem promising.

Like honesty, fortitude may require at least the option of forgiveness to deal with past hurts. Fortitude is the courage to persevere in a commitment in the face of adversity. Many have reached the fork in the road of a troubled relationship where perseverance necessitates either forgiveness or some form of denial.

We have found in our counseling practice that clients often face a crossroad in therapy when they first sense the pain or anger they feel toward their parents. Some clients will vigorously defend their parents, even when it is obvious that they have significant hurt or resentment. Facing the emotional pain in our hearts can be frightening. But the possibility of experiencing forgiveness offers some clients the fortitude to continue in therapy when turning back feels like an easier way.

Summing Up

In the story at the opening of this chapter, Rick faced a moral dilemma. What would it look like for Rick to choose to forgive his father? First, Rick could acknowledge to himself and to others that he considers his father's actions wrong. Such a position will probably mean that Rick will always regret his father's relationship to the family. But Rick can choose in mercy to cancel the moral debt his father owes him. Rick cannot make decisions for other family members, but he can decide how to handle his own moral dilemma.

We would not expect Rick to forgive in one sitting. The moral realities of relationships are messy, and so is the process of healing. Rick will have to decide how he wants to relate to his father, a decision that is separate from his decision to forgive. Forgiveness does not mean that Rick can or should accept repeated moral failures on the part of his father without consequences to their relationship. Forgiveness also does not mean that Rick will simply forget the history of his father's behavior and never mention it again. He may decide at some point that the door is open to address the topic with his father.

Forgiveness does mean, however, that Rick has relinquished his tenacious demand that his father stand permanently condemned. Forgiveness offers the hope of moral freedom to those in the grip of bitterness and despair.

Our ability to think about forgiveness can help us resolve the dilemmas created by competing moral imperatives regarding our response to hurts. In the next chapter we will look in greater detail at our ability to think rationally about forgiveness.

Three

Forgiveness & Rational Thought

S
O JIM IS GETTING MARRIED?" PHIL ASKED NERVOUSLY. HE knew he was raising a sensitive topic for Mary, for Jim had hastily broken off their engagement the previous year just three months before the wedding. Jim had been less than honest with Mary about the other woman in his life, and he had made no effort to stay in touch following their breakup.

"Yeah . . . next weekend," Mary said.

"So, how do you feel about him, Mary?" asked Cindy.

"Well, it's been difficult. I hated him for quite a while. The pain and embarrassment were unbearable at first. But I gradually came to see that forgiveness is better than hate. I still care about Jim, despite how he has acted. Someday we might be friends again. How would you guys look at it?"

Phil said, "I can't stand to keep a grudge against anyone. I feel so guilty staying mad. I always feel better letting go of my anger."

Cindy was more blunt. "I would have been really mad if I were you,

Mary. But whenever I go to Mass angry with someone I'm reminded that I have to forgive others if I want to be forgiven."

Three people, three different reasons for forgiving. What accounts for their different styles of reasoning? In chapter one we said that forgiving involves the whole person. Does it also involve the way that we *reason?*

In this chapter we explore ways people think about forgiveness based on the area of psychology that studies cognitive development. Cognition is thinking and imagining. Models of cognitive development generally suggest that as humans develop biologically they also develop cognitively. People at higher levels of cognitive development reason more complexly (or rationally) than do people at earlier stages. Applied to morality, this would mean that differences in moral reasoning about relational issues, such as Mary, Phil and Cindy's conversation, may represent different stages of cognitive development.[1]

Robert Enright and his colleagues at the University of Wisconsin have described how reasoning about forgiveness develops. We will review the foundational work on cognitive moral development by Jean Piaget and Lawrence Kohlberg (two pioneers in the field) and then describe Enright's model of development of reasoning about forgiveness.

Cognitive Development

Jean Piaget was a Swiss biologist and philosopher who made some important contributions to the study of child development.[2] Piaget observed children at play and became interested in how children responded to stories involving moral dilemmas. He noted that the moral reasoning of younger children (ages three to seven) was guided by their parents' authority. That is, because parents control the consequences of actions, they thereby determine what the child considers right or wrong.

Morality based on parental authority gradually changes at the age of eight (sometimes earlier) to morality guided from within. Children move from determining morality based on the consequences of their actions to moral reasoning about their *motives*.

Key to Piaget's understanding is the development of fairness and sharing. We have all seen young children struggle with sharing when confronted by the need to share with other children or to take turns. The ability to take the perspective of another person is a crucial part of social development and is closely tied to sharing with others.

As a child begins to share, she can understand rules not just because of consequences they produce but because rules represent concerns about fairness toward others. In Piaget's understanding of cognitive development, people mature in the sophistication of their abstract reasoning from black-or-white, right-or-wrong thinking to considering numerous points of view.

Exercise 3-1
Teaching Children to Share

Parents and teachers can use the following to teach children how to share:

☐ Highlight taking turns with preschool children, and reward children with praise when they cooperate with sharing toys.

☐ Model unselfish attitudes by congratulating the success of players on the other team in competitive games. Encourage school-aged children to root for their teammates. Reinforce unselfish play in sports.

☐ Involve adolescents in service projects for the elderly or disadvantaged and underscore the benefits of giving to others.

Moral Development

In the United States Piaget's model of cognitive development gained attention in the 1960s largely through the influence of Harvard psychologist Lawrence Kohlberg. Kohlberg extended Piaget's work by formulating a six-stage model of moral development based on a person's capacity for abstract moral reasoning. Like Piaget, Kohlberg was interested in *how* people reason, not their specific decisions.

Cognitive psychologists such as Piaget and Kohlberg assume that humans are rational and can use reasoning to carry out plans. Thinking guides behavior. The goal of moral development from the cognitive approach, therefore, is to stimulate *wisdom,* which is taken to mean rational thinking. In Kohlberg's model a person must go from stage 1 to stage 2 before advancing to stage 3 or higher. Kohlberg considered the stages of moral development to be universal and consistent with all major world religions.

Kohlberg's hypothesized six stages are organized into three levels. At each level, different considerations influence the moral decisions that a person makes. To say that a person is at a certain level of moral development means that most of his or her reasoning about moral judgments is characterized by that level. The levels are preconventional (prior to considering social convention), conventional and postconventional.

Preconventional level. At the preconventional level (stages 1 and 2) people determine right and wrong solely on the basis of how certain choices make them feel. Remember our opening vignette. Phil weighed the personal costs and benefits in terms of his own feelings in deciding whether to forgive. Staying angry at others made him feel bad, and "letting go" of his anger made him feel better. He reasoned as we might expect a child to reason—at a preconventional level (stages 1 and 2). He thought mostly of himself, not others.

Conventional level. At the conventional level (stages 3 and 4) a person determines right and wrong on the basis of expectations from one's family, peers or nation. The person wants to maintain the approval of others or to uphold the laws that protect an orderly society. Cindy demonstrated conventional moral reasoning. Her forgiveness was influenced by her religious community (for example, what her church usually said about forgiveness) and a sense of duty to keep a moral commandment. Kohlberg believed that most adults usually use conventional moral reasoning.

Postconventional level. At the postconventional level (stages 5 and 6) a person has internalized self-chosen moral principles. These principles, according to Kohlberg, include valuing the dignity of all people and striving for solutions to moral dilemmas that are equitable for everyone involved. The appeal at this level is to one's conscience. Mary displayed postconventional moral reasoning in her personal commitment to forgiveness over hatred. She forgave because she saw her offender (Jim) as a person of worth despite his flaws.

To summarize, the preconventional thinker asks "What is best for me?" The conventional thinker asks "What is best for my group?" The postconventional thinker asks "What is best for humanity?"

Developmental Growth

Models of cognitive development, such as those of Piaget and Kohlberg, suggest that growth from one stage to the next is caused by mental tension. For example, Cindy, who said she cannot remain angry at people when she is at Mass, might experience tension if her priest read the biblical account of Jesus angrily clearing the temple. Cindy might find it confusing to reconcile her view of her religious tradition with information that opposes that view. That tension could push Cindy to search for moral principles rather than external authority to guide her.

Tension can occur simply from hearing other points of view that represent different stages of moral development. That is why ethics courses in high school, college or graduate school often have class members suggest their solutions to moral dilemmas. The guiding assumption is that the tension produced by hearing views other than one's own will challenge people toward more complex moral reasoning.

Kohlberg's model has led to several thousand studies, and substantial support for the general developmental progression has been gathered across diverse cultures. But not all studies support the cognitive model. In chapter four we will critique the cognitive developmental approach to morality. First, though, we will apply the theories of moral development to forgiveness.

Stages in the Development of Forgiveness

Robert Enright has probably done more than anyone else to broaden his fellow psychologists' understanding of forgiveness.[3] Enright and his colleagues have formed what they call the Human Development Study Group at the University of Wisconsin. They suggest that Kohlberg's model of moral development corresponds in many ways to a developmental progression of six soft-stages (or styles) in people's understanding of forgiveness. Their research has indicated that individuals often show reasoning at two adjacent stages, so it is misleading to consider a strict separation of stages. That is why they prefer the designation "soft-stages" or "styles."

Whereas Kohlberg's model of moral development focuses on justice, Enright's model focuses on mercy, which is the forswearing of revenge. You will recall from chapter two that justice and mercy are often in conflict with each other. Yet justice and forgiveness are related to each other. Both involve being able to look at things from another's perspective. Enright and his colleagues consider only the sixth and final stage (love) to fully meet their definition of forgiveness. Let's look at Enright's six stages and how we might help people who are at these stages of reasoning to forgive.

☐ *Stage 1: Revengeful forgiveness.* At this stage forgiveness is possible only if the offender is punished at least to the degree of pain or damage his or her offense has caused.

☐ *Stage 2: Restitutional forgiveness.* At this stage forgiveness can occur out of guilt for holding a grudge or if the offender offers restitution.

Evaluation of stages 1 and 2. Enright and colleagues do not consider these first two stages to qualify as forgiveness because they are motivated by the demand for punishment or reward, both of which characterize preconventional moral reasoning. Forgiveness involves canceling a debt, not exacting payment or avoiding one's own guilt. At stages 1 and 2 the person confuses punishment (retributive justice) and compensation (restitutional justice) with forgiveness.

The concept of restitution, which is implicit in stage 2 reasoning, is an ancient one that involves the practice of an offender paying back his or her victim for the damage caused. Restitutional forgiveness sometimes emerges as a pattern in marriages and other relationships.

I (Steve) met with a couple for marriage counseling who attempted to resolve most of their conflicts in this manner. Whenever there was a disagreement, the conflict would escalate until one person became verbally hostile, usually the person with the more stressful day. Then the partner who did the better job of keeping his or her cool was in the bargaining position. He or she would craftily demand that the other partner "pay up." The restitution might take the form of going to a certain restaurant, giving a back rub or watching a favorite television program. Although this approach helped the couple manage their different tastes in food and entertainment, the offending party usually resented the manipulation. Restitution, though it can sometimes be good, is not forgiveness.

Application of stages 1 and 2. Children at the preconventional level of forgiveness should be encouraged to forgive because of the personal rewards gained or punishments avoided. Parents can illustrate forgiveness by asking a child (older than age seven or eight) to help them weed their garden or by observing someone else's garden. The parent can describe how the garden is like the heart, and occasionally people hurt or offend us. When our anger turns to bitterness it becomes like a weed in the garden of our heart. If we pull the weeds, our garden can stay healthy and alive. But if we allow bitter weeds to grow, eventually our garden becomes ugly and weeds choke the life out of the vegetables in our garden. Forgiveness is like pulling out the weeds.[4]

☐ *Stage 3: Expectational forgiveness.* Forgiveness is offered in response to social pressure.

☐ *Stage 4: Lawful expectational forgiveness.* Forgiveness is offered in response to societal, moral or religious pressure.

Evaluation of stages 3 and 4. Stages 3 and 4 correspond to the conventional stages of moral development in Kohlberg's model. Forgiveness is stimulated by social pressure. A person might forgive in an effort to meet the expectations of family or peers (stage 3) or to obey the commandments of moral or religious institutions (stage 4). In either case forgiveness does not come from within. Enright and colleagues suggest that individuals whose approach to forgiveness is characterized by stage 3 or 4 moral reasoning are likely to hold onto feelings of hurt and anger toward their offender, since forgiveness is incomplete.

Application of stages 3 and 4. To help children who reason at the conventional level to forgive, ask them to name the opposite of forgiveness (possible answers: revenge, bitterness and anger). This can help children understand the definition and clarify misunderstandings. Then ask children, "Who is hurt by unforgiveness? Who is helped by forgiveness?" Try to help the children to see how forgiveness benefits others, even those not immediately involved in the conflict.[5]

☐ *Stage 5: Forgiveness as social harmony.* Forgiveness is granted to restore social harmony and right relationships.

Evaluation of stage 5. At stage 5 the person forgives on the condition of restoring social harmony. The individual using stage 5 reasoning can take the cognitive perspective of other people and can also envision himself or herself as a member of systems—families, communities and other relationships—that can be changed. Whereas in previous stages a person requires that certain conditions be met *before* the person forgives (revenge, restitution, social pressure), at stage 5 the person expects that social harmony will occur *after* he or she forgives.

Application of stage 5. Explain to children (older than age seven or eight) that the water in a clear jar represents a family or groups of friends. Then put a drop of red food coloring into the water. As the water turns pink, tell the children that the red is the hostility of unforgiveness that can "color" relationships between people or groups of people. Flesh out the illustration by describing how small grudges can lead to major feuds (such as the story of the Hatfields and McCoys). Ask how forgiveness can prevent all-out warfare. You also might use some of the techniques that we describe in chapter nine for helping people see things from another person's perspective.[6]

☐ *Stage 6: Forgiveness as love.* Forgiveness is unconditionally offered because it promotes love and increases the likelihood of reconciliation.

Evaluation of stage 6. Stage 6 is complete forgiveness. At stage 6, principles take precedence over social concerns. Forgiveness is offered without regard to prior conditions being met or consequences forgiveness may produce. Forgiveness is unconditional.

In our opening vignette Mary modeled an internalized commitment to forgiveness representative of stage 6. She did not demand changes in Jim before she offered forgiveness. She said that she hoped reconciliation could occur at some point, though she would probably say that Jim might need to change before they could enjoy a meaningful friendship.

How Forgiveness Develops

How do people move from one stage of reasoning about forgiveness to the next? In a cognitive developmental model, the mechanism thought to cause change is an underlying *script*. A script is a mental framework that works like the script of a play. When a person encounters a situation, he or she activates the corresponding script and assigns the character roles accordingly.

For example, when I (Steve) go to a restaurant, I usually follow the same general script. I sit down, look at the menu, decide, order, eat, converse (if I'm not alone), pay my bill and leave a tip. Notice that the last feature of the script, leaving a tip, involves the role of the waiter or waitress. I do not usually give much thought to what percentage tip I will leave but simply apply my rule of thumb—15 percent. My script, or mental framework, for eating at a restaurant saves mental energy.

My former boss, Gary, had a more complicated script for eating at a restaurant. After he was seated and the waiter or waitress brought our menus, he would engage that person in spontaneous, and often humorous, conversation. He would usually find out the person's name and something about him or her. Then he would frequently involve the person in his meal selection by asking for an opinion about various items on the menu. Throughout the meal, as the waiter or waitress returned, Gary might ask further questions about the person's work. This communicated a sense of dignity and interest in the person as an individual. By the end of the meal, one usually had the feeling that Gary had made a new friend. Gary would likewise leave a 15 percent tip (sometimes more) but would have communicated much more than common courtesy.

This illustrates the way scripts work in interpersonal settings.[7] Scripts have a guiding assumption. A person's script of forgiveness governs how he or she might deal with an emotional injury.

Piaget viewed the script of forgiveness as guided by the assumption of *ideal reciprocity. Reciprocity* is treating in a like manner. Ideal reciprocity follows the motto "Do as you would be done by." So for Piaget forgiveness emerges when a person moves beyond the literal reciprocity of "an eye for an eye" to the ideal of treating others the way we would like to be treated.

Enright and his colleagues disagree with Piaget. They view the script of forgiveness as being guided by the assumption of *abstract identity*. Abstract identity involves the view that despite all else, my offender is a human being of inherent worth like myself—a person with whom I can identify. This involves looking beyond the hurtful context to achieve unconditionality, which requires significant abstract reasoning.

The restaurant example illustrates the difference between these two scripts. I tend to approach those who serve me with an assumption of ideal reciprocity. I expect to receive courteous service, so I try to be courteous. Even when the service or the food is less than ideal, I leave my standard tip. Gary, on the other hand, approaches people in a restaurant in a manner that parallels abstract identity. He treats people with dignity, respect and humanness. His spontaneous interest and lively conversation move well beyond the simple courtesy of social rules to valuing individuals through love.

Research on the Development of Forgiveness

Psychologists are not satisfied with a theory that sounds good on paper—they want evidence to support the theory. Several questions are of primary concern. First, do people really develop reasoning about forgiveness according to the model outlined by Enright and his colleagues? Second, do the stages of reasoning about forgiveness show a similar pattern in a variety of cultures? In other words, are the stages of reasoning about forgiveness universal, as Kohlberg suggested about the stages of reasoning about justice? Third, are people who reason at the higher stages actually more forgiving than are those at the lower stages? Although research on the development of forgiveness is still in the early stages, we will describe the results of some preliminary studies conducted by Enright and his colleagues.

Developmental patterns. Enright's group approached the first question by asking participants (grades four, seven, ten, college and postcollege adult) in Wisconsin to consider two stories that posed a moral dilemma wherein a person was emotionally hurt by the actions of another character.[8] They asked participants what would help the offended party forgive: revenge, restitution, peer and authority pressure or the desire for restored social harmony. If Enright's model for how reasoning about forgiveness develops is correct, older participants would reason about forgiveness at higher stages than would younger participants.

In two studies Enright's group found that style (or stage) of forgiveness increased with age. Participants were also given a test of their reasoning about justice that fit Kohlberg's model. The researchers found that those higher in their level of reasoning about justice tended also to be higher in their level of reasoning about forgiveness. This finding supports the notion that reasoning about justice and forgiveness may require common skills in being able to see things from another's viewpoint, or social perspective-taking (more about perspective-taking in chapters nine and ten).

Crosscultural support. Psychologists are impressed not with one or two studies, but with multiple studies that yield similar results, especially if those experiments are carried out in different cultures.[9] Tina Huang and Robert Enright did a similar study in Taiwan and found the same trend for forgiveness—children's reasoning about justice was related to their forgiveness style. Younghee Park and Enright also found a similar trend in Korea.[10] These findings provide some cross-cultural support for Enright's model of how people reason about forgiveness.

Higher-order forgiveness. In a second study, Huang and Enright wanted to find out whether higher reasoning about forgiveness was related to lower blood pressure and less negative emotion, such as anxiety and anger.[11] Specifically they wanted to test the idea that stage 6 forgiveness is more complete than stage 4 and results in less residual negative emotion related to a past hurt.

Participants who were assessed as being at stage 4 (forgiveness out of obligation) and stage 6 (forgiveness out of love) and who had all suffered an interpersonal hurt necessitating forgiveness in the past three years were selected to be in their second study. The participants were asked to tell the story of their interpersonal conflict while their blood pressure was monitored. Expert raters watched videos of the participants telling their stories and counted the number of times the person displayed a "masked" (or fake) smile and how often he or she looked down at the ground. Emotion researchers believe that these facial expressions reveal that someone is trying to conceal negative emotions.

What is particularly interesting about Huang and Enright's second study is that whereas stage 4 and stage 6 forgivers did not differ in the level of emotional distress they reported, they did differ on the tests that did not rely on the participants' personal reports. Stage 4 participants displayed more masked smiles and looked down more frequently than did stage 6 participants. Stage 4 participants also registered slightly higher blood-pressure levels at the end of the first minute of the conflict-telling session (though, admittedly, the size of this difference was not considered significant by normal scientific standards).

These results suggest that those with a higher level of forgiveness may retain less residual negative emotion regarding an interpersonal conflict than those at a lower level of reasoning about forgiveness. They may also suggest that forgiveness leads to reductions in blood pressure and negative feelings. Such findings imply that forgiving may promote health. (We will say more about forgiveness and health in chapter thirteen.)

How Children Learn Forgiveness

The cognitive developmental approach to forgiveness suggests several ways to encourage the development of forgiveness in children. These include stories that present dilemmas, role models and role plays.

Stories that present dilemmas. Kohlberg and his colleagues advocated the *plus-one* approach to moral development using stories that describe moral dilemmas.[12] Pose a story in which a character faces a moral dilemma to a child or group of children. In a group of children, some will be at higher levels of reasoning, and some will be at lower levels. By asking various children what the main character in the story should do and why, some children will be exposed to views at levels of moral reasoning higher than their own. Kohlberg assumed that children will be challenged by reasoning at the level that is one level higher than their own, hence "plus-one."

Stories that present a dilemma can also be used with one child and an adult who inquires about the child's reasoning. The adult can offer a rationale at the next higher level of moral development. For example, a child whose attitude reflects an orientation toward personal rewards (stage 2) can be encouraged to think about the importance of mutual consideration and social responsibility (stage 3). Most people may find it difficult to understand the reasoning of a stage greater than one level higher than their typical functioning. Use high-interest dilemmas with children, such as those involving sports, games or dating. We have described three such dilemmas in exercise 3-2.

Exercise 3-2
Dilemmas That Illustrate Levels of Reasoning About Forgiveness

These are examples of dilemmas that might be used to challenge children to improve their reasoning about forgiveness.

1. You are playing a game with some neighborhood friends. One of the kids tries to cheat but apologizes when you catch him or her. How should you respond?

☐ Stage 2 reasoning: Forgive because it will ruin your day to stay angry. Keep playing as long as there is no more cheating.

☐ Stage 3 reasoning: Forgive because it is important to accept apologies from friends or family members.

☐ Stage 4 reasoning: Forgive because it is good to forgive and bad to hold a grudge.

☐ Stage 5 reasoning: Forgive because it helps friends get along. Staying mad ruins the fun for the whole group.

☐ Stage 6 reasoning: Forgive because you want to give respect to others.

2. Your school's archrival, Central Junior High, has just pounded your athletic team in the season opener. Several of the hotshot Central players taunted you and your teammates on their way to the locker room last week. How should you respond?

☐ Stage 2 reasoning: Forgive because bitterness could get in the way of your performance in future games. Use your frustration to improve your skills.

☐ Stage 3 reasoning: Forgive because good sportsmanship is a team rule. Your team has to keep a good attitude even if other teams do not.

☐ Stage 4 reasoning: Forgive because it's wrong to hold grudges even if others are wrong. Forgiveness is the right thing to do.

☐ Stage 5 reasoning: Forgive because it prevents the league from becoming chaotic. What will happen if all the teams in the league start taunting and hating one another?

☐ Stage 6 reasoning: Forgive because you are committed to treating others with respect even when they have not treated you with respect. Respecting others is more important than preserving pride.

3. Your best friend has started dating the boy you have always

wanted to go out with. She knew you liked this person, yet she betrayed you anyway. You have avoided her for two weeks, but now you are supposed to work with her on a committee at school. What should you do?

☐ Stage 2 reasoning: Forgive because you will feel better if you are not mad every time she is around. Forgiveness will allow you to enjoy the committee and perhaps even enjoy your friend.

☐ Stage 3 reasoning: Forgive because forgiveness is an important way your family resolves conflict. Forgiveness that you have seen modeled in your family can be transferred to school.

☐ Stage 4 reasoning: Forgive because it is right to forgive. If you forgive others, you will be forgiven.

☐ Stage 5 reasoning: Forgive because the work of the committee will benefit. Forgiveness will prevent factions among your circle of friends.

☐ Stage 6 reasoning: Forgive because you are a person who values others even when they are selfish and inconsiderate. By forgiving you remain a person who offers the respect to others that is important to you.

Stories that present dilemmas involving interpersonal conflict can be used to promote the further development of forgiveness. One important skill in resolving interpersonal conflict is the ability to generate alternatives. Researchers have found that aggressive children often have a limited ability to generate alternative courses of action when offended by a peer, so they lash out.[13] Parents and teachers can use dilemmas to help children consider problems from more than one perspective and come up with different strategies for resolving conflict.

For example, your son gets smacked in the face with a ball while playing a game at school and responds by punching the other child. Ask your son, "What would have been some other ways to respond?" Try to get him to come up with several alternatives. Then pick a positive alternative to fighting and plan the steps for that response your son can use the next time he faces a similar situation.

Adults can encourage children to view problems in relationships in terms of mutual goals rather than the needs of only one person. This is often difficult for adults themselves. For example, in dilemma 3 the victim would need to realize that her (or his) friend has goals of enjoying the committee and having an active social life. Perhaps they can agree to work together on the committee since they cannot share the boyfriend (at least not without further problems). Children will benefit if adults frame forgiveness as a strategy to achieve collaborative goals and long-term relationship satisfaction.

Role models. Kohlberg stressed the importance of parental role modeling in helping children develop their moral reasoning.[14] Consider how interpersonal conflict is resolved in your family and in your outside relationships. Do you distinguish between hurtful behaviors that are accidental and those that are intentional? Parents should distinguish between accidents and intentional actions in their child discipline.[15] For example, a ten-year-old who accidentally spills his milk at the dinner table can be asked to help clean up the mess rather than be sent to his room. When parents distinguish between accidental wrongs and intentional wrongs, children can learn to consider the motives of others.

My (Steve's) own father modeled empathy and taking the perspective of others characteristic of the higher stages of forgiveness. He would often tell stories of his early relationship with his father, which involved startling incidents of violence, verbal abuse and neglect. For much of his life my father wrestled with significant emotional hurt and hostility toward his father. But as he told these stories he would add that he had realized in adulthood that certain situational factors had made my grandfather's life difficult.

My grandfather was a farmer who had to rent his land during the Great Depression. He raised and supported six children after his wife died of cancer. My father's oldest brother, Curtis, spent much of his own childhood so sick that he had to be hospitalized, which created further emotional and economic problems for the family.

As I listened to my father, I never got the impression that he excused his father's wrong behavior or denied the seriousness of what my father had suffered. Rather, I learned the value of considering the perspective of others and how empathy for his own father's struggles helped my father to forgive.

Role-plays. Role-plays are another great way to encourage children to develop empathy (seeing things from someone else's perspective). Use dramas or skits involving interpersonal conflict to stimulate moral reasoning at a higher level.[16] For example, a child is having trouble with a classmate who is teasing him or her. The child is asked to role-play the mean classmate. The parent can then play the role of the child and demonstrate an appropriate response, such as ignoring the other child, politely asking him or her to stop teasing or reporting the teasing to the teacher. After modeling appropriate behavior, the parent should help the child talk about the advantages of not retaliating.

The child can also be challenged to consider what might contribute to the classmate's behavior. For example, a parent can ask, "Do you think your classmate is lonely and doesn't know how to make friends?" or, "Do you think people have made fun of your classmate in the past?" Several options can be considered, but what is important is that children learn to consider the perspective of the other person. This can also help prevent children from viewing an offense against them as due to personal deficiencies.

Summing Up

The rational approach to forgiving is powered by the moral sense that we discussed in chapter two. When we understand that a wrong has been committed—against us or by us—we want to see it righted. Forgiveness is one option that we consider for righting such wrongs.

As our cognitive ability matures, we can think about forgiveness better. Movement toward forgiveness requires growth in moral reasoning from a focus on personal rewards and punishments at the earliest stages to the later stages characterized by the social perspective of role models and group rules. The most mature form of reasoning about forgiveness arises from an internalized commitment to the dignity and worth of all people.

The rational approach to forgiveness suggests that development will be most likely to occur when we consider moral dilemmas for which our current stage of reasoning proves unsatisfactory and when we are provided with an example of moral reasoning at a higher stage. The cognitive developmental approach highlights the ways people change their thinking about forgiveness and emphasizes the potential of educational interventions to produce growth and well-being.

Exercise 3-3
Rate Your Own Reasoning About Forgiveness

In chapter one you identified some hurtful situations about which you have not been completely able to forgive the other person. Choose one of these, and write as many reasons as you can think of within a five-minute period why you should forgive the person.

Examine each reason in light of the stages and levels of development we have described in this chapter. Classify your reasoning by stage. At which stage do you find the most reasons? That might be the stage at which you are currently reasoning about forgiveness.

Now select the next higher stage of reasoning (in the event that you tested at any stage lower than stage 6—forgiveness as love). Try to list some additional reasons that would be characterized by that higher stage of reasoning.

Evidence shows that taking a rational approach can help us become more forgiving. Thinking about how forgiveness can help balance the competing moral imperatives that govern our response to hurts (that is, we are pressed to be both just and merciful)—and using our rational powers to think about forgiving is indeed helpful for empowering us to forgive. But thinking rationally isn't all there is to being able to forgive. The rational approach has some limitations. In chapter four we will focus on some of those limitations.

Four

Forgiveness &
Rational Thought
Limitations

*I*T IS JULY 26, 1987. FATHER LAWRENCE MARTIN JENCO IS STAND-
ing blindfolded in front of an elevator in a secret prison
somewhere in Lebanon. He is finally being released after
nineteen months as a hostage of Shiite Muslims. In an
adjacent room, fellow hostages Terry Anderson and Thomas Suther-
land are not going home. Jenco's captivity has included severe beat-
ings, cruel confinement to a three-by-six-foot closet and painful eye
infections due to filthy blindfolds. He has gone months without being
outside or being allowed to bathe. Now, after repeated broken promises of release, he is going home.

Two of Father Jenco's captors stand behind him. One of the
captors, Abu-Ali, warmly calls Jenco "Abouna," which means "dear
father." It is a name that evolved over the course of Jenco's captivity.
On the morning of his kidnapping a guard had taken his prized
silver cross given to him on the twenty-fifth anniversary of his
priesthood. Now Father Jenco feels the surprise of the cross being

slipped into his hand. The gift of the cross symbolically closes the circle of his captivity.

The other captor gently begins to massage Father Jenco's shoulders. Jenco remembers the morning of his kidnapping when he stared into the hateful eyes of the same man threatening him with "You are dead!" Father Jenco now senses a loving apology in his compassionate touch—a nonverbal request for forgiveness. What could be going through Father Jenco's mind in such a moment? What mixed emotions would be stirring his heart?[1]

His book *Bound to Forgive* describes an encounter with yet another captor shortly before his release. Sayeed, a guard who had beaten Father Jenco several times, asked the priest if he remembered the first six months of his captivity (when most of the abuse took place). Father Jenco responded that he did remember all the pain and suffering Sayeed had caused him and the other hostages.

"Abouna, do you forgive me?" Father Jenco recounts his reaction:

These quietly spoken words overwhelmed me. As I sat blindfolded, unable to see the man who had been my enemy, I understood I was called to forgive, to let go of revenge, retaliation, and vindictiveness.

And I was challenged to forgive him unconditionally. I could not forgive him on the condition that he change his behavior to conform to my wishes or values. I had no control over his response. I understood I was to say yes.[2]

In chapter three we described the rational approach to forgiveness. This approach is fueled by our ability to understand how forgiveness helps us balance the imperatives to respond both justly *and* mercifully to the hurts we receive. The work of Enright and his colleagues has contributed a great deal to our understanding of forgiveness.

Father Jenco faced an incredible challenge, yet he chose to forgive. What level of reasoning about forgiveness does his response reflect? Though the rational approach has considerable support in psychological research, it has some important limitations: it is too cognitive, may not predict action and is too individualistic.

Too Cognitive

Psychologists are concerned with cause-effect relationships. When an event occurs, such as one person forgiving another, we want to know what *caused* the forgiveness. Most psychologists would concede that human behavior is complex and includes many causes. But is there a *primary* factor that causes forgiveness? If so, what is that factor?

Different camps in psychology put forth competing explanations for what aspect of the person is the primary factor that leads to forgiveness. A few days ago I (Steve) found myself intensely angry at another person. An acquaintance had publicly mocked a friend of mine about her figure the last time I had seen him. I was at a party with him and could feel the rage churning in my stomach. What would help me forgive?

The rational-developmental approach to forgiveness emphasizes the way I think about the offender. But what about the role of emotions? How do emotions affect my ability to forgive him? What about my behaviors? Would the way I act toward him affect whether I could forgive? What about my environment? How do the people around me affect whether I forgive him?

Advocates of a rational approach to psychology such as Piaget, Kohlberg and Enright do not rule out the influence of emotions, behavior or the environment, but they do consider our rational powers to be primary.[3] Nevertheless we need also to consider the role of emotions, behavior and culture on moral development.

Shared laughter versus unforgiveness. Father Jenco described an unusual incident that occurred early in his process of forgiving his captors. One of the guards was telling the story about his sister visiting Switzerland and attempting to order chicken in a restaurant without knowing the correct word in any of the European languages. She tried imitating what she wanted by clucking and flapping her arms like a chicken. The entire restaurant burst into laughter, as did the guard while retelling the story. Father Jenco recounts his reaction: "Hearing the story in the guard's fractured English made it even funnier. I believe our laughter and smiles helped change attitudes: enemies were becoming friends."[4]

What was the catalyst for this change in Father Jenco's attitude? Sharing laughter with this guard allowed him to begin to see his captors differently. Empathy for the humanness of his captors warmed his cold heart and began to change his thinking. Positive emotions can erode unforgiveness. Have you ever been angry with a parent or partner when suddenly joy bursts onto the scene? A friend makes a joke. You watch a funny movie together. It's hard to hold onto hate when you are sharing joy with the target of your animosity.

My wife, Danielle, and I (Steve) locked horns in one of our worst arguments shortly after moving into a new apartment. We reached an impasse after several minutes of verbal sparring, so I offered a psychological interpretation of what I thought her problem was (spouses of counselors will know what I'm talking about). Danielle found my interpretation about as helpful as the flu. She strongly counseled me to reserve my own counsel for my paying clients. Then she stormed out of the bedroom, slamming the bathroom door behind her to shut out my lecturing. I hated her getting the last word!

Several minutes passed with Danielle in the bathroom and me sitting on the bed stewing. Then I heard the knob on the bathroom door rattle. It rattled again. I remembered noticing the day before that the bathroom door would stick when closed all the way and realized Danielle was stuck in the bathroom. I wish I could say there was something besides joy in my twisted heart at that moment. Glee might be closer to the truth. I knew how to get the door unstuck but was in no big hurry to do so. I began to laugh on one side of the door, and I could hear Danielle laughing on the other side. As I opened the door to the bathroom, laughter opened the door to forgiveness.

Empathy. Psychologist Martin Hoffman is a leading researcher on the relationship of empathy to moral development. Hoffman suggests that moral actions such as forgiveness develop through moral motivations, not just thoughts. Where the rational approach emphasizes reasoning, Hoffman emphasizes moral motives.[5] Empathy is an emotion that can motivate actions such as forgiving.

According to the rational approach our thinking guides our emotions and behavior. Is that always the case? As I felt hostility toward the guy at the party, the principles of forgiveness came to my mind. I remembered with indifference that I was working on a book about forgiveness. My angry heart felt like a clenched fist.

Hoffman believes that emotions such as empathy affect the moral principles we select as the basis of our reasoning during a moral dilemma. At the party I actually felt empathic anger on behalf of my friend who had been verbally abused. Empathy for my friend led me to think about the moral principle of retributive justice (revenge) and a moral condemnation of the offender. My emotions guided my thinking.

The day after the party, when I was having breakfast with a friend, a discussion arose about this obnoxious offender. One person recounted having complimented the guy about his daughter. The offender cheaply attributed his daughter's complimentary quality to the good genes of "his side of the family." The story fueled my contempt. The person telling the story, though, gently concluded, "It's too bad when people have so much personal insecurity that they can't receive a compliment."

The empathy and sorrow in my friend's voice sent a wave of guilt through my heart: *How could I be so cold? And when I'm working on a book about forgiveness!* My rational mind fought back: *Insecurity is a poor excuse for hurting others!* But the genuine empathy of the other person was forcing me to wrestle with more than my angry feelings and condemning thoughts. My conflict was emotional and cognitive.

Comprehending that you are capable of the same ugliness that you are condemning in another can penetrate a cloud of hatefulness. Have you ever been in the midst of an argument, your thoughts or your voice screaming condemnation at another because he or she doesn't care? *You do hateful things,* you might be thinking. Or "You're insulting," you might say (insultingly). Or "You always put me down," you might say, putting the other person down. Suddenly, with the sharpness of a lightning flash, you realize that your mind and mouth have betrayed you: you have the same flaws as the person who hurt you.

Attachment. Attachment engages our emotions and can influence our thinking about relationships. Attachment is the bonding that occurs between two people, such as a mother and a newborn infant. Attachment theory is a psychological theory that emphasizes the role of the bond between a caregiver and a young child in the development of the child's ability to trust others.[6] A young child needs to sense that the world is safe and that a caregiver will soothe him or her when distressed.

Attachment theorists believe that the relations between caregivers and children lead children to develop a working model that will be used to understand relationships later in life. A working model is like a cognitive prototype or script (see chapter three). If I said to you, "Picture a dog," you would probably form a prototype of dog in your mind. I picture Zac, my brother's former black labrador. I know there are other types of dogs, but my working model is set by the dog with which I have the most personal experience.

According to attachment theory, we each have a working model of relationships that is shaped by our early experiences with primary caregivers. If we experienced rejection, distance or smothering from our primary caregivers, our working model of relationships will be negative. We may expect to be treated the same way by others. This expectation could lead us to avoid intimacy or cling to others in a effort to combat the insecurity and anxiety that we fear.

The working model of attachment theory is similar to the rational approach: they both emphasize cognitive development. An important difference, however, is that attachment theorists see our working model as rooted in our emotional reactions to early relationships. Our view of relationships is not simply logical; it is also emotional. Attachment theorists view the rational approach as too exclusively logical. Cognitive development is driven by *relationships,* not just reason.

Traci and Gene offer an example of working models in relationships. Gene became bothered shortly after their wedding whenever

Traci came home in a bad mood. Eventually Gene started to overreact if Traci came in the door tense or upset. All Traci had to do to set Gene off was to complain about the traffic or the bills that had arrived.

Gene later explained: "I knew I was responding to more than just Traci. Then one day, when I was about to gripe at her for her mood, I remembered the way my dad used to come home from work. He always had a scowl on his face and a grievance against my mom." Gene realized that he had formed an emotion-laden picture of relationships and was responding to Traci on the basis of that picture. His emotional ties to the old model of relationships shaped his thinking about his marriage.

Gender. The rational approach to forgiveness may not apply equally well to both genders. Carol Gilligan offered the first major critique of Kohlberg's model of moral development on the grounds that women tend to approach moral issues differently from men. Her book *In Different Voice* suggests that women focus less on abstract rational principles and more on interpersonal aspects of morality in comparison to men. In her interviews with women, Gilligan found that women frequently requested more information about the particular circumstances of people in moral dilemmas. She proposes an *ethic of care* for the foundation of moral development as an alternative to what she considers Kohlberg's male-oriented *ethic of justice.* Gilligan's ethic of care emphasizes empathy as the primary moral motive, as does Martin Hoffman.[7]

Blythe McVicker Clinchy is a psychologist who builds on Gilligan's critique of Kohlberg by looking at the ways women approach moral dilemmas. Clinchy distinguishes between *separate and connected knowing.*[8] If you know anyone who likes to play the "devil's advocate" in a discussion, you are familiar with separate knowing. The heart of separate knowing is to detach or to separate oneself from the person or topic under consideration. Separate knowing is like the objective and critical thinking of a scientist and is consistent with the rational-developmental approach. The separate knower is also like an attorney who wants evidence and justification for moral positions.

Connected knowing is based on attachment. The connected knower tries to stand in the other person's shoes to understand better his or her point of view. Connected knowing empathically explores opposing points of view. Having understood the person behind a moral position, the connected knower may find that position wanting. Clinchy found that most women use both separate and connected knowing, but lean toward one of the two. The empathic and interpersonal aspects of connected knowing are consistent with the moral development of many of the women in her studies.

It would be simplistic to assume that the moral development of all women could be described by Gilligan's ethic of care or Clinchy's connected knowing. Many women rely on abstract principles of justice and separate knowing in forming moral positions. But the rational-developmental approach may need to be qualified by these issues of gender.

We believe that forgiveness integrates an ethic of justice with an ethic of care and combines separate and connected knowing. You may remember from chapters two and three that forgiveness can balance the imperatives to be just and merciful. Forgiveness requires that we hold our offender morally accountable (justice), but forgiveness also entails a commitment to caring about that person's welfare as a human being (care). Separate knowing allows us to stand back from a situation and evaluate a moral offense. Connected knowing enables us to empathize with our offender and affirm the relationship.

Self-esteem. When we are hurt or offended by someone in an interpersonal relationship we often experience an attack on our self-esteem. When I (Steve) was in sixth grade I was initiated into the high-stakes world of romantic relationships. The girl's name was Jennifer. Our romance was negotiated tribal style. Her friends met with my friends and agreed that we would "go together." Our first date was the movie *Battlestar Galactica,* and I was dressed to kill in rust-colored, bell-bottom corduroys and a matching button-down shirt with gold disco stripes. We were chauffeured to and from the theater in my mom's green station wagon with the simulated wood-grain paneling.

I guess I should have seen the end coming. But when Jennifer dumped me the next week (through messengers, of course), I was shocked. My shock turned to humiliation when I found out that her reason was not my poor taste in movies or the parental escort. Rather, my friends had betrayed me by divulging to Jennifer my darkest secret—I did not know how to roller-skate. In the social fast lane of junior-high romance, a nonskater might as well be a leper. The roller rink was where all the important social transactions took place, and Jennifer must not have been ready to settle down to a relationship based on science-fiction movies.

In the aftermath, as I tried to put back together the pieces of my life, I remember thinking, *I didn't really want to go out with her anyway. I don't really like her or her friends.* I began to focus on Jennifer's negative qualities, such as how fickle she must be, and how it would be more fun to watch movies without wearing those sharp bell-bottom cords (with the matching shirt). I was trying to recover my self-esteem by telling myself that I was in control, for my first romantic rejection had left me feeling helpless and undesirable.

Psychologist Roy Baumeister studied how people describe their negative experience in romantic relationships of being spurned by a person they were attracted to or turning down someone attracted to them. His participants wrote brief stories about specific experiences and how they felt.[9]

The stories of people being spurned by a would-be lover (the Steves) showed a primary motive of recovering self-esteem. People often described feeling led on and viewing their would-be lover as mysterious and confusing. There often seemed to be an effort in the stories to find a problem with the would-be lover rather than with oneself. In my case, my insecurity over my inability to roller-skate was so threatening that my self-esteem could only be protected by focusing on Jennifer's deficits. (Fortunately, now I have grown far beyond that—so far that I hardly ever mention Jennifer's dirty sneakers.)

Baumeister also notes that those participants who had to turn down someone who was attracted to them (the Jennifers) were not aware of having led anyone on. Frequently they were annoyed by the persistence of the rejected seekers (the Steves).

These findings suggest that the way we perceive conflict in romantic relationships depends on what position we are in. Being rejected may be such an assault on our self-esteem that our rational thinking is clouded by an effort to recover positive feelings about ourselves. This would mean that interpersonal conflict, especially in relationships pivotal to our identity, may engage emotions not accounted for by the rational approach alone. The process of forgiveness is especially complicated when someone has been hurt in a romantic relationship (or quest for a relationship). The passions of the heart can make it difficult to gain the objectivity of the rational approach.

Exercise 4-1

What Factors Besides the Rational Help Us Forgive?

Pick one of the people you would like to forgive for having hurt you in the past—perhaps a single time, perhaps many times. *Honestly examine your relationship with the person* and think about your past in light of what you have learned in this chapter. To help you examine your relationship, answer the following questions:

☐ Have you shared times of laughter with this person? Recall a specific time when you laughed together. If you can't recall a time, is there any possibility that you will ever share laughter with the person?

☐ Can you empathize with the person? Can you see that you are capable of harming others—intentionally or unintentionally? Can you understand the person's human fallibility?

Examine your past to determine your attachment style. Most attachment theorists classify attachment styles into three types: (1) anxious-ambivalent, (2) avoidant and (3) secure.

1. Anxious-ambivalent attachment styles are often developed in babies whose care was interrupted (perhaps by parental divorce in the toddler years) or who had multiple caregivers (such as many changes in day-care arrangements). Caregiving was usually inconsistent. Anxious-ambivalent adults often have problems seeing things

from other people's points of view and may have low levels of commitment in relationships. Usually they fear losing established relationships. They may be angry or passive toward their parents. They often fall in love easily and feel intense jealousy.

2. Avoidant attachment styles are often developed when caregivers reject babies. Avoidant attachment results in adults who are often isolated and lonely but deny grief, sadness and anger. They sometimes feel detached from deep feelings of any kind and feel that they can never get the love they need. They often are compulsively self-reliant and competent, but they tend to be perceived as hostile, provocative or emotionally detached.

3. Secure attachment styles are often developed through relatively consistent caregiving. Secure attachment results in the ability to form and maintain most relationships but to have an appropriate self-reliance. Securely attached adults usually worry about losing the security of personal relationships, but they are generally satisfied with their relationships. They can seek support and give support to people in intimate relationships.

Is your attachment style as an adult playing a part in being unable or unwilling to forgive the person who has harmed you? As you scan the list of people who may have harmed you, do you notice that the offenses that bother you are dominated by a single type of offense? Perhaps you often feel betrayed. Might your attachment style be anxious-ambivalent, stemming from inconsistent caregiving due to a parent who was moody, alcoholic or frequently unavailable? Perhaps you often feel rejected and misunderstood. Might your attachment style be avoidant, stemming from childhood experiences of rejection?

Consider how your gender might influence your response to hurts. As a woman, you may highly value relationships and find that unkindness deeply affects you. As a man, you may find that miscarriages of justice bother you enormously. Although gender differences may explain your natural tendencies, there are limits to how much effect they have. The individual characteristics that you inherited and learned may overshadow gender characteristics.

Evaluate your self-esteem. We each have arenas in which we are confident and those in which we are insecure. When a blow is dealt to either area, it can have a devastating impact. When the area of our confidence is attacked, it undermines our sense of effectiveness. When the area of our insecurity is attacked, it strengthens our sense of worthlessness. Did the person hurt you in a particularly vulnerable area—one of great strength or weakness? If so, your reaction is likely to be strong.

May Not Predict Action

A second limitation of the rational approach to understanding forgiveness is that moral reasoning does not always lead to moral action. Do people who reason at the higher levels actually act differently from people whose reasoning is primarily at the lower stages?

Kohlberg was more interested in the way people think about a moral dilemma than in what they decide to do or what they actually do. Two different people might both say that a person should forgive a spouse who cheats on them, but Kohlberg is interested in differences in how the two people reason about this dilemma, not in their decision or whether they carry out their decision.

Several psychologists have examined the relationship between moral reasoning and moral behavior. Their findings have been inconsistent.[10] One of Kohlberg's former students reviewed fifty studies and found that people higher in moral reasoning tended to be higher in moral behavior. Other researchers have found that the connection between moral reasoning and moral behavior is not clear-cut and depends on factors such as the situation or family dynamics. Most of us would probably concede that there are times when we reason on a higher moral plane than we act. I may be able to explain that the moral principle of forgiveness is unconditional love, but when I am cut off in rush-hour traffic I sometimes act like Darth Vader and want to love someone alongside the head.

Over several decades psychiatrist Robert Coles has interviewed hundreds of children about their views of morality. Coles describes impressive moral responses from children too young to have even achieved stage 4 reasoning in Kohlberg's model. He opposes the view that moral development arises primarily through increased abstract reasoning ability and warns of the danger of such an elitist model. Morality and intelligence are not the same, he argues. It is not hard to think of intelligent public figures who have used their reasoning ability to lie or violate public trust in other ways. Increased cognitive ability can lead to more sophisticated reasons for hatred and violence as easily as it can lead to love or forgiveness.

Coles thinks that we best understand the moral life by looking at actual behavior rather than at verbal responses to abstract dilemmas. Why? Because unlike our moral reasoning, our behavior affects other people. Moral reasoning must be translated into some form of behavior when we encounter our enemies on the street.[11]

Also, our actions can change our thinking. During my freshman year in college I lived next to an obnoxious guy I could not stand. I found him to be selfish and arrogant, and he was quickly falling out of favor with the rest of my fraternity. I became so annoyed by him that I turned to a drastic measure—I offered to buy him dinner at a great restaurant. There was no sound reasoning behind my behavior; I just knew I had tried everything else I could think of to handle my annoyance.

The night we were to go out I almost decided to cancel—I felt like doing anything but taking this guy out for a good meal. But something happened to me over dinner. I did not really enjoy him very much or come to any great insight. But my hostility subsided. Grudges I had carried against him seemed less important. I forgave him.

Sometimes our behavior can change because of how we think about another person. Of course there can be danger in doing good deeds to an offender who is abusive or needs serious confrontation. But our own moral behavior, such as holding our tongue when we feel like gossiping about our offender, can lead to a deeper moral understanding.

Too Individualistic

The rational approach to morality focuses on morality *within the individual.* We will look at the individualistic biases that underlie the rational stage model and how research has demonstrated that these individualistic biases weaken the rational model as an explanation of how forgiveness occurs.

Philosophy. Every model of human development has a guiding philosophy of what healthy human functioning should be like. That is especially true in an area such as moral development. Kohlberg's model of moral development was largely influenced by the Enlightenment philosopher Immanuel Kant. Kant stressed the power of human reason. Kant's emphasis on human reason led to the de-emphasis of two other influences—God and community.

Kohlberg's philosophy of morality is human-centered: he assumes that morality is defined within the individual. God or spiritual realities are not thought to define a moral order. Reliance on spiritual powers for moral direction puts one at the conventional (stage 4) level of reasoning. Determining morality for oneself as an individual is viewed as the highest level of moral development.

The stage model of the rational approach also reveals its individualistic bias by devaluing community as a source of moral direction. Dependence on the social expectations of one's family, peers or religious community represents conventional (stage 3 or 4) reasoning. The highest stage in Kohlberg's hierarchy involves moving beyond the influences of others.

The devaluing of both spiritual realities and social community as influences on moral reasoning places cultural limitations on the rational-developmental approach, which Kohlberg considered universal. Some cultures are collectivistic rather than individualistic. In collectivistic (or communal) cultures, group harmony is valued over individual expression. The needs of individuals are subject to the needs of the group or community. Likewise, many cultural groups look to spiritual realities to provide moral direction. To assume that individuals should define what is moral, rather than God or one's community, biases the rational stage model against some cultures and religious groups.

Research. Some research shows that Kohlberg's model of moral development discriminates against religiously conservative persons. Religiously conservative persons tend to score lower on Kohlbergian tests of moral development than do others of comparable age and education.[12] Conservative religion tends to emphasize *conserving* tradition, so it is not surprising that some religious people usually respond to moral dilemmas with stage 4 reasoning: they look to their religious communities for direction.

Psychologist P. Scott Richards was interested in the factors that influence this tendency, so he studied fundamentalist students in training for ministry. They usually preferred stage 4 responses to moral dilemmas.[13] Were they *unable* to understand higher level responses, such as Kohlberg's model suggests? Not at all. Richards interviewed the seminarians after they had been tested. He found that they preferred the stage 4 responses and thought those responses were more moral even when they understood the stage 6 responses.

Richards concluded that Kohlberg's hierarchy is biased against some theologically conservative religious individuals. These individuals may have a concern about the broad societal impact of allowing every individual to define his or her own morality, so they favor the role of God and religious communities in defining what is moral. Many conservative religious individuals also consider certain scriptures (e.g., the Koran, the Bible) to be divinely inspired so the religious meaning ascribed to these scriptures sets them apart from human moral principles. Kohlberg's model assumes that there are no such divine resources. Yet in Western cultures many people who can reason at postconventional levels of cognitive development look to divine resources (scriptures, prayer, prophecy and so on) for moral direction.

Summing Up

The development of forgiveness is complex. We have multiple motives for forgiving. Father Jenco is an excellent example.[14] At one point he decided to "annoy his guards with love." He was displaying a vengeful forgiveness (stage 1). At another point he remembered the warning of South African author Alan Paton that "hate is corrosive and that one who hates does terrible things to one's own character and personality."[15] Father Jenco was then motivated to forgive for the reward of catharsis and by guilt over not forgiving, which represent stage 2 in Enright's hierarchy. He remembered how a fellow priest advocated forgiveness (stage 3), and he frequently meditated on Jesus' command to forgive (stage 4). Father Jenco also described being transformed from viewing his captors as enemies to forgiving them as his brothers (stage 6).

This one man was motivated toward forgiveness by personal rewards, by obedience to his God and religious community and by the principle of love. His story of forgiveness does not follow a neat step-by-step sequence of moving from one stage to the next. Rather, each of these motives—the personal, social and spiritual—seems to have interacted to provide multiple dimensions to Father Jenco's forgiveness.

When we forgive, we may think rationally and we may understand and employ forgiveness more easily if we have developed our convictions about why forgiveness is important. Yet there is much more to forgiveness than reason. Reason is one ingredient in a recipe for forgiveness. When mature reasoning about forgiveness is mixed with other ingredients, the combination will be a powerful one that can help us to forgive.

We will look at more of those ingredients in chapters to come. But first we need to add to the recipe, so we will take a step back and think about two ways in which the ingredients, once combined, help create forgiveness. In the next two chapters we will examine *how people change.*

Five

Forgiveness &
Your Response
to Hurts

ORGIVENESS REQUIRES CHANGE—CHANGE IN HOW WE RE-
spond to the hurts we receive. Two words that are crucial
to how we need to change in order to forgive are *repentance* and *transformation*. In this chapter we focus on repentance. In the next chapter we will look at the importance of transformation.

Repentance as a Result of Self-Examination
Repentance is a commitment to abandoning inauthentic or unethical
ways of acting toward other people. I (Mike) recently saw a Russian
film called *Pokaiane* (a Russian word for "repentance"). This film is
set around the death of a small-town Russian mayor, Varlam Aravidze.
After the burial his relatives keep finding his body in their backyards.
Soon they discover that a woman named Ketivan is exhuming the
body daily. She is taken to court to be tried for her bizarre penchant
for digging up the mayor's body.

During the scenes of Ketivan's trial, we realize that this film is no comedy—it is an attack on the life of the Georgian-born Joseph Stalin, a model for the deceased mayor. As it turns out, Ketivan's father was sent to the gulags deep in the forests of Russia. The film contains footage of family members looking for the names of their loved ones carved into the ends of logs that were felled in the forest when the prisoners were forced to work. This was how many victims of Stalin's gulags attempted to communicate to their families.

During her trial, Ketivan's sanity is questioned because her behavior seems pointless and strange. The defendant contends, "Aravidze is not dead."

Seeing his chance, the prosecutor pounces. "Then you believe he's alive?"

She retorts, "Yes he is! For as long as you continue to defend him, he lives on and continues to corrupt society."

The point? For lasting change to occur in Russian society, Russian citizens must repent for the past. Those who abused others must repent, and those who stood by and did nothing must also repent.

In *Pokaiane* we expect Ketivan to be convicted of her crimes, only to find that she indicts everyone else for theirs. Initially, the spotlight of blame is on Ketivan as she is brought to trial. But during the trial everyone, including each member of the audience, is forced to look at his or her own heart. We are forced to grieve over the indifference and bitterness that led to the rise of Stalin's brutality and over the destruction of twenty million Russian citizens.

In the previous four chapters we encouraged you to *think*. We discussed what forgiveness is and is not, and we discussed how good and valuable forgiveness can be for individuals and for our world. We outlined some of the cultural pressures that influence our views of forgiveness and the value that we ascribe to forgiveness. We discussed the importance of nurturing our "moral sense" as a precursor to thinking well about forgiveness. We discussed rational approaches to forgiveness.

But thinking isn't enough. Simply understanding forgiveness will not create lasting change. Neither will moralizing, exhorting or describing how good forgiveness is. Forgiveness requires a fundamental change of heart—a turning away from old ways.

When we want to forgive another person, we usually know who has the problem—the person who injured us. We rarely think that there might be something about which we should repent, or even think differently. Like the Russian people in *Pokaiane* we might be surprised to find that in cases where someone has treated us unjustly we also have some repenting to do. Repentance is a two-way street.

This suggestion might produce outrage: *For what actions are we, the victims, supposed to repent? What thoughts and conclusions are we supposed to reconsider?* The usual reactions that we get to the statement that the victim has some repenting or reconsidering to do are anger and resistance.

Earlier in life, I (Mike) was doing volunteer work for a church. A friend told me that my supervisor was spreading harsh rumors about me to the pastoral staff behind closed doors. I was floored. I had a difficult time believing that this supervisor, who had appeared so benevolent and friendly, could have betrayed me, especially when I perceived my behavior and attitudes to have been above reproach.

It did not take long for me to fan up a fiery indignation. Soon I distrusted every word, look and action that my supervisor directed toward me—and toward anything and anyone that I cared about. I genuinely perceived the man to be abusive and pathological. I even attempted to sour other people's interactions with him. I nurtured elaborate fantasies of revenge and retaliation. I compared my miserable condition to his seemingly triumphant and unavenged life of villainy.

In the midst of my indignation, my friends challenged my views. I was gently poked and prodded into considering the possibility that I needed to examine my own heart. A direct suggestion that I needed to repent of something would have hit me like a bomb. I would have rebelled against it. *Are you saying that I have done something wrong to invite this guy's assault upon my reputation?* Yet my friends' subtle hints made their way onto the back burner of my mind and heart.

Much later, when my outrage had died down, I examined my heart. I discovered that I had deceived myself. In a moment of clarity I realized that I had allowed my suspicion that this man had betrayed me to cloud my judgment, reason and emotion. I did not even bother to investigate the truth of my friend's suggestion that my supervisor had spoken ill of me. I was trying to cope, but I wasn't doing it very successfully.

This set of realizations laid bare my heart. I realized that I had not examined the thinking and acting that I was using to make sense of the imagined betrayal. Soon thereafter it dawned on me that my strategies required dramatic revision if I was ever to forgive. But of what was I to repent?

It is important to repent of the right things. If we attempt to repent of that which does not require repentance, we end up locked in self-made cages of shame. Therapist Sheldon Cashdan tells a story of a client named Celia with whom he was working.[1] Celia had been sexually abused repeatedly by her father during childhood and had never dealt with the pain of these experiences. Cashdan describes how he eventually led Celia into telling her story of the repeated incestuous episodes. He then describes how he discovered Celia's deep and pervasive shame over the offense.

Celia had stored within her heart remorse and shame because of her (wholly inaccurate) perception that somehow she had been responsible for her father's atrocities. In her efforts to repent of the wrong things (like seducing her father), she had created for herself a cage with no door. She could not repent enough for something that she had not done, so she carried inappropriate shame and guilt through much of her life.

Although it would be inappropriate to repent of actions over which we have had no control, there is much of which we can repent productively. If we are to learn to forgive, most of us must repent of the strategies that we use to cope with our hurts and our insistence upon obtaining revenge.

Repentance Requires Changing Our Coping Strategies

Interpersonal hurts create stress. We can think of stress as demands that tax our psychological or physical resources and for which we have few good automatic responses. Because it is somewhat out of the ordinary for us to be seriously hurt by another person, we have few good automatic responses for dealing with the hurt. Stress tells us that we need to do something to get our lives back into balance.

Some stress can be good. It lets us know that we need to make changes, especially in situations that we see as important to our survival or well-being. If we did not feel any stress when we were hurt by others, we would be coldly detached from the world and from other people. *When we are hurt by others, it is supposed to feel stressful.*

We should be concerned, though, about the strategies that we use for coping with the stress of an interpersonal hurt and damaged relationships. How do you cope when a person hurts you unfairly and intentionally? You might brood and sulk, avoid the offender, hold a grudge, try to get revenge, pretend that the offense was not a big deal, make life miserable for the person who hurt you or gossip about the person. Perhaps you blame yourself. Perhaps you blame God. There are probably more options, and some of them appear in exercise 5-1.

Exercise 5-1

Some Strategies That Won't Help You Deal with Hurts

What unhelpful strategies do you use to cope when you have been hurt by someone else? Check all that apply.

☐ Overlook the hurt; pretend it never happened.

☐ Spend a lot of time thinking about how unfair it was.

☐ Plan on getting revenge.

☐ Tell myself that it's no big deal.

☐ Smooth over the conflict.

☐ Realize that he or she did not mean to hurt me.

☐ Use drugs or alcohol to numb the pain.

☐ Overeat.

☐ Try to find someone to replace him or her.

☐ Try to save the relationship at all costs.
☐ Re-create the event in my mind.
☐ Dream about contacting a hit-man.
☐ Become emotionally numb.
☐ Gossip about the person.
☐ Convince myself of how evil he or she is.
☐ Rethink all the aspects of the relationship.
☐ Find new activities to fill up my time.
☐ Badger the person until he or she will talk about it.
☐ Send nasty letters.

If your forgiveness strategies aren't working, then you may want to look for some ways to act differently. But first you might need to repent of your old strategies. Repenting is like making room for new furniture by getting rid of old furniture that you no longer need.

One Saturday afternoon I (Steve) found an unusual way to cope when someone has injured me. Our vacuum was broken, and I reluctantly took it to a vacuum dealer to see about getting it repaired. As I was explaining the problem to the dealer, he abruptly snatched the vacuum out of my hand and quickly looked it over.

"Yeah," he interrupted me, "I know the problem. It'll be $39.95. When do you want to pick it up?"

"Thirty-nine ninety-five? That seems like a lot," I replied.

"That's what it will cost to repair it," he countered.

"I think I'll check some other places," I said as I reached for the vacuum.

As my wife and I walked out the door of the shop, he scoffed, "That piece of junk isn't even worth $39.95!"

Once home I eagerly looked up that vacuum dealer's phone number, then dialed. When I heard the man's unmistakable, whiny voice say "Hello," I offered him a vigorous "Bronx cheer" (also called "raspberry" or "razz"). After hanging up the phone, I turned to see my wife in shock. I was shocked myself. But I gained momentary satisfaction from my way of coping with this encounter (evening the score).

Three Popular, but Ineffective, Coping Strategies

Most people employ ineffective strategies to deal with interpersonal hurts. Three of the most common are (1) holding grudges or entertaining fantasies of revenge, (2) being cynical and (3) assigning the blame for all of our problems in life to our offender. These coping strategies might make a person feel better in the short run, but they often are roadblocks to forgiveness.

Cultivating bitter grudges and fantasies of revenge. In the episode with my supervisor I (Mike) received cold comfort by nurturing my bitterness and fantasies of revenge. They became crutches, even friends. I *liked* them. They were fun. I spent time with them. When I was feeling particularly victimized, fantasies of getting even with my supervisor (usually through dramatically confronting and humiliating him in front of *his* superiors) comforted me.

Somewhere in the depths of our hearts, we get something out of nurturing fantasies of revenge. They keep us from being hurt again by the same person in the same way. They inspire anger, which makes us feel more powerful. They give us the mirage of raising our self-esteem because we are lowering the esteem in which we hold the other person.

Yet such entertainment has a cost. A heavy payment is exacted for the hours that we spend in the cinema of our bitterness and vengeful fantasies. A Chinese proverb says, "The one who pursues revenge should dig two graves"—one grave for the offender, one grave for yourself. Researchers now accept that bitterness, cynicism, mistrust, hostility and revenge take a substantial toll on mental, physical and relational health. Revenge consumes energy. It takes mental and physical fuel to supply energy to the movie house of our vengeful fantasies. And our energy is limited. We don't have the energy to sustain our fantasies of revenge for very long before other parts of our lives begin to die from lack of nourishment.

Susan insisted that she did not have any resentment toward her family members despite sometimes feeling "a little rejected." "I'm just not aware of any anger," she insisted. She was getting a bit tired of her counselor asking about anger.

The counselor tried a different approach. "Do you ever have any daydreams about interactions with your family?" he asked.

"Well, yes . . . I guess so," Susan responded with hesitation. "Sometimes I think about what it would be like to go home and tell the whole family I have a terminal illness."

Revenge fantasies take many forms, but the common denominator is a desire to control or punish those who have hurt you. One way to change fantasies of revenge is to identify how your implicit beliefs about the importance of revenge might keep you locked into your insistence on revenge. Exercise 5-2 can help reveal these beliefs about revenge.

Exercise 5-2

Thoughts That May Underlie Your Desire for Revenge

The desire for revenge can be motivated, at least in part, by one or more of these beliefs:[2]

☐ We must demonstrate that we are not afraid of the person who hurt us.

☐ We must convince our offender that we have greater worth and value than our offender supposedly believes. If we think that the offender's actions were statements about the offender's lack of respect and esteem for us, then the desire to avenge ourselves can be a desire to demonstrate that we have greater value and dignity than the offender believes. *By taking revenge,* we think, *I am able to show my offender that I am not a worm who can be pushed around.*

☐ *If I avenge myself, I will restore my honor.* If we perceive that the offense took away from our value and worth, then our desire to seek vengeance might be based on a desire to restore our self-worth.

☐ If we do not seek revenge, we are condoning the offender's actions. *By not hurting the person who hurt me,* we might think, *I will communicate that I do not care if the offender hurts me again.* We think, *It would be wrong to let my offender get away with hurting me.*

☐ People who do wrong must be punished. We may believe that

through punishing the offender we can help break their callous attitudes toward us and increase the likelihood that they will repent of their hurtful behavior.

Of the people who have hurt you (identified in chapter one), think of one person upon whom you desire to wreak revenge. Examine your thoughts. See if you can detect beliefs that contribute to your desire for revenge and thus your inability to forgive. Based on what you know about forgiveness, consider how forgiveness can accomplish the same goals that you are trying to accomplish through a desire for revenge.

Being cynical. When we are intentionally and severely hurt by another person, our view of the world tends to change. In our assumptions about life, most of us carry around an expectation, or script, that life is basically fair. This "just world" script may contain beliefs such as these:

- ☐ "Do unto others as you would have them do unto you."
- ☐ "What goes around comes around."
- ☐ "They'll get what's coming to them."[3]

When we are hurt by others we question our just-world script. We see people who did not follow the Golden Rule. We find that offenders, abusers, racists or betrayers have not received what is coming to them. When the just-world script is challenged, we may conclude that the world is not just. The script is shredded, our bubble is broken. We begin to think that the entire world is unjust. We become cynical.

Even people we once viewed as neutral or benevolent may appear to have ulterior motives. As a result of our shattered just-world script, we may assume that significant others in our lives are motivated to the same forms of betrayal that we experienced at the hands of our offenders. This can lead to distortions in our interpersonal world that extend far beyond the relationship with the offender.

Our just-world scripts may be changed when we're badly hurt. Yet the real world is much more complex than our altered just-world scripts would suggest. In some ways offenses against us are like alarm clocks that force us to face the fact that the world is not completely just. But *there is some justice.* It would also be inaccurate to assume that life is completely blind to issues of justice and injustice.

To break out of the cynicism that our shattered just-world script creates, we must search for examples of justice in the present. We must hope that somewhere in the future our desire for justice will be fulfilled. We must also work for justice in our communities right now. We see things differently when we try to make a difference.

Cultivating biased assignments of responsibility. Some people seem to blame their offenders for all their problems. That is especially true in troubled marriages. But good counselors do not allow one spouse to be pinned with all the blame because it makes marital problems worse. Similarly, forgiveness is often hampered by too much focus on the offender's responsibility.

Timothy Boyd has suggested an exercise called the "barometer of responsibility" for helping people measure their contribution to a conflict.[4] We have adapted this exercise in exercise 5-3.

Exercise 5-3
Barometer of Responsibility

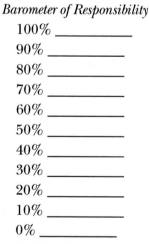

1. Write "now" beside the point on the barometer that represents the extent to which you believe your offender is responsible for the difficulties in your life.

2. Consider the amount of energy you have invested in ineffective strategies for dealing with your hurts (such as entertaining fantasies

of revenge, bitterness, upward comparisons and altered just-world scripts). Can you see that you, too, contributed to your current problems? Does your perception of your offender's relative contribution to your current difficulties change? If so, write "intermediate" at this new point on the barometer.

3. Consider the contribution of other factors (such as your current mood, the mistakes of other people, a lousy job, a horrible boss, financial problems) to your current problems. Can you see that your difficulties are not wholly due to the person who hurt you plus your own involvement? Does your perception of your offender's relative contribution to your life situation change? If so, write "new" at this new point on the barometer.

No excuses for the offense. We do not wish to diffuse the responsibility that the offender must bear for the ways that he or she injured you, especially in cases where the offense was severe. But as you know in moments of calm reflection, the offense is not the only important event in your history, and it is not the sole contributor to the struggles and difficulties of life. By reminding yourself of this truth, you can attain a more accurate *felt* estimate of the relative impact of the offense. This more accurate estimate will help you forgive.

Summing Up

For the people in the movie *Pokaiane*, putting Stalin's memory to rest was not possible until they had parted ways with their own methods of coping with his crimes—their own complacency, insensitivity and denial. They had to repent of these ways of living if they wanted to be changed by forgiveness.

I also had to repent before I was able to forgive my supervisor for his betrayal. By repenting I learned some things about myself. I learned about my suspiciousness and tendency to hold grudges. I learned that I too often jump to conclusions, rehearse the hurts in my mind and nurture fantasies of revenge. Until I looked at these and other ineffective strategies for handling my hurt, I could not forgive my supervisor. After considering and rejecting my own coping strategies and looking for new behaviors, I made room in my heart for forgiveness. Repentance is difficult, but it allows forgiveness to grow.

In this chapter we talked about repentance as *abandoning old coping strategies*. Without eliminating the unhelpful responses to our interpersonal hurts, we cannot develop the long-lasting habits, thoughts, behaviors and emotions that will lead us into becoming more forgiving people. Repentance also has a positive side—replacing old ways of acting with new ways of acting. We will discuss new ways of acting as we go along.

S i x

Forgiveness &
Transformation

A s an athlete I (Ev) am okay. I'm not great at any given sport, but I'm probably better than average at most. I couldn't always say that I was an "okay athlete."

As a coordinated child, I excelled at backyard baseball. But when I tried to play on a little league team, I struck out the first two times at bat and was benched in the final inning. I couldn't face the team as a failure. I was embarrassed. So I bypassed free-agency and retired from my baseball career at age eleven.

When I tried basketball, Michael Jordan's reputation as greatest ever was safe. I had a minus two-inch vertical leap. And at five-foot-two and ninety-five pounds in junior high, I figured I was never going to play professional football. Good decision. I graduated from college at five-eleven, 145 pounds. When I turned sideways, I disappeared. (Regrettably, I no longer have this problem.)

As puberty slammed into my body at age fourteen or fifteen, I began to have coordination problems. I remember walking up the stairs at high school and, for no apparent reason except perhaps a breeze, falling against the stairwell. That was the final straw. Something snapped in my mind. I saw myself as hopelessly uncoordinated. I had gone through a transformation.

After that, it didn't matter that in high school, college and the Navy I competed in basketball, volleyball, handball, racquetball and tennis. I still saw myself as a bumbling athletic failure.

That changed in one day when I was thirty-six years old. I actually won an open men's tennis tournament in Richmond. It was the first tournament I ever won that, in my mind, counted. It transformed the way I looked at my ability in sports. Instead of thinking about my losses, I began to think more about my victories. I revisited my sports history and revised it. I suddenly could see my adolescent lack of coordination as a normal event in a body that was rapidly changing instead of proof-positive of my permanent klutziness.

In a similar way, forgiveness is a transformation. If you forgive a friend for a grievous hurt, you look at the friend through radically different eyes.

What Do Transformations Have in Common?

Musical ability. I have thought about the changing points in various areas of my life. One occurred in my self-concept as a trumpet player. I was filled with confidence as I played a trumpet solo in the state-wide eighth grade solo contest. Halfway through the solo, though, my lip spasmodically tightened and the trumpet squealed as if in pain—then again two-thirds through the song and once again at the climactic crescendo. At the end of the performance I walked off the stage, locked myself in a warm-up room and cried. It seemed to be the thing to do at the time.

My director eventually coaxed me out and escorted me to see the judge, who gave me his evaluation orally instead of in writing. He awarded me a superior rating and uttered some calming platitudes about nervousness, which I refused to listen to. I knew, despite what anyone said, that I was a terrible trumpet player.

My director scheduled me to play my solo at the spring concert—in front of an auditorium full of people, including my parents. I was not a happy camper. But my director was insistent—he did not care whether I wanted to perform or not. So, knowing that the world would quickly find out my incompetence, I dreaded that concert.

The night of the concert, though, I played almost flawlessly. My outlook on my musical ability changed as dramatically as turning on a light switch. As I walked off the stage with applause ringing in my ears, I knew that I could be imperfect and still have people appreciate what I did.

Marriage. Since I was a virgin when I married Kirby, I doubted whether I would actually be able to have sex. I faced the marriage bed with anticipation and terror, so when Kirby and I arrived at the motel I immediately attacked. Kirby wriggled out of my grasp, though. She had in mind a more romantic way to consummate our marriage than a quickie to ease my concerns.

Throughout dinner I worried about making love. I could hardly eat. Then we walked on the beach, and I confessed my fears to Kirby. Finally we went to our room and made love. It was beautiful. I'd like to tell you that my mind was completely on pleasing my beloved, but that wouldn't be correct. I was relieved. Unburdened. Things would never be the same again.

Becoming a Christian. When I married Kirby she was a Christian and I wasn't. I always wanted to please God but could never figure out where Jesus fit into the picture. So in that first year of adjustment to marriage, we tussled about our religious differences.

Eventually Kirby and I attended a marriage enrichment course at a local church. During that course I got to know Pastor Tom Allport, a roly-poly teddy-bear of a man with a ready smile and obvious love for everyone, even—to my surprise—me, a committed unbeliever in what he most valued.

It was love that won me over. I could see real love in both Kirby and Pastor Tom. I finally accepted Jesus' love for me as reflected in them. Suddenly my entire experience of myself was transformed. I felt simultaneously free and accepted. I felt joined to others more intimately than ever before, yet simultaneously independent of rules that had previously bound me. The fences had abruptly moved back, revealing a wide-open, beautiful country.

Lessons from Examining My Transformations

Thinking about these turning points in my life, I came to some conclusions. For the most part, my life has progressed in a relatively continuous fashion. I feel like much the same person I was in my teens, thirty-five years ago. But in a few areas—my self-image as an athlete, as a musician, as a lover of my wife and as a Christian—there have been substantial turning points. Those turning points set me on new courses. Some dramatically changed the way I looked at my life. In an instant I was changed, never to see the world the same way again.

Not all transformations occur instantly. Some happen over time and are discovered unexpectedly. We drive all night and suddenly realize that dawn has come. For example, when I discovered that someone could love me—Kirby—I didn't experience a cataclysmic event. I just opened my eyes to a new day.

Some transformations spin us one-hundred-eighty degrees and shove us in the opposite direction. Others turn us one degree and only years later do we see the vast difference that one degree made.

Although each transformation took place in one area of my life, each affected other areas. My new self-confidence as a tennis player spread to my swimming. Before I won that tennis tournament, I never swam. (I was one of the few people to get out of the Navy without passing the swimming test. I was sick that day.) After winning the tennis tournament, I began to swim laps.

Forgiveness is a turning point. Sometimes it is stopping dramatically, skidding to a halt and running in the opposite direction. At other times it is simply veering aside. In either case the change lands us in a different place than we started—like Dorothy opening her black-and-white Kansas door into multicolored Oz.

Abrupt transformations sound like magic, not very scientific. But in this book we have tried to present an interesting approach to forgiveness that is based on science. *Are* abrupt transformations scientific?

Lessons of Science

The remaking of physics. Traditionally progress in science was thought to occur by the gradual accumulation of data—scientific brick upon brick until an edifice was complete. In 1962 a philosopher of science, Thomas Kuhn, proposed a new way of thinking about changes in science. He proclaimed that many major changes occurred through revolution, not evolution.[1]

"Normal science," Kuhn said, operates by accumulation of scientific facts. Experiments are done not hoping to disprove a theory but seeking to support it. When experiments don't come out as expected, as sometimes happens, scientists are upset. They redesign and replicate the experiments to find what the problem was. As scientists solve little problems, science progresses.

But sometimes pesky problems accumulate. If scientists can't solve the problems, the field can experience a crisis. Problems can be dealt with in one of three ways: (1) someone can eventually explain what is happening within "normal scientific" understanding; (2) scientists can tacitly agree to forget the problem until there are better methods to address it; or (3) someone can propose a new way of looking at the field, as when Newton and Einstein reconceptualized the physics of their respective day.

Personal problems as scientific revolutions. Let's apply Kuhn's observations about science to examining life. We each develop a way of looking at life. When our view of life is working well, it's "normal living" (analogous to "normal science"). We are able to predict what is going to happen, and our predictions seem to work out. Sometimes, though, our predictions go awry. We think people will like us, but they reject us. We think we can control our moods, but we get depressed and can't seem to shake the sadness. We think we have a habit under control, but we find that it is an addiction. We think we can control our children, but they continually defy us.

Each of those predictions is a failed personal experiment. Like personal scientists, we keep trying to solve our problems in the ways that have always worked for us. When those ways don't work, we often seek help from a friend. If the friend can't help, we seek help from family members, clergy and perhaps a mental health professional.[2] These helpers try to help us solve our problems within our usual way of viewing ourselves, others and the world. If that doesn't work, though, we sometimes have a personal crisis. We need a transformation to break out of crisis.

That transformation might be dramatic, such as a conversion to vegetarianism, a different religion or social activism. Or the transformation might be a renewal of earlier enthusiasm, such as a renewal of Christian faith or recommitment to a profession. Either a one-hundred-eighty-degree or a one-degree transformation can knock us for a loop, jarring us from a personal crisis into a more productive direction.

Interpersonal injuries as scientific revolutions. Normal interactions with a friend are normal science. A betrayal, a rejection, a violation of expectations by the friend is a failed interpersonal experiment. At first we might ignore the failure, hoping it was a once-only happening. But if problems continue, they can lead to a crisis in friendship. Unforgiveness is a loss of faith in the relationship—a crisis.

To resolve the crisis that occurs when another person hurts us, we can do the same things that scientists do to resolve scientific crises. We can (1) ignore the problem, (2) declare that the problem is one that will somehow heal in the future and stop worrying about it now or (3) be transformed by looking at the relationship differently. The third option, forgiveness, is a scientific revolution in a relationship.

Chaos Theory

Even now modern science is in crisis. Science simply cannot explain some phenomena. Have you ever wondered why weather forecasters cannot predict the weather accurately more than two days into the future? It is because weather is a noncontinuous system. A system is continuous when a change in one area produces a related change in another. If you add a hundred pounds to a camel's back, its back sways one inch. Add five hundred pounds, it sways five inches. Then add a straw and the camel's back collapses. The system changed from continuous to noncontinuous.[3]

When two weather systems flow past each other, small changes can produce vast, noncontinuous transformations in local conditions. A few miles' difference may yield either a cool, sunny, high-pressure day or a blustery, snow storm. The path of the weather doesn't act completely at random—it won't snow in July in Richmond, Virginia. There are limits on how unpredictable a system can be.

Practical applications of chaos theory. A couple of recent applications of the science of chaos have been suggested in psychology. Falling in love has been looked at as a noncontinuous event. People meet, feel an attraction and start to share activities. For many people, though, at some point the relationship suddenly changes—they are in love. Love is a noncontinuous change in their relationship.

The dissolution of marriages, too, has been seen as a noncontinuous transformation. John Gottman, a psychologist at the University of Washington, studied more than two thousand couples intensively over a period of twenty-five years.[4] He found that when marital relations go bad, they gradually worsen. A little disagreement here leads to a criticism there, which leads to a bigger disagreement and so forth. At some point, though, things dramatically change.

Gottman thinks he knows the straw that breaks the marriage's back. When the ratio of positive to negative interactions falls lower than five to one, people start to think negatively about their marriage. Having fewer than five positive interactions for every negative interaction seems to be akin to putting dark glasses on the partners, making them look at the negatives rather than the positives. If the positive interactions don't quickly increase, the marriage is in grave danger.

Forgiveness and chaos theory. Forgiveness and unforgiveness are also noncontinuous transformations. In a normal relationship, a person receives an unbearable hurt, and the relationship changes from good to bad or from bad-but-tolerable to intolerable. A noncontinuous transformation occurs.

In normal circumstances, relationships operate under the principle of forbearance. Forbearance involves ignoring the inevitable hurts that occur in any relationship. If the hurt cannot be ignored, it is generally forgiven quickly and forgotten. Generally, love—willfully valuing the other person—characterizes the relationship. Participants in the relationship see each other through rose-colored glasses. Negatives are minimized and positives are attended to. Feelings of hope that the relationship will be maintained at a positive level characterize both people, who are happy with the relationship.

We have illustrated this in figure 6-1. At the beginning of the graph, the person focuses on the mountaintops and ignores the valleys in the relationship.

No Middle Ground

Figure   6-1.

The relationship, however, may go bad. Perhaps a traumatic event occurs. Friends might disagree over an important issue or a married person might discover a partner's secret affair. That big event might push the person beyond a threshold. A threshold is the bottom plate of a doorway, signifying entry into a new room. The new room is different. The threshold of hurt signifies a drastic change in the relationship.

In other cases the threshold may be reached more gradually. Perhaps over time small hurts accumulate, like weight added to the back of the camel. Finally, the straw breaks the relationship. Or perhaps a period of high stress might lower one or both partner's threshold, and an event, which under normal circumstances would have little effect, could take on catastrophic proportions. The threshold is crossed, and the entire flavor of the relationship changes—like adding salt to formerly sweet tea. The people don dark glasses, seeing only the darker side of each interaction. Negative interactions increase and positive interactions decrease. Feelings of discouragement, dissatisfaction and depression characterize the relationship.

"I just didn't see it coming," Sonya recounted to her counselor with tears streaming down her face. "After eleven years of marriage, I can't believe he could leave without warning. Our marriage had its problems, but there were no major conflicts. One day we were arguing about the money he spent on his fishing trip, and he said, 'That's it! I'm finished!' That was a year ago, and now he's filing for divorce," she explained.

Once the dark glasses of unforgiveness are donned, the relationship will almost certainly deteriorate unless another transformation occurs that moves the person from bitter to better—forgiveness. Forgiveness is a transformation that frees the one who was hurt (see figure 6-1). Thoughts, feelings and acts of kindness are freed like a child frees a captive bird.

In one of Elsie Homelund Minarik's Little Bear children's books, Little Bear finds a robin with a broken wing. He nurses it back to health, but it doesn't thrive. It can't fly in its cage, and it can't sing to mark the territory it doesn't patrol. Finally, Little Bear must free the robin. It is overjoyed because now it can enjoy the life it was meant to live. The robin returns year after year to see Little Bear, and so do its children.

Forgiveness is freeing the robin. Negative judgments are condemned to irrelevance. Anger, resentment and unforgiveness vanish
into the stratosphere. Forbearance returns.

Unforgiveness Is a Wall

"Something there is that doesn't love a wall," wrote Robert Frost in
"Mending Wall," his poem about the Cold War tensions with the Soviet
Union.[5] "I let my neighbor know beyond the hill; / And on a day we
meet to walk the line / And set the wall between us once again." The
forces of nature come against a wall and erode it. A stone falls, then
another. But the neighbors walk the wall together, keeping the wall
between them. The neighbor says, "Good fences make good neighbors," whereas the narrator says, "Before I built a wall I'd ask to know
/ What I was walling in or out."

We try to erode the wall of unforgiveness as the elements erode a
natural wall—gradually. Our philosophy is like Lewis Smedes's:
"When the mortar of hate goes, the wall [of unforgiveness] eventually
crumbles."[6] But "eventually" can be a long time, and we can allow our
life to pass in bitterness while waiting for unforgiveness to erode. The
forces of nature may be against unforgiveness, but we walk the wall
and replace the stones of anger, hate and unforgiveness even as we
sense the mortar wash away. We put enormous energy into maintaining our unforgiveness. It makes us feel stronger and empowered. It
makes us feel righteous. So we rebuild the wall. "Good fences make
good neighbors," we mumble under our breath.

The Berlin Wall is an example of unforgiveness. The wall was erected
and guards stood on each side, patrolling the wall and the neutral zone
between East and West Berlin. No people were allowed to cross from
East to West for fear that they would not come back. In the same way, in
unforgiveness we don't allow acts of kindness toward the person who
offended us because we fear that they won't be returned.

Yet look at the fate of the Berlin Wall. People decided abruptly that
it had to come down. People did not simply ignore it—a transforma-

tion occurred. They kicked down the wall, pounded it into chips and dust with sledgehammers and dismantled it piece by piece.

Summing Up

In relationships, hurts may build up. A final hurt can change the entire relationship, making it appear hopeless and completely negative—like the straw that broke the camel's back. Like scientific revolutions and chaotic transformations of weather, relationships can quickly flip-flop into unforgiveness.

The good news, though, is that forgiveness can change the relationship just as quickly. A bleak and hopeless relationship can be transformed by a single event—such as one person forgiving the other or one person experiencing a large change in his or her life. A little psychological "push"—as delicate as the sweep of a butterfly's wings—at just the right time and place can produce a cascade of forgiveness and change. Ponder these changes by studying exercise 6-1.

Exercise 6-1

Sudden Transformations in Relationships

Forbearance: Business as Usual

☐ Love

☐ Rose-colored glasses (focus on the positive)

☐ High ratio of positive-to-negative interactions

☐ Forbearance (little hurts overlooked, quickly forgiven and forgotten)

☐ High hopes

☐ Feelings of happiness and satisfaction

Threshold: Plunge into Unforgiveness

☐ Accumulation of small hurts or one large hurt pushes the person over the edge

☐ Ratio of positive-to-negative interactions drops below five to one

☐ Dark-colored glasses (focus on the negative)

☐ Hope is lost

☐ Feelings of discouragement, dissatisfaction and depression

☐ Chaos reigns

Retransformation: Restoration of Relationship

☐ Someone takes the initiative to forgive

☐ The forgiver changes

☐ New rose-colored glasses

☐ More positive, less negative behavior

☐ Hope reblooms

☐ The other person eventually notices the changes

☐ Forgiveness may spread to the other person

☐ Forbearance returns

In the past two chapters we examined how people change in order to forgive: forgiveness occurs through repentance, and forgiveness occurs through transformation. In the following chapters we will examine the specific domains of who we are that must change if we are to become better at forgiving.

Exercise 6-2

Reflect on Your Successful Past Experiences with Forgiveness

Thus far we have concentrated on difficulties you may have had in forgiving others. Most likely, though, you have successfully forgiven others many times. Ponder the times you forgave someone who hurt you. List occurences you can remember which you forgave. (Those might be hard to remember, because when we forgive we often have a sense of closure and may not easily remember the occasions later.)

For the events you can remember, describe how the forgiveness took place. What did you do when you forgave? Did the experience seem like a noncontinuous or a continuous change?

Once you have described several experiences, see if you can detect a pattern. Were most episodes of forgiveness continuous or noncontinuous?

One thing you can learn by examining successful instances of forgiving is that *forgiveness can happen*. If you are having difficulty forgiving someone now, take heart in the knowledge that you have forgiven in the past and can forgive in the future.

Seven

Forgiveness, the Brain & the Mind

WHY ARE WE SOMETIMES SWEPT LIKE A BOBBING FISHING boat into a hurricane of unforgiveness? We struggle to forgive, leaning into the awesome wind as hurt and hate slosh over the gunwales and threaten to swamp us. We creep ahead, are blown back.

Then we try to forgive. The sea is calm, and we float serenely. We think we have conquered the storm, but then the eye passes, and we are blown back into the destructive force of unforgiveness, hate and bitterness.

Why is forgiveness so hard? Why does hatred so often return when we think we have banished it? Why do hurtful memories intrude into our thoughts, imaginations and emotions?

At one level the answers lie within the operation of brain and mind. Both unforgiveness and forgiveness involve the way our mental and emotional experience is organized. If we understand the mental ebb and flow of unforgiveness and forgiveness, we can understand why it is sometimes so difficult to forgive.

John's Tragedy

"My father never understood me." John was fifty-three. His counselor had heard about John's father six times in eight counseling sessions and wondered how often John told someone about his father's cruelty.

"I could never do anything right in his eyes. He pushed me to excel, drove me, berated me when I relaxed and then criticized me for not achieving what he expected. It was always 'You've got to work harder, John. Do your best, John. You can do better, John.' "

One year earlier, at the peak of his power, John ran a huge corporation. He was self-assured, handled conflicts with employees daily, negotiated million-dollar deals. His father's drive had paid off in John's success. He lived on a prison ship of luxury, rowing to the unremitting cadence of a long-dead father who could not be silenced: "You've got to work harder, John. Do your best, John. You can do better, John."

But John was miserable. "I couldn't take the sound of his voice."

One night John blew a neat, powder-seared hole in his head with a small-caliber pistol. He destroyed brain tissue and lived. After a remarkable recovery, he entered counseling because he did not want, again, to feel the powerlessness of being compulsively driven to succeed.

"I could always hear my father's voice. I was an anxious perfectionist, eager to please, hard working, but never able to measure up."

Then one day came a breakthrough. John forgave his father. "Suddenly, after an argument with my own oldest son, I understood that my father wasn't trying to drive me crazy. He loved me and wanted the best for me, like I wanted the best for my son. I knew that in my heart," said John, "not merely in my head."

Determined to forgive and forget, he vowed to stop thinking about the past. He worked at it. But one month later his hard-won changes had slid back into the ooze of unforgiveness.

"Why didn't it last? Why was my forgiveness temporary? At first it seemed like it would last forever. But I had flashbacks. I'd remember one particular time when I was a teen. I worked for my father at his meat packing company. He sent me into the freezer one day to organize it. I suppose it hadn't been organized in years. I spent three days, eight hours a day in sub-zero temperatures, shifting boxes and gritting my teeth as I scraped frost off boxes to see what was supposed to be inside. When I finally finished, I called my father down to see. He looked at the freezer for about ten seconds and then pointed to a frozen steak that had fallen out of a box somewhere onto the floor. He said, 'How many more of those did you lose?' and then walked off. That sums up our relationship."

"Besides the occasional flashbacks, I did okay except for a few times. I'd stop for a drink on the way home from work, and I'd get to drinking and thinking—playing the reruns in the late-late show of my mind—and I'd get angry all over again. It was as if I had never forgiven him at all."

The Brain

Why didn't John's forgiveness last? We find part of the answer in John's reliance on his rational mind. There is much more to forgiveness than simply the ability to think rationally.

The brain is made up of three parts: the brainstem, which governs basic survival; the midbrain limbic system, a web of structures that govern emotion, motivation and much of the memory; and the cortex (of two hemispheres), which directs sensation, motor behavior and higher order thinking. The left cortical hemisphere primarily (but not exclusively) controls language, and the right cortical hemisphere primarily (but not exclusively) controls visual imagery. The differing physical structure of different parts of the brain is responsible for rational thought, images and emotions. The interconnections of those thoughts, images and emotions at conscious or unconscious levels make up the mind. It is the complexity of those interconnections that makes forgiveness so difficult to experience and maintain.

John's brain has kept him embroiled in unforgiveness. His left cortex rationally understands himself as one who was irreparably hurt by his father. His right cortex supplies images of his troubled relationship with his father. His emotions were stirred up when he was hurt time and again, and those emotions burned permanent memories into his mind. All parts of his brain feed information to each other. His whole brain works together to keep him stuck in unforgiveness.

Anger can captivate a person and imprison him or her in unforgiveness and bitterness. Sergeant Jacob deShazer was a bombardier in World War II. His plane was shot down over Japan, and deShazer was imprisoned in a Japanese prisoner-of-war camp. As so often happens in war, the guards were cruel, and deShazer soon began to hate his guards. He fantasized choking the life from them. His rage reproduced itself larger and larger with each day until he lived for a single reason—to exact revenge on the guards who had made life miserable for him.

DeShazer's anger was working overtime, pumping out neurochemicals and hormones that intruded into the cortex and directed his thoughts continually to revenge. He was in an emotional and mental prison that was as constricting as were the metal bars that penned him into a five-foot-square cell.[1]

Like Jacob deShazer, John was imprisoned, and he could feel the bonds of unforgiveness and bitterness choking the life out of him. A bullet to the brain seemed the only way out. But now John has hope—hope that he can somehow find the understanding to prevent being strangled again by his mind.

The Mind

The mind predicts. How does the mind organize our memories? To function well in the world we each need to be able to predict the future. When the alarm rings in the morning, we need to predict that punching the switch will turn it off. We need to predict that if we swing our legs over the edge of the bed they will touch the floor and not cast us into a bottomless pit. We must predict the future during every waking minute if we are to act.

To predict, our mind takes input from left brain, right brain and midbrain and integrates words, images and emotions at conscious and unconscious levels. Consciousness devises rational explanations for experience, and those rational explanations focus our eyes on certain experiences so that we can predict. For instance, John created an understanding of his life—a "story"—that gave his father's words a central role. John saw himself as driven by his father's criticism and demands, and from the time he formulated that understanding of his experience he behaved as if it were true.

John recalled vivid visual images of his father's fault-finding in the freezer. Those images were consistent with John's rational story. Like John, we all consciously recall and rehearse important visual images that seem to describe more than a simple memory. Like a full-scale model—a prototype—that an engineer makes to demonstrate how a machine will operate, those images are *mental prototypes* of other experiences. For John, the vividly remembered freezer episode was a prototype of his interactions with his father.

John reacts emotionally to his story of victimization and the images of his father's rejection, both of which bolster a cycle of unforgiveness. John could forgive easier and have it last longer if he changed his prototypical image or refused to indulge it. Yet he believes that the image is accurate and true, and he keeps reimagining it. It hurts to think about the rejection, but he returns to it repeatedly. It is like eating jalapeño peppers. It hurts, but in a way that John might not even understand fully, it feels good.

The mind protects itself from threat. The mind protects itself in a way similar to how the body protects itself from threat. When you have a sore finger, you are careful not to strike it and reinjure it. You know that it is especially tender, so you alter your normal behavior to keep from knocking it. Imagine organizing your entire life so that you protect yourself from physical pain.

People with back pain do it all the time. They don't lift heavy objects, they place their hands on their thighs when they bend over, and they learn different ways to stoop and lift. Their tender back is never far from their mind, and they change their behavior and lifestyle to insure that they never injure their back again.

The mind is similar. Some emotions are unpleasant, and we try to avoid them. We avoid thoughts, images and situations that might lead to feeling those emotions. We organize our mental life to avoid particular types of psychological pain. *The unconscious mind protects itself out of fear and pride.* Fear might prevent us from examining our hurts.

☐ We might fear that thinking about our pain will reopen old wounds and cause us to bleed again.

☐ We might fear that we'll lose love. If we admit that someone hurt us, we think that we'll reject him or her.

☐ We might fear that we'll get angry and lose control. That is especially true of men. Terrified that their anger will be unleashed, they withdraw into a chamber of silence.

Pride might prevent us from examining our hurts too.

☐ We might be too proud to admit that we can be weak enough to be hurt by someone.

☐ We might be too proud to admit our weakness and vulnerability. Hurts might disrupt our sense of self. If we admit that our boundaries can be pierced, we may feel weak and vulnerable.

☐ We might be too proud to admit that we could be wrong.

John blames his father for his troubles. The louder John talks, the more he makes himself believe that his father made him the way he was yesterday and the way he is today. John paints his father in darkest black hues so that he doesn't face his own weaknesses. When John's counselor asked him how he might have contributed to his father's critical, judgmental lack of acceptance, he got angry with the counselor: "You're just like him. You can't understand me. You have to find a flaw. You blame me instead of allowing my father to take the rightful blame for what he did to me all my life. I was a kid. He was the adult. He should have known better."

John can't even consider that he might have done anything to contribute to his father's criticism. Wounded, he unconsciously protects the wound. Bleeding the blood of honest self-examination is too traumatic for John. It is easier to attack. When John consciously tries to give up unforgiveness, his unconscious mind drags him back.

Holding onto unforgiveness is a protective defense. But whereas defenses protect, they also constrict. A castle that defends people from attack simultaneously confines people. If the limitations are ultimately harmful or if the actual threat is mild (even though it is perceived as being great), then the castle needs to be abandoned.

It is not easy to abandon our mental castle. When we try to exit by the door of rational thought, emotion drags us back. When we try to escape by changing the prototypical images, our unconscious defenses wall us in.

Exercise 7-1

Exploring the Castle

It takes courage to poke into the dark corners of a castle. Pick one of the hurts you identified in chapter one and answer these questions:

1. What are you saying to yourself that justifies holding onto the hurt? Are you saying that the person who hurt you is a terrible person? Are you thinking that you deserve better? Identify as many thoughts as you can.

2. Does an image recur? Do you replay a scene on the late show in your mind? What happens in the scene? Write your description.

3. What emotions do you feel as you think about the person and the hurtful act? Usually people feel a mixture of emotions. Strong ones, such as anger, tend to mask the more muted ones, such as distress over being hurt or disappointment because a relationship did not meet your expectations. Think about all the emotions you feel concerning the hurt.

4. Examine your defenses. How do you protect yourself from pain? Do you solicit support by showing others your distress? Defenses are natural protection that we all employ, but they slow down healing. Don't rush in by trying to knock down the defensive walls all at once. Sometimes those walls serve a good purpose. Sometimes, though,

they wall in a moral infection. You'll need to decide how they are working for you.

5. What other barriers prevent forgiveness? Is pride at work?

At this point don't try to muster up an attitude of forgiveness. Simply explore your thoughts, imagination, feelings and defenses. Later you may want to try to change your experience.

Locked into Unforgiveness

Unforgiveness is like a thorny pyrocanthra bush, sending runners underground to emerge as other wicked, thorny pyrocanthra sprouts scattered around the original bush. Even when we root out the original pyrocanthra bush, the runners remain in an underground web, and where we least expect it another little bush pops up to stab us.

The thorny runners of unforgiveness form a web throughout our unconscious mind. Hate, anger, bitterness and unforgiveness can pop up (into consciousness), stimulated by a thought, image or feeling. When we tell ourselves a story about how we are a victim of undeserved hurt, anger and righteous indignation empower us. The story we tell ourselves requires continued suffering, but it also helps us predict the future and protect ourselves (we hope) from a similar hurt.

So when new information—perhaps a kindness done by the one who hurt us—tries to contradict our "story" from the rational left cortex, we smother it amid a matted blanket of contrary reasoning. We fear that to change our familiar story of unforgiveness leaves us less able to predict the future and protect ourselves.

When we develop a new image of ourselves as potentially forgiving, the prototypical unforgiving image overpowers and crushes it. When the spark of a new, more positive emotional experience ignites, soggy old emotional experiences snuff it out.

How to Forgive

If we want to change from being unforgiving to being forgiving, we must change our mental and emotional experience. That is more complex than simply deciding to forgive or having one emotional experience of forgiveness or having one memory transformed dramatically. Changing requires that we transform our thoughts, images, emotions and memories—all of these—lest we relapse into unforgiveness.

Moving from unforgiveness to forgiveness requires courage. Robert Coles, in a lecture about his experience with the civil rights movement, related the story of Ruby, one of the first black children to integrate the southern schools in the 1960s.[2] Coles, a Harvard child psychiatrist and professor, was stationed in New Orleans and had the opportunity to meet with Ruby regularly to discuss her experiences. He describes the climate of tension, where each day a black child in a white dress walked calmly to school surrounded by federal marshals in gray coats to protect her from a jeering, taunting crowd of adults.

One day Ruby stopped before entering the school and said something aloud. The crowd went wild with anger, and for a while it looked as if there would be violence, for the crowd perceived Ruby to be talking back to them.

Later Coles interviewed Ruby. "What happened at school today?"

"Nothing happened."

"The teacher said you said something to the crowd."

"I didn't."

"Ruby, your lips were moving. What was going on?"

"I was talking to God," she said.

Each day, when the federal marshals began the walk to the school, Ruby stopped and, before coming into contact with the crowd, said a prayer. That day she had forgotten to pray. When she neared the building and heard the crowd, it reminded her. So she stopped and prayed, and the crowd mistook it for insolence.

"What did you pray?" asked Coles.

"I say, 'Father forgive them, for they don't know what they're doing.' " When Coles urged her, she went on: "When Jesus was looking at that mob, that's what he prayed. . . . It was my grandma's idea. And it was my mama's idea. And it was my dad's idea. And it's my idea too."

That's the type of courage required by forgiveness.

Forgiveness doesn't happen all at once. As we might expect, most people don't tear down all of their protective walls instantaneously. They take down one set of walls first and, over time, remove other levels of protection. Some people take down the rational walls first. They see the need to forgive and decide rationally to forgive. Other people may experience a transformed prototypical image. For instance, John might learn to imagine his father pointing out the frozen steak that he missed, and then John might imagine himself criticizing his own son. By connecting his prototypical image of his father with an empathic image of himself, John might lose some of his bitterness.

Exercise 7-2

Talking to Yourself as a Way of Promoting Forgiveness

To move from unforgiveness to forgiveness you must change your thoughts. Some of today's most effective counseling techniques involve catching ourselves talking negatively to ourselves. Donald Meichenbaum, founder of cognitive-behavior modification, recommends that you try to change your negative internal dialogue in five steps.[3]

First, recognize when you are speaking negatively with yourself. Second, interrupt the conversation. Third, substitute more positive thinking. Fourth, reward yourself for making the change. Fifth, reassure yourself that you will have a positive impact if you persist in trying to change your thinking and deal with the thoughts that cast doubt on the effectiveness of your efforts.

Use this kind of self-talk to modify unforgiveness. Follow the same steps:

1. Recognize when you are speaking bitterly or having unforgiving thoughts.

2. Interrupt that talk or those thoughts.

3. Substitute an understanding that you have hurt others in the past and that you need forgiveness. Try to see things from the other person's point of view and empathically feel with the person who hurt you.

4. Congratulate yourself for any change. Don't wait until you are perfectly forgiving; that time of perfection probably will never come. Reward progress.

5. Reassure yourself that you are freeing the other person from bonds of being hated or unforgiven, even as you are freed.

Still other people may have an emotional experience, and the defensive walls crumble from inside. Protective walls of unforgiveness can come down like the Berlin Wall. Apparently the Berlin Wall was as firm as ever, but change had occurred over time from within the East German system, and one day people were hammering at the wall, taking pieces of it away with them as souvenirs.

Other walls are removed after delicate negotiations between countries. Meetings between Jews and Arabs have continued for years. Beginning with the Camp David accord in 1978 between Egypt and Israel, both sides have come countless times to the bargaining table to remove the walls of violence, hostility and unforgiveness that has divided them for centuries. Yet, as of this writing, walls of separation remain.

Forgiveness is not just destruction. Forgiveness is not simply tearing down walls. It is also building new structures. Forgiveness as a *rational decision* reprograms parts of the mind, replacing old reasoning with new; forgiveness as an *altered prototypical image* reprograms different parts of the mind; forgiveness as an *emotional experience* reprograms still other areas of the mind.

Exercise 7-3
Building Zone

Do you think too many negative thoughts about an emotional injury? Are you trying to snuff out those thoughts?

Imagine that I said this to you: "Don't think about the lemons. Don't think about the tangy-sharp taste of the juice. Don't think about the pungent, acrid smell." If I went on and on about what you should try not to think about, do you suppose you would think about lemons? Almost certainly—*unless* you thought about oranges or some other fruit. If you have a clear focus for your thoughts, you can concentrate on that focus.

If you are having trouble getting thoughts of hurt and judgment, or even self-condemnation (because you can't forgive), out of your mind, you need a positive focus. Write ten positive statements you could say (and truly believe) about the person who hurt you. That won't erase the pain that the person inflicted; it won't right the wrong that the person perpetrated. But it might help balance the ledger.

When a person has been injured—perhaps a strained muscle in the foot—it is natural to focus on the injury. As the injury heals, though, one should try not to limp. Limping can cause secondary problems. Similarly, after an emotional injury, a person doesn't want to limp along emotionally by either overemphasizing the negative or the positive. Those who are overbalanced on the negative side should build up the positive.

Complete healing of hurts through forgiveness depends on changing the rational, imaginal, and emotional parts of the mind and destroying the foundations of conscious and unconscious psychological defenses of inappropriate self-protection. Incomplete forgiveness (leaving old structures intact and failing to build new helpful ones) results in contaminated information flow and opens the possibility of relapse.

Though Sergeant Jacob deShazer hated his Japanese captors with his mind and soul, he experienced forgiveness through reading how another person forgave. A Bible was smuggled into the Japanese prison. DeShazer read it, not because he believed it but because it was against the rules and he was into disobedience. But in the pages of the gospels he saw an example of forgiveness that touched him to the core. He read about Jesus, crucified, dying, muttering, "Father, forgive them, for they know not what they do."

Such love transformed deShazer's thinking. It provided a powerful image. It reorganized his experience of who he was and who he could be. When a guard slammed a cell door on deShazer's bare foot, deShazer didn't rail against the guard. He prayed for him.[4]

Learning how other people forgive can motivate us to forgive those who harm us—not by what we can get from forgiveness but by seeing the gift of forgiveness that we can give others, seeing the nobility of forgiveness in the face of injustice, seeing that for us it is the right thing to do. Forgiveness sets the captive free. Jacob deShazer was not freed from prison until the war's end, but he was freed from his hatred and bitterness before then. If he had died in the POW camp, his soul would have been free from hatred.

Summing Up

Forgiveness is an act that involves much more than the rational thinking discussed in chapters two, three and four. Forgiveness involves repentance and transformation in several other domains of our personality. To forgive we must change our memory. To forgive we must improve our empathy—the human quality that links our private experience with the experiences of others. To forgive we must change our motivations to help others. To forgive we must change the stories that we tell ourselves about how we fit into the world. In the next four chapters we will explore ways to change our memory, our empathy, our motivations and the stories that guide our lives so that we can become better at forgiving.

Eight

Forgiveness & Your Memory

VERA'S FATHER, AN ALCOHOLIC, REJECTED AND PHYSICALLY abused her during his periodic alcoholic binges. The epitome of his cruelty occurred when he arrived home drunk on the night of Vera's senior prom and forbade her to attend. So she slipped out. He caught her and blackened her eye, then forced her to call her date and say she was ill.

After graduation she left home and did not go back. Thirty years after her high-school graduation, she received a call from a childhood friend with whom she had kept contact. Her father was dying of cancer. Would she visit him? She was thrown into crisis over the decision. Hurts resurfaced.

Vera had described the senior-prom incident many times to her friends, her fiancé (who had later married her) and her children. Over time she had nursed and rehearsed it until she could almost evoke tears from an audience. Clearly she had not forgotten the incident, but time had bandaged the emotional rawness. The mere thought of facing her father again after all those years ripped the thinly adhering scab from the wound and exposed the hurt in all its almost-fresh gore.

She did not want to see her father. She couldn't. She wouldn't. But what did he look like? Would he apologize? Had he asked for her nurture in a moment of needy pain? Wouldn't it be delicious to ignore his summons? But how would he know that she was rejecting him if she didn't go? What if he was sorry? How could she find out? Should she forgive him if he was sorry? Could she? What if she forgave and then forgot? Wouldn't that make her a doormat to any abuse anyone else ever dealt out?

"I Don't Want to Forgive and Forget!"

Some people may not want to forget or forgive a hurt. Despite feelings that perhaps they *ought* to forget or forgive a hurt, they may hang onto anger and resentment because those emotions empower them. Chapter seven noted that Sergeant Jacob deShazer, after repeated abuse by his captors, hated them and lived only in hope that he could someday kill them. Desire for revenge was spurred on by self-righteousness. Anger, resentment and lust for revenge drove deShazer to get up in the morning and to persevere despite hardships. He refused to forgive because he felt that hatred kept him alive, gave him a will to fight.[1]

We also may not want to forget because by forgetting we spoil our tragic self-image. In Charles Dickens's novel *Great Expectations,* Pip, when still a lad, meets Miss Havisham. Miss Havisham is a woman whose heart has been broken, so she has become arrested in space and time, held forever in the past by memories. She was half dressed when she found that her fiancé had rejected her. So she sat for years half dressed for her wedding, with the clocks stopped at twenty minutes until nine. Dark, distressed, disturbed, distorted, decaying, Miss Havisham doesn't want to forget. She introduces herself to Pip like this:

"Do you know what I touch here?" she asked, laying her hands, one upon the other, on her left side.

"Yes, ma'am." . . .

"What do I touch?"

"Your heart."

"Broken!"[2]

Her broken heart screams for revenge—on men.

Miss Havisham has adopted a beautiful orphan, Estella, and has reared her to break the hearts of men. Estella is an expert. She captivates Pip's heart and, near the end of the novel, reveals to Pip that she is going to marry another—Bentley Drummle, a brute—thus denying herself to worthier men, as Miss Havisham has trained her.

Pip is crushed, but not thinking of himself he begs Estella not to throw herself away on Drummle—to no avail. Says Estella: "You will get me out of your thoughts in a week."

> "Out of my thoughts! You are part of my existence, part of myself.
> . . . Estella, to the last hour of my life you cannot choose but remain
> part of my character, part of the little good in me, part of the evil.
> But in this separation I associate you only with the good, and I will
> faithfully hold you to that always, for you must have done me far
> more good than harm, let me feel now what sharp distress I may.
> O God bless you, God forgive you!"[3]

Hate and unforgiveness are like addiction. They make us feel better immediately, but in the long run they destroy. They have as much control over us as prison bars. As if addicted, the person can never be freed unless dependency is realized and admitted. Often that admission comes through pain.

Miss Havisham, as she watches in horror Estella's cruel rejection of Pip, unconsciously lays her hands on her heart and keeps them there. By seeing Pip's pain, she empathically begins to feel pain in her broken heart once again. She sees her need for forgiveness for what she has made of Estella—and perhaps her need to forgive the man who, many years before, hurt her.

Putting the Hurt Behind You

Many people *want* to forget painful or hurtful memories but don't think they can. Most people see themselves as passive recipients of memories. They think, *What can I do? I can't change the past. I merely remember what happened to me.*

Memory works in such a way that sometimes we simply forget. We don't make an effort to forget, but all the same the memories sometimes fade away effortlessly. We forget meaningless trivia, or names escape us.

Despite the difficulty we sometimes experience as we try to remember facts, memory is surprisingly resistant to forgetting. Remember that high school Spanish you took? Chances are you forgot a fourth of your vocabulary shortly after the test you took. On the other hand, even if you haven't thought about your high school Spanish for years, you probably still can recognize almost 60 percent of the vocabulary you learned in high school.[4] Further, with a little review you could relearn the forgotten words much faster than you could learn new words. Those "forgotten" words aren't gone. They are playing hide-and-seek with you in your mind.

Memories stick around. If that is true even for high school Spanish, which you might have had little occasion to use for years, then imagine how hard it would be to forget an emotional trauma.

To put a painful memory behind you, you must act. You must make a conscious decision. The memory won't conveniently slip your mind overnight. You must exert effort. You can't forget painful hurts, and trying to do so usually fails. It's like trying to *not* think about lemons. You can't do it. By actively resisting a memory, you keep plucking at its strands.

University of Virginia Professor Daniel Wegner has conducted much research on persistent thoughts.[5] In one line of research, he had undergraduate students imagine a white bear. Then he told them to try not to think about the white bear. Each time they thought of the white bear, they had to ring a bell.

What happened? The more the students actively tried not to think about the bear, the noisier it was. Wegner had students think aloud as they were trying to forget about the bear. Students usually tried to distract themselves. A sample might sound like this.

"Okay, I don't want to think about—white bear [bing]. Table. Yeah, table. Grain in the table. Spill mark. Must have been a glass. White bear [bing]. Look at the wall. White. White bear [bing]. Picture. Describe the picture. Amsterdam. Houses along the canal. White bear [bing] . . ."

So it went. Unwanted thoughts popped unbidden into the students' minds. Trying actively to suppress thoughts and memories generally won't work. In fact, the strategy is counterproductive.

Why We Can't Merely Forget Hurts

We can't easily forget hurts because it is adaptive to remember a painful experience. By remembering we are more likely to avoid a similar hurt. We can see why hurts are memorable if we look at the advice of memory experts on how to study for a test (see exercise 8-1). Hurts are natural and powerful aids for memory.

Exercise 8-1

How to Remember Better

Here are several ways to remember information better. These are strategies used by memory experts and by students to help them remember information that is important to them.

During learning,

☐ associate what you wish to remember with emotion.

Once you've learned information,

☐ *overlearn the information.* Continue to practice even after you know the material perfectly.

☐ *replay it.* Think about the material often. Thinking several times about the material is better than spending the same amount of time all at once.

☐ *refresh the memory.* Once you've learned something, use it today if you want to remember it tomorrow. The less time since the last recall, the better you'll remember.

Make recall easier by

☐ *integrating it* into your self-concept, concept of others and concept of the world. The more the information is a part of the way you see life, the better you will be able to recall it.

☐ *elaborating on it.* Don't just think of the material; think of how it is connected to other areas of your life, how it is related to other things you know.

☐ *tying it to images* (mental pictures) *and other emotions* (such as depression, anxiety, more anger, resentment, bitterness and so on). By associating the information you want to recall with other images and emotions, you involve different parts of the brain and open up different memory cues.

☐ *ruminating on its meaning for you.* You will remember things that matter to you more than things that aren't very important to you.

☐ *experiencing similar emotions.* Each of the primary emotions is associated with events that happened to you in that emotional state. If you become angry, you'll be more likely to remember other things that made you angry.

Ignore contrary evidence:

☐ Information that interferes with information you want to remember should be disregarded.

Hurts are emotional. Because we remember emotional times, memory experts can improve memory by associating things with emotional experiences. Hurt activates emotion spontaneously—strong emotions such as anger, fear, distress, even rage, terror and depression. Those experiences make lasting impressions.[6]

Further, similar emotional states experienced later cue our memory for the previous event, even though the current experience has nothing else in common with it. Thus, when a student rejects my (Ev's) teaching, my mind may flit immediately to my father's rejecting face or to the pain of being rejected by my first love.

Hurts are connected to other memories. We think about hurtful events again and again. We associate them with other events so that we know what to avoid in the future. We try to make sense of the pain so that we can work our explanations into the understanding of our lives. We then rehearse the story—refreshing our memory repeatedly and overlearning the memory.

Memories of hurts exist within a web of interconnections, and like a complex spider web, plucking a single strand sets the entire web in motion. For example, on the day that my first love broke off our two-year relationship, she gave me a Christmas present—a soft, blue sweater. Even today, the sight of a blue sweater can trigger memories of that rejection.

Hurts are associated with ongoing events and people. People who hurt us are usually the ones we spend time with. A stranger who ignores me doesn't hurt me, but a father who ignores me may wound me deeply. By nature, the people who have the power to wound us are the very ones we see and talk to day after day. Every time I see those people I am reminded of the painful hurt they inflicted. I may know that I should separate their actions from their personality, but a person's actions cling like a wet T-shirt. When I see the person, I see the T-shirt and might once again feel the pain.

Hurts are personal. Remembering impersonal information is difficult. Memory experts relate abstract information to their personal lives. When we are hurt, it can't get much more personal.

Thus hurts are emotional, are connected to other memories, are associated with ongoing events and people with whom we interact daily and are intensely personal. It is no wonder that hurts are so hard to forget.

Memories Are Often Inaccurate

The irony is that our memories aren't very accurate. Studies have shown that our memories are molded, shaped and distorted by a variety of things. In one study, people who saw a movie of a car wreck developed different memories of details because of the questions they were asked about it. People who were asked "How fast do you think the cars were traveling when they *smashed into* each other?" estimated greater speeds (and imagined seeing broken glass when there was none) than people who were asked "How fast do you think the cars were going when they *hit* each other?"[7]

People who were asked how "frequently" they had headaches reported three times as many headaches as people who were asked how "occasionally" they had headaches. People who were asked "How *long* was the movie?" answered, on the average, 130 minutes, but people who were asked "How *short* was the movie?" answered, on average, 100 minutes.

If memory can be distorted so easily, why are we so certain our memory is accurate? How do these inaccuracies creep in?

Once we have an emotional experience, we *think* about it. We label it, and we recall, not just the mood, not just the visual image, but also the *words* we used to describe the event to ourselves. As we tell and retell the story to ourselves and to others, we may embellish the story or impoverish it. Before long our memory of the event is changed through retelling. Because the change is so gradual we are always sure that the event occurred *exactly* like we currently remember it. Rather than being like a videotape recording that is replayed when we remember the event, long-term memory is more like growing successive generations of plants, each of which differs from the last, though it shares the genetic make-up of the previous generation.

There are two major understandings of the nature of memories.[8] According to one theory, each time a person remembers an event, he or she is growing another generation of plant. The seed of the previous plant is used to make the new plant. Thus the seed of bitterness can lead to increasingly bitter memories, but the seed of forgiveness can lead to memories that are richer and fuller. According to the other theory, the memory of the event remains unchanged, but, once the event is remembered, the person combines the most recent memory of the event with previous memories to derive a sort of "average" picture. Either way, the seeds of bitterness or forgiveness influence the person's later memories of the event.

Hate, anger, resentment and bitterness are chains that bind us to the past. Even if the person who hurt us dies, we usually feel trapped with the lingering pain. If your father hurt you as a child, like Vera's did when he forbade her to attend her senior prom, then your father's death would prevent any reconciliation. Death won't loose those chains of pain. The chains of memories of painful hurts become twisted with self-serving inaccuracies over time. We may try to toss off the chains by forgetting, but forgetting won't loose those chains. Only forgiveness will.

How Changes in Memory and Forgiveness Affect Each Other

Forgiving changes the soil (emotional climate) and also irradiates the memory-plant, changing the structure of the memory. For example, I (Ev) remember an incident from my graduate school experience. One of my professors was a *clinical* psychologist, and he clearly discriminated against us students in *counseling* psychology. I kept behavioral records of the number of times he looked at counseling students versus clinical students, the number of times he called on them, the number of times he said positive and negative things to them. The pattern of bias was consistent and marked. Naturally, I earned a B in the course. That was not a tragedy. But it is the kind of self-serving, petty grievance that most of us thrive on occasionally. I certainly did.

For years after I graduated, I harbored resentment against that professor. I knew that the grade didn't matter, yet whenever I thought of that professor—which I did probably more often than I thought of any other professor—I saw him smirking and avoiding the eyes of the counseling students. In time I became convinced that I needed to forgive the professor. He didn't want or care about my forgiveness, but my memories of him kept me in bondage to hurt.

At first I tried the rational approach. I listed reasons for and benefits of forgiving. I knew that unforgiveness was making me bitter. With each realization, I clipped a small barb from the multibarbed hook of unforgiveness, but I could see that the rational approach alone would probably never take away the power of those emotional images.

I examined myself. Was I biased against anyone? How about clinical psychologists? *Ouch*. It hurt to realize that my biases were deeper than I realized. I was like Miss Havisham in *Great Expecta-*

tions, holding my heart that had been pierced by the discovery of my own bias. That realization of my own bias helped me understand my professor better.

I visualized myself standing by the professor who had hurt me while I confessed my biases to God and received his forgiveness, which I didn't feel I deserved. After that I could no longer imagine that professor the same way because I could see myself with the same wet T-shirt, with a bias logo on it. I didn't forget, but I remembered differently. My image of the harmful scene was forever transformed, and in the wake of transformation, forgiveness floated in.

Forgiving may discharge the emotion, which breaks the connecting strands between anger, depression, fear and the memory. Psychoanalytic therapists tell us that dealing with a troublesome hurt—not merely denying it, suppressing it, repressing it or venting emotion—relieves the emotional pressure to relive the hurt. It is as if a festering wound has been lanced and the infectious pus drained. Forgiveness is the scalpel that punctures the hate and hurt to release the infection of resentment and bitterness. Then healing can begin.

Changing Our Story to Promote Forgiveness

When we write a new story about ourselves, others and the world—as I did when I visualized myself and my professor both with biases—we permit forgiveness to enter. When a memory of a hurt is one of the centerpieces of our personal story that connects self-image, other-image and world-image, then whatever experiences we have are attached to the organizing story, like adding strands to a spider's web. When we forgive, much of the story becomes not forgotten but transformed in memory, and the pain becomes irrelevant. Changing our story helps put memories behind us.

As we construe our experiences differently, we build new associations farther from the original memories. We are like spiders spinning webs far from the section in which some nasty debris is lodged. The strands leading to some memories may break one by one because of disuse until only one or two strands still connect to the old memories that don't fit with our new story. The old memories are now isolated and we remember them less frequently. (We will discover more about changing our stories in chapter ten.)

Having forgiven, we have two pictures of a hurtful event—one of a person clothed in evil who has unfairly harmed us, and another of ourselves in similar evil garb, standing beside the needy person. We can shine our mental spotlight on either picture. We can choose the one we want to look at.

The captivity of Israel could have forged a national consciousness of the Jews as a servile people. Yet the Bible focuses not on the many years of Jewish slavery but on God's action in liberating the Jews from slavery. In the Passover celebrated each year, the Jews tell the story of God's liberating power. They focus on the triumphs in their difficulties, not the past from which they were liberated. They focus on God's victories, not the hardships of forty years of wandering in the wilderness. They focus on entering the promised land, not the years of war after they got there. They choose what to focus on.

When we forgive, we are freed from having to focus on our chains of hatred and anger, our victimization. Instead we can choose to focus on ourselves as victims or as overcomers of difficulties. On the basis of the stories that connect our memories, we can control much of what we think, and we can choose to have certain experiences or refuse those experiences.

In *Great Expectations* Miss Havisham sees the emotional pain she has, through Estella, inflicted on Pip. After forgiving the fiancé who had hurt her, Miss Havisham *chooses* to seek forgiveness from Pip. Forgiving others sets her free to seek forgiveness. After she helps Pip in some financial matters, she gives him a tablet.

"My name is on the first leaf. If you can ever write under my name, 'I forgive her,' though ever so long after my broken heart is dust—pray do it!"

"O Miss Havisham," said I, "I can do it now. There have been sore mistakes, and my life has been a blind and thankless one, and I want forgiveness and direction far too much to be bitter with you."

She turned her face to me for the first time since she had averted it, and to my amazement—I may even add to my terror—dropped on her knees at my feet, with her folded hands raised to me in a manner in which, when her poor heart was young and fresh and whole, they must have been raised to Heaven from her mother's side.

To see her white hair and her worn face kneeling at my feet gave me a shock through all my frame. I entreated her to rise, and got my arms about her to help her up, but she only pressed that hand of mine which was nearer to her grasp, and hung her head over it and wept.[9]

Miss Havisham no longer was fettered to her dark room. The clocks could move past twenty minutes until nine. She could choose to clutch her bitterness or seek forgiveness for the cruel acts that sprang from her own pain. In choosing forgiveness, she not only grants forgiveness to the one who had hurt her but is also able to receive forgiveness.

How to Forgive by Changing a Memory

Focus on what is true. You mold your own dreams. You can help change your story, not by making up things that aren't true, not by fabricating faith and hope where none exist, but by seeing what is true. Choose, like Israel, to see God's acts of trustworthiness in the midst of your troubles. Choose, like Miss Havisham, to see where you have harmed others and seek their forgiveness. Choose, like Ruby, the black child who was one of the first to integrate a southern school, to pray for your tormentors each day: "Father, forgive them, for they don't know what they are doing."

Recall a person who hurt you. Your pain is real, not something you imagine. Your pain, though, keeps *you* trapped and binds *you*, not the person who hurt you. Unforgiveness makes you suffer more than the other person. Resolve to be free of unforgiveness. You can be. That's what is true.

Recall a specific memory as vividly as possible. You can't forgive a person in the abstract. You can't grit your teeth and say, "I forgive," and expect much to happen. You'll keep replaying hurts in the underground

cinema of your mind. You can know that you need to forgive, assert
that you want to forgive and even understand how to forgive. But
healing doesn't involve mere rationality. It also involves imagery and
emotion.

To forgive, search your memory banks and find that emotion-
wrenching, hurtful image. It hurts merely to recall it, but you need to
re-experience that painful moment in your mind. Only as it becomes
sharply focused, only as it draws forth the jab of remembered pain is
it ripe for modification. (You may want someone to sit with you if the
memory is traumatic.)

Develop empathy for the one who hurt you. Part of forgiving occurs when
you (who were hurt) realize that you have hurt others. Forgiving is
not forgetting. Forgiving requires that you acknowledge the other
person's actions as harmful, then empathize with the person. For
instance, you can understand how your parent could have inflicted
hurts on you by understanding that you are capable of hurting those
who depend on you. Understand that the person who harmed you is
a fallible, needy human, prone to fail as we all do. You may have done
nothing to deserve the hurt you received, but in some ways you have
hurt others and need forgiveness yourself. In seeing your own guilt
and admitting it to yourself, you can free yourself to forgive.

Imagine, feel and think how forgiveness would change the memory. Steel
yourself for recalling a painful time, but know that you cannot be
harmed by the past. The past is done and gone. If you feel upset by
your memory, shift to another thought, get up, walk around and do
something active. Healing won't come by torturing yourself with
emotional memories but in modifying those memories until you are
released from the pain. Once you know that you are in control of your
memories, you can proceed to imagine the past.

See in your mind's eye the painful scene unfold.[10] Imagine the
perpetrator cloaked with the evil or the evid deed. Acknowledge the
deed as bad. Be thankful that the deed is past. But see, too, yourself
and the less noticeable cloak of hurtfulness you wear. You didn't cause
the hurt that the other inflicted, and your actions did not justify the

other's evil actions. Yet you know that you have hurt others—unintentionally and intentionally. You know that you need forgiveness for your acts of witting and unwitting cruelty so that you can understand the other person's humanness.

Sense the other person's neediness. Sense the other person's bondage. Imagine yourself releasing the other person from the evil that weighs him or her down. As the weighty cloak of hurtfulness lifts, you can see it lift from your own shoulders as well. You can feel the chains fall off. You can feel your freedom.

You didn't *have* to forgive the person who harmed you, but in strength you *chose* to forgive. By forgiving you aren't forgetting or denying the hurtfulness, but you are placing the hurtfulness in a hot-air balloon and releasing it from its moorings so that it does not overshadow you any longer. Best of all, in forgiving you can better receive forgiveness.

Realize that forgiveness takes time. When changes are made, they are often unseen, much like a bone that is healed beneath the skin. You may be reluctant to test a newly healed broken bone by putting the bone under stress. But if you don't, your muscles could atrophy. Healing of a broken bone requires having faith that the bone is healed and placing it under stress again.

Healing a broken memory similarly requires having faith that the transformed memory is healed and then walking in faith. But, just as you would not run a marathon right after a broken leg bone had been set, you should not expect yourself to run directly from healing to wholeness. You'll need some time before full use is restored.

Consider whether reconciliation is possible and desirable. Forgiveness does not necessarily mean that you'll reconcile with the one who hurt you. In many cases, reconciliation with someone who has grievously injured you is not possible. For example, a parent who hurt you may have already died, a divorce and remarriage of an ex-spouse may be finalized or an abusive partner may be incarcerated. In none of those cases would you be able to reconcile and restore the relationship. Reconciliation and restoration wouldn't be called for or be possible.

Reconciliation depends on the offender renouncing his or her previous hurts, confessing those sins and taking steps to insure that such hurts are unlikely in the future.

Exercise 8-2
Applying What You Have Learned to Change Your Memory

We can never forget emotional hurts. The memories lurk in a web of connections and associations with other memories. But we can transform our memories so that they are never the same and so that they lose their sting.

You can apply the following six-step method to transform your memory of a particularly painful event. In the text we discussed each step. Now it is time for you to apply it to a particular memory. Select a memory of an occasion in which you were hurt.

1. Focus on what is true: you have been hurt; your pain is real; your unforgiveness makes you suffer as you recall the injustice; you can change your unforgiveness by modifying your memory.

2. Recall a specific memory as vividly as possible. Visualize the whole painful ordeal.

3. Empathize with the person who hurt you by trying to understand the person's point of view, by understanding that you are capable of hurting others and by feeling with the other person.

4. Imagine, feel and think how forgiveness would change the memory.

☐ Imagine a modified scene that incorporates your own human frailties. Remember, though, that you did not cause the person to hurt you. The other person had many choices about how to behave. You are not responsible for his or her choices, which may have been innocently insensitive or truly evil. Nevertheless, try to incorporate an image of healing and forgiveness into your memory.

☐ Free yourself by releasing the other person from the evil that weighs him or her down.

☐ Think about the choice you have made to forgive the person. Don't minimize the evil the other person might have done, but focus on your choice to release the person from the evil.

5. Realize that forgiveness takes time.

6. Consider whether reconciliation is possible or desirable. Reconciliation goes beyond forgiveness. Reconciliation may be neither possible nor desirable. Do not feel that you must reconcile with a person whom you have forgiven for a hurt.

Vera's Story

With terror Vera decided to visit her father on his deathbed. Before leaving, though, she needed to reconsider her past. The tears she shed in the two days after she heard that her father wanted to see her were enough to convince her that she had not escaped the past. She feared what would happen when she saw her father face to face—that her rage would flow over him like lava, encasing him in ashes and entombing him. She didn't want that to happen. She wanted to free him and herself from the past.

She made up her mind to forgive her father. At first she worried that forgiveness revealed a fundamental weakness in her character—a reluctance to confront evil honestly. After a couple of days, though, she decided that in forgiving she *was* confronting evil—and defeating it—instead of letting it drag her through continued anger and despair.

Vera imagined the afternoon of her prom. She saw herself, nervous, pulling her dress repeatedly from the closet and holding it in front of her to see its shimmer. She saw herself start when the front door slammed, heralding her father's arrival home. She saw him leaning against the doorway and heard him call her a tramp and forbid her to go to the prom. She felt the slap of his words and the slap of his hand when he caught her trying to slip away that night. Finally she saw herself crying into her pillow, trying to avoid another belting, as her father railed throughout the house.

Vera knew that her father's behavior had not been in response to her. She hadn't provoked him to anger. She hadn't behaved shamefully. She had in no way contributed to the debacle. Instead she imagined her father as a pitiful man enslaved to a vile habit, and for the first time in years she felt compassion for, not fury at, his weakness.

Not that I've been such a saint, thought Vera. *I've been arbitrary with my children. I've made bad decisions with my husband. I've overeaten and overcontrolled. I'm a slave to my habits as he was to his. I have good intentions but can't pull off my self-improvement projects. Not even close. I guess we're both a bit mixed up.*

Then, in an act of supreme courage and strength, Vera imagined herself saying to her father, "I forgive you. I understand the evil you did to me, but I choose to set you free." The image of her father shouted back and raised his hand to strike her, but Vera concentrated not on him but on her own choice of forgiveness.

Exhausted, she stared blindly across the street. She had remembered without rage and had forgiven. It was the hardest thing she had ever done, but she felt better for having done it.

When she stood at the side of his bed later that week, gazing down on his emaciated frame, it was easier than she had thought to see his weakness. His physical strength had ebbed and, in her mind, so had his ability to reach through the years to torment her. *I forgive you, Dad,* she thought. She still didn't trust what would happen if she said it aloud, but she knew in her heart that she was free.

Summing Up

We can never really forget past hurts. It is pointless and counterproductive to try. But we can change our memories. Forgiveness can occur if you remember your injuries, confess your own part (if any) in the injuries, empathize with the person inflicting the injury and then relinquish retribution and embrace forgiveness. As Lewis Smedes has said so eloquently, "You enslave yourself to your own painful past, and by fastening yourself to the past, you let your hate become your future. You can reverse your future only by releasing other people from their pasts."[11] Putting aside the old ways of remembering our hurts is the repentance that helps us to forgive. Once these changes in our memory occur, we are more likely to experience a transformation in our ability to forgive.

N i n e

Forgiveness &
Motivation

*M*AY 13, 1981—ST. PETER'S SQUARE. TELEVISED IMAGES DIS-
played Pope John Paul II spread out in the seat of his
car, struck by an assassin's bullet. The world watched
as the lifeblood of the Roman Catholic church's
spiritual leader ran down his white cassock. A Turkish Muslim named
Mehmet Ali Agca was apprehended. Later he was tried and sentenced
to life in an Italian prison for the attempted assassination of the Pope.

Christmas 1983—Rebibbia Prison in Rome. More than two years had
passed. The same two men, would-be assassin and his intended victim,
met again. *Time* magazine told the story:

When the Pope arrived in his cell, Agca was dressed in a blue
crew-neck sweater, jeans, and blue-and-white running shoes from
which the laces had been removed. He was unshaved. Agca kissed
John Paul's hand. "Do you speak Italian?" the Pope asked. Agca
nodded. The two men seated themselves, close together, on
molded-plastic chairs in the corner of the cell, out of earshot. At

times it looked almost as if the Pope were hearing the confession
of Agca, a Turkish Muslim. At those moments, John Paul leaned
forward from the waist in a priestly posture, his head bowed and
forehead tightly clasped in his hand as the younger man spoke.
Both Agca and John Paul had some time to think between May 1981
and December 1983. The Pope has came to Agca to speak words of
forgiveness:

> For 21 minutes, the Pope sat with his would-be assassin. . . . The two
> talked softly. Once or twice, Agca laughed. The Pope forgave him
> for the shooting. At the end of the meeting, Agca either kissed the
> Pope's ring or pressed the Pope's hand to his forehead in a Muslim
> gesture of respect.

What the two men discussed will remain in confidence. John
Paul emerged from Agca's cell, and only said, "I spoke to him as a
brother whom I have pardoned, and who has my complete trust."[1]
The story of John Paul and Mehmet Ali Agca is one of the most
inspiring public examples of forgiveness in this century. What could
have motivated such a powerful display of forgiveness? What human
motivation could be powerful enough to move someone to forgive a
would-be assassin? What human motivation could be powerful
enough to inspire the Pope to refer to his would-be assassin as his
"brother"? What can psychology can tell us about the psychological
forces that can powerfully motivate our desire to forgive?

Exploring Motivations for Forgiveness
Motives are forces (e.g., biological drives, instincts, unconscious desires,
needs, external incentives or social rewards) that move us to action.

Many forces may motivate us to forgive:
☐ the desire to be free of anger, revenge and hostility
☐ the desire to show gratitude to God for forgiving us
☐ pride
☐ love for the offender and desire for a restored relationship
☐ fear of the offender
☐ the desire to protect our own health

☐ the desire to appear magnanimous
☐ concern for the welfare of the offender
☐ the desire to be obedient to parents or religious/moral authorities
☐ the desire to avoid violence

Although all these motivations may be legitimate in some sense, psychologist Mary Trainer's research suggests that some motives for forgiving are better than others. We have adapted an exercise for you (9-1) that will help you recognize your own motives for forgiving.

Exercise 9-1

Reasons for Forgiving

Pick a person that you want to forgive. Indicate whether the reasons for forgiving listed below are true of you; that is, does each reason express why you want to forgive? Circle T for "true" or F for "false."

1. Forgiveness is my best revenge. T / F

2. I am the kind of person who never harbors resentment against someone who hurts me. T / F

3. I felt compassion toward _____ when I realized how much he/she had suffered. T / F

4. By rising above the hurt, I could show _____ that I was still "on top." T / F

5. I feel I am mostly to blame and therefore should forgive immediately. T / F

6. I didn't want hard feelings between us anymore. I wanted us to be friends. T / F

7. By forgiveness I can show that I am morally superior. T / F

8. I feared that others would look down on me as bitter and resentful if I didn't forgive. T / F

9. There is more to _____ than was evident in our hurtful encounters. _____ has a good side too. T / F

10. I pitied _____. He/She is such a weak person; _____ can't help the harm he/she does. T / F

11. Persons I look up to (priest, minister, rabbi) told me I should. T / F

12. I realized that _____ is human like me. We all make mistakes. T / F

13. I felt that _____ was no longer worth my attention, upset and anger. T / F

14. I felt that I should make myself forgive since God expects us to. T / F

15. Both _____ and I participated in the hurting process. I felt drawn to mutually forgive and be forgiven by _____ and by God. T / F

Trainer interviewed divorced men and women who had been painfully hurt during the dissolution of their marriages about their attempts to forgive their ex-spouses. She identified three motives that people have for forgiving: *expedient forgiveness, role-expected forgiveness,* and *intrinsic forgiveness.*[2]

Expedient forgiveness is forgiving in order to get something. Examples of things people might get from forgiving include freedom from negative thoughts and emotions, freedom from stress-related symptoms and a better reputation in the eyes of others. Expedient forgiveness is a means to other ends.

Role-expected forgiveness is motivated by the expectations of others or God. Though there's nothing wrong with forgiving "because authority figures have told us that we should forgive," in role-expected forgiveness the expectations of authority figures have not been internalized. Therefore role-expected forgiveness is a compulsion.

Intrinsic forgiveness is a free decision to change hostile attitudes, thoughts and feelings on the conviction that forgiveness itself is important. Intrinsic forgiveness flows from the heart. In the story of Pope John Paul, we might see the Pope's ability to call Agca his brother and the restoration of his trust in Agca as evidence that his forgiveness for Agca was a product of intrinsic forgiveness.

Expedient and role-expected motivations are not very powerful motivators. It is difficult to get excited about the hard work of forgiving if your motivation is to look good in the eyes of others, to avoid punishment or to benefit yourself.

Think about it. Underneath expedient and role-expected motivations for forgiveness are ideas such as "I would like to keep hating you, but my pastor [or priest or rabbi] tells me I must forgive" and "If hostility were not so bad for my heart, I would love to continue dreaming up ways to get revenge." Clearly these motivations are not motivations to forgive at all. *They are motivations to avoid the pain of unforgiveness.* "We all know we should forgive," expedient and role-expected motivations inform us, "so let's get it over with quickly." It is like eating canned spinach—not tasty but good for us. If we are to forgive intrinsically, we must turn from our reliance on expedient and role-expected motivations and develop intrinsic motivation.

How do we gain intrinsic motivation? What could transform us into people who can view our former enemy as a brother (or sister)? We believe that intrinsic motivation comes primarily from adopting a psychological perspective called *empathy.* That belief is one of the central tenets of this book.

Empathy is an emotional response that matches the subjective experience of another person. Put another way, when we feel empathy for a person who is hurt, we feel bad with them. When we feel empathy for a person who is excited about having won an award at school or work, we feel happy or excited with them. When we use the word *empathy,* we are referring to a quality that involves both thought and feeling: when we are empathic, we can *think* and *feel* what it must be like to stand in another person's shoes. The person exists for us as a *person,* not as an anonymous stranger or nameless, faceless monster.

In the rest of this chapter we will examine how we can develop empathy as a way to develop an intrinsic motivation to forgive. But first let's find out what your answers in exercise 9-1 tell you about yourself. Score your true and false answers by completing exercise 9-2.

Exercise 9-2

Scoring Your Motivations to Forgive

1. Assign yourself one point for each "true" answer for items 1, 4, 7, 10 and 13 in exercise 9-1. Write the total in the blank below:

_____ Expedient Forgiveness

2. Assign yourself one point for each "true" answer for 2, 5, 8, 11 and 14. Write the total in the blank below:

_____ Role-Expected Forgiveness

3. Assign yourself one point for each "true" answer for 3, 6, 9, 12 and 15. Write the total in the blank below:

_____ Intrinsic Forgiveness

The higher you score on *expedient* and *role-expected* forgiveness, the worse are your present chances of forgiving the person you identified in exercise 9-1. People with expedient motivations are more likely to hold a grudge and experience negative feelings and less likely to forgive, help or communicate goodwill toward someone who hurt them. People with high role-expected motivations for forgiving are more likely to have hostile feelings and less likely to have positive feelings, communicate with or help someone who hurt them.

The higher your scores on *intrinsic* motivation for forgiveness, the better are your present chances of forgiving the person who has hurt you. Intrinsic motivations lead to more forgiveness, more positive feelings, decreases in hostile behavior and greater desire to communicate good will.

Remember that no one's motivations are pure; at any given time we all are probably motivated by a combination of intrinsic, expedient and role-expected motivations. Remember also that this is only an approximate measure of your motivations. Other motivations may also be involved in your desire to forgive.

Where There Is Empathy, There Is Intrinsic Motivation to Forgive

Psychological research, as well as our own experience (and probably yours as well), tell us that, when people confess something they have done that hurt us, we find it easier to forgive them.[3] Think about your own experience for a moment: what happens inside you when someone who has hurt you says "I'm sorry for what I did. It was a lousy thing to do to a friend"? Doesn't forgiveness (usually) come easier?

Why should a friend's confessing and apologizing make our forgiveness easier? When an offender confesses and apologizes for hurting us, that interaction allows us to develop a new picture of our offender. A noncontinuous transformation occurs. Instead of seeing him or her through lenses of anger and bitterness, the person's humility and apology cause us to see him or her as fallible and prone to evil acts, not as the devil; we see him or her as in need of mercy, not revenge. The offender appears broken and contrite. Our offender is more human—more like us. We are moved.

In our own research, we examined whether the relationship between apology and our capacity to forgive a person is due to our increased empathy for an apologetic offender. It appears that much of why people find it easier to forgive an apologetic offender is that *apology and confession increase their empathy for their offenders, which changes their ability to forgive.*

What if your offender will not confess and apologize?

☐ "The person who hurt me is not alive anymore. How am I going to forgive someone who can't apologize?"

☐ "The person who hurt me doesn't care. She will never be able to confess that she did something wrong."

☐ "My husband threatened to kill me. I'm afraid of having any sort of contact with him. It seems too dangerous."

Unfortunately many of the people who hurt us never apologize. Perhaps they are too afraid or too proud. Perhaps they are dead or have moved away. You cannot rely on a contrite, apologetic offender to gain the empathy you need to forgive. But you can develop empathy in other ways.

Developing empathy for one's offender is like gardening. Before you can grow anything, you must break up and turn under the soil. Weeds must be pulled and rocks and roots removed. After the soil is soft and free of obstructions, you can plant seeds that will lead to good fruit. To gain empathy, we must experience repentance and transformation. We must repent by pulling up the stones and weeds that inhibit the growth of empathy, and we must be transformed by planting the psychological seeds of empathy.

Pulling Up the Impediments to Empathy

The fundamental attribution error is a stable principle from social psychology: *People tend to think about themselves and the causes of their own behavior according to different guidelines than those they use to think about others and the causes of others' behavior.*[4]

Imagine that I am your college professor. If I were to arrive late each day to a course that I was teaching, I might explain my chronic lateness in terms of outside circumstances that made me late—the terrible traffic on the interstate, a broken alarm clock, an out-of-town friend who called as I was leaving home. You, however, would tend to explain my chronic lateness in terms of my personality or traits. You might label me as "absent-minded" or "disorganized" or "self-absorbed" or perhaps even as "selfish." The principle of the fundamental attribution error also suggests that if I observe *your* chronic lateness, I will probably explain your behavior in terms of *your* personality (you are lazy and disorganized), not in terms of outside circumstances acting upon you (the traffic was terrible).

This double standard of judging others in terms of their personalities while we judge ourselves in terms of the terrible circumstances that we have suffered is pervasive—that's why it's called the *fundamental* attribution error. The pervasiveness of this error in judgments has consequences for developing forgiveness through empathy.

"You are the most critical person I know," Ben accused his wife as the counseling session heated up.

"Oh, that means a lot coming from you, Mr. Encouragement. What about your ranting and raving about my family?" countered Sharon. She pounded her fist on the chair arm.

Ben looked away. "Well, I-I've been under a lot of stress at work lately." Ben found it easy to explain Sharon's negativity as due to the type of person she is, but he attributed his own criticism to a stressful situation in life.

However, it is not reasonable to explain the hurts that we cause in terms of our circumstances while we explain the hurts that others create as a function of their personalities. We cannot simply explain the sins of others against us by concluding that they are brutes, monsters, unfeeling cowards or any other description, while we allow ourselves off the hook: "No one understands the kind of pressure I am under"; "If you had my childhood, you would have done the same thing." If we want to be people of integrity, we cannot allow ourselves to explain away our own failures while holding others responsible for theirs. How do we defeat this double standard when we judge the causes of other people's behavior?

Psychologists Allan Fenigstein and Charles Carver found that people who are attentive to their inner feelings—people with a high degree of self-awareness—are more likely to explain the causes of their behavior in terms of their personality or stable traits. Fenigstein and Carver asked students to imagine themselves in hypothetical situations. Some students were made aware of themselves by the ruse that they were hearing their own heartbeats as they pondered the situations, whereas others believed that they were simply hearing unrelated noises. Those students who believed they were hearing their own heartbeats saw themselves as more responsible for the situations than those who believed they were hearing extraneous noises.[5]

As the Fenigstein and Carver study illustrates, we are likely to consider our personal contribution to our actions when we are made aware of ourselves. Although many would say that our culture's biggest problem is that we think *too much* about ourselves (certainly in self-serving ways), it is probably true that most of us do not take time to focus on the ways that we hurt others independently of the outside influences on our behavior. A four-step method for reducing the effects of the fundamental attribution error on your ability to empathize with the person who hurt you appears in exercise 9-3.

Exercise 9-3

Uprooting the Fundamental Attribution Error

Reducing the effects of the fundamental attribution error on your capacity to empathize with your offender is crucial. Here are four steps for "uprooting" the fundamental attribution error.

1. *Consider your attributions about your offender.* How much do you believe that the person hurt you because "that's the way he or she is"? Are there external pressures that might have made the offender act as he or she did?

2. *Consider your attributions about your own behavior.* To what degree did you provoke the offender's behavior? How did you respond? Do you think that you are capable of offending someone the way you were offended? If you did, how would you want to be perceived?

3. *Take a "moral inventory."* Spend some time thinking about the hurtful things you have said to, done to or thought about other people. Think about these actions as you stand in front of a mirror during quiet reflection or by writing them down so that you can see them.

4. *Evaluate.* Did you develop a greater sense that you are as "responsible" for your hurtful behavior as your offender is for his or hers? Are you able to see that you are in the same moral condition as your offender? If so, then you have reduced the fundamental attribution error.

Planting the Seeds of Empathy

Once we have repented by removing the major hindrance to empathy—the fundamental attribution error—we can plant four seeds that will lead to a transformation in our ability to empathize with the person who hurt us: (1) recognize our common identity with the offender, (2) recognize our own tendency to hurt others, (3) revise our story about the offender and (4) recognize the potential influence of religion.

Recognize our common identity. Uprooting the fundamental attribution error allows us to experience that we share a similar human identity with our offenders, despite our surface dissimilarities. The notion of *identity* has been applied to forgiveness by Robert Enright at the University of Wisconsin.[6]

The ability to recognize identity in the social realm allows us to see past some differences between persons, such as gender, ethnicity and religion, and to affirm that each person has inherent value that merits our respect. Enright and his colleagues argue that identity allows us to focus on something outside the hurtful context of an offense. We can see past the details of insensitivity, betrayal and hurt and can appreciate the fact that both offender and victim are inherently valuable and have worth that should be honored, *even when the offender has failed to honor the worth of the victim.* If all the dissimilarities are taken away—differences in upbringing, our psychological and physical differences, our inherited dispositions and our diverse experiences—we recognize that we stand in the same condition as our offenders. We have hurt others with our actions in the past and have also needed forgiveness.

Recognize our own tendency to hurt others. Dealing with our common identity with our offenders raises an important reality—regardless of how we have been hurt by others, we have also hurt others. Lewis Smedes writes about our tendency to overlook our own hurtfulness in this way: "We always feel like innocent lambs when someone hurts us unfairly. But we are never as pure as we feel."[7]

Gaining empathy for one's offender requires that we take an "inventory" of our own history of hurting others. Read the story of Corrie ten Boom, who was confronted by her similarity to someone who hurt her deeply. In her book *Tramp for the Lord* Corrie tells of encountering a former guard from the Nazi concentration camp where she and her sister had been incarcerated during World War II. After she preached a message in a German church of God's offer of forgiveness to everyone, the guard approached her and asked her for forgiveness on behalf of all the people he had hurt in the concentration camp.

Corrie did not feel the power to forgive. She did not want to forgive him. But she did forgive him. She reminded herself that God promised to forgive her sins. She recalled many of her offenses against others. In many ways she was like the old soldier. She had been forgiven much. Now it was her turn to help another human who was seeking forgiveness. Acting on faith, she stretched a hand out to the guard and felt a rush of energy radiate down her arm. "I forgive you, brother!" she cried. "I forgive you with all my heart."

That moment of realizing her own need for forgiveness was a turning point in her profound decision to forgive the German man. On the surface they could not have had less in common. Corrie was a Dutch woman and a victim of the Holocaust. The German man was a perpetrator of Holocaust crimes. But they both needed forgiveness. *Recognizing their common need for forgiveness* was the difference between forgiveness and unforgiveness.[8]

Take time to complete the activities described in exercise 9-4. Think of one incident from the past when you needed forgiveness from another person. Recall how it felt to realize your need for forgiveness. Then think for a moment about the person who hurt you most recently. Could it be that in some small or symbolic way the person is experiencing the same need for forgiveness?

Exercise 9-4

Recalling the Need for Forgiveness

Think back to a time when you hurt someone or did something wrong and needed forgiveness. It might be an incident from childhood, an episode in your marriage or a time when you felt a need to be forgiven by God. Perhaps you said something hurtful to a friend or parent. Now that you have that incident in your mind, describe what you did.

1. What were the circumstances? Did you get caught, or did you "get away with it"? Did you feel guilty?

2. When you realized your guilt and need for forgiveness, did you experience any bodily sensations? What did it feel like in the pit of your stomach? Did you ever have sweaty palms? Could you "feel" your guilt and need for forgiveness in other parts of your body?

3. What emotions did you experience as you realized your need for forgiveness?

4. What did it feel like (or would it have felt like) to ask the person you hurt for forgiveness? What did it feel like (or would it have felt like) to receive forgiveness from that person?

5. Is it conceivable that the person who hurt you could have experienced (or could experience in the future) some of the same sensations and emotions that you felt when you realized your guilt and need for forgiveness in the past?

Revise your story about the offender. How would you tell the story of the person who hurt you—not the story of the hurt itself or the events that led up to the hurt but the story of that *person*? It could be making a tremendous difference in your capacity for empathy.

At a conference I (Mike) attended, one presenter struck me as pompous and self-absorbed. He stared off into space when he spoke, carefully crafting wordy sentences. He highlighted the parts of his talk that he believed to be most profound with appropriately placed strokes of his Sigmund Freud beard. He belittled and dismissed sincere questions from his audience. I disliked him intensely.

Then I experienced a shift in my thinking: *Whose son is he? Does he have his own family? I wonder if he has ever grieved over the loss of a loved one. I wonder if he has ever sacrificed things he wanted to do so that he could make his family more comfortable and happy. What has been disappointing about his life? Does he like himself?* Suddenly the pompous, self-absorbed professor no longer seemed contemptible. He was not even simply a self-absorbed academic. He was more complicated than that. He was human. I felt some tenderness for the man, *even though I knew nothing about him.*

Only the "story" I was using to make sense of the man had changed. Yet as the story changed I identified with him. I felt empathy. I no longer felt comfortable deriding him. He was too much like me.

When you find yourself angry and unable to forgive someone who has hurt you, try to examine the mental story that you rehearse about the person who hurt you. Then revise that story by asking yourself, as I did, about the tender, human details of the person's life. You might find that you acquire a new empathy for the person and thus a new, intrinsic forgiveness for the person who hurt you.

Recognize the potential influence of religion. Research suggests that traditional religious belief and participation may help us to forgive. On average, people with a religious or spiritual outlook appear to be more motivated to forgive. Research also suggests that many religious people tend to place forgiveness, community and right relations with others higher in their value systems than do nonreligious people. Religious people are also more likely than nonreligious to use forgiveness to deal with the hurts they encounter (and also to ask for forgiveness when they hurt others).[9] Our clinical experience has taught us the same lesson that research demonstrates: a religious outlook motivates many people to forgive intrinsically.

Some of our most recent research suggests that religion helps many people to forgive by helping them to empathize with their offenders. Chris Rachal and I (Mike) surveyed more than two hundred people who had been hurt by another person. Not only did we find that more religious people (people who reported praying and attending religious services regularly) were more empathic and more forgiving toward their offenders, but we also found that religious people were more forgiving because *their religious involvement helped them to be empathic toward the people who hurt them.*[10] As a result of their greater empathy, many religious people were better able to forgive.

Some religions (including, though perhaps not limited to, Judaism and Christianity) have resources that give people power and inspiration to forgive. However, individuals draw on religious resources too infrequently. Find out whether your religious tradition has anything to say about forgiveness (and empathy). In some religious traditions you might find resources to increase your motivation to forgive.

Evaluation: Does empathy really help? Our empirical research supports the notion that empathy may indeed lead to greater forgiveness. We have conducted several studies in which we found that empathy for the people who hurt us is strongly related to our ability to forgive those people. To test the importance of empathy for forgiveness even further, we did a research study to find out if promoting empathy for one's offender through a clinical intervention also promoted forgiveness for one's offender. We conducted weekend seminars with participants who had been hurt by a significant person in their lives. One-third of our participants were involved in a seminar that encouraged empathy toward their offender. Another third of our participants were involved in a seminar that encouraged forgiveness strictly for its power in reducing revenge and other harmful effects. The final third of our participants were in a waiting-list condition and did not participate in a seminar.

We found that, over time, our seminar based on empathy was superior to the other seminar and to the waiting-list control group. (The seminar based on the reduction of revenge was better than no seminar at all.[11]) Thus it appears that not only are empathy and forgiveness related, but improving your empathy may also improve your ability to forgive.

What If You Have Too Much Empathy?

Although our research suggests that there is an important relationship between empathy and forgiveness, could there be some instances in which identifying with the plight of the offender on an emotional level becomes counterproductive or downright harmful? We believe so.

Distraction from the work of forgiveness. If you were to see someone who appeared to be hurt on the side of the road or interacted with someone who needed a small favor or heard what you thought was a painter falling off of a ladder in the next room, it might be helpful to empathize with the person you perceived to be in need. That empathy might help you stop the car to see if the person needed help, to do the small favor or to investigate the suspicious sounds.

Imagine, though, that you had such a strong emotional reaction to the plight of someone else that you were actually *overwhelmed* with emotion. You might become so distressed that you could no longer focus your attention on another person but only on your own feelings. Similarly, in generating empathy for the person who hurt you, it is necessary to avoid so much empathy that you are more focused on your own distress than on your offender's need to be forgiven.

In practice people probably only rarely experience an "empathy overload," but to ensure that you don't, observe whether your empathy moves you toward the person who hurt you or farther away. Useful empathy should increase your desire for things to be right between you and your offender, whereas excessive empathy will draw your focus off your offender and onto yourself.

An overidentification with evil people. During the early 1980s Frances Toto of Allentown, Pennsylvania, made five unsuccessful attempts to kill her husband, Tony. When Tony did not die from bullet wounds to the head and chest, Frances tried to finish him off with chicken soup laced with barbiturates. After Frances served four years in prison, Tony welcomed her home with open arms. He explained, "I don't understand why people break up over silly things. I think people need to sit down and talk."[12]

Empathy and compassion toward our offenders should not be confused with trivializing the awful offenses we sometimes encounter. Healthy forgiveness does not arise from denial of serious problems in a relationship or from empathizing with evil behavior. We do not prescribe that form of empathy. Abusers often use empathy to *refute* the value of the people they abuse. The use of empathy as a means to forgiveness is intended to *affirm* our common worth as human beings, in spite of the atrocities that people commit.

Summing Up

Pope John Paul forgave Mehmet Ali Agca. Corrie ten Boom forgave the old German guard. We can never know completely what motivated them to forgive, but what seems clear is that both Pope John Paul and Corrie ten Boom were intrinsically motivated to forgive their offenders. They forgave from the heart, and they came to see their abusers as their "brothers." Although Pope John Paul and Corrie ten Boom may have wanted to rid themselves of their hatred or to be faithful to their religious beliefs, they forgave primarily out of concern for the other person. They participated in forgiveness for its own sake. They knew that forgiveness was important, and it flowed from their hearts.

We develop intrinsic forgiveness by developing empathy. Empathy is a psychological force that allows us to feel *with* another person. How do we develop empathy for someone who has hurt us? First we must repent of our tendency to make the fundamental attribution error. Next we must allow our perspective to be transformed by recognizing our common identity with the offender and our common tendency to hurt others, revising our story about the offender and exploring religious resources. Empathy can transform us into people who forgive intrinsically—people who forgive from the heart.

Ten

Forgiveness &
Stories

THINK BACK ON THE BOOK THUS FAR. WHAT DO YOU REMEMber? Naturally we want you to remember the main points: that forgiveness is not easy; that forgiveness is morally good; that it involves rational thought, images, emotions and even unconscious motivations; that it requires empathy for the offender; and that it promotes healthier relationships. What comes back most strongly, though, are probably the stories we have told. You might recall the story of how Miss Havisham finally forgave her fiancé, how Sergeant deShazer forgave his Japanese captors, how Corrie ten Boom forgave the former Nazi prison guard and how Pope John Paul II forgave his would-be assassin.

People enjoy stories. Teachers are often confounded when former students can remember almost none of the content of a course but can recount even the most trivial stories told by the teacher years before.

I (Steve) reflected on one of my former teachers as I prepared to teach my first college course. This professor taught the only education course I ever took, and he made quite an impact on me. I wanted to understand what principles of effective teaching I could glean from this man. But I, too, could remember only the engaging stories he told. He told stories about his personal and professional struggles and failures. He told us stories about difficult choices and profound joys in his life. Some nights the stories led the class into deep laughter. Other nights this teacher's stories led to tears. As I reflected on these stories, it occurred to me that if I wanted students to take something away from my class, I needed to tell stories.

Stories and Identity

Why are stories so powerful and so easy to remember? It is because our lives and relationships seem to unfold like stories. Theodore Sarbin is among the many contemporary psychologists who see the story as a basic metaphor for a person's identity.[1] Such psychologists view a person's identity as his or her "life story." Each of us constructs a life story when we remember events from our past or dream about our future. We need to make sense out of our life story, to find a coherent plot. So we identify with certain stories or characters provided by our family, culture or religion.

Stories are powerful because we identify with the characters. When I was a child I loved the story of the Alamo. I was captivated by the image of Davy Crockett heroically refusing to surrender the fort to the enemy and fighting to the death. I would often pretend that I was Davy Crockett defending the Alamo. Through that story I identified with a character who taught me about loyalty.

Psychologist Kirk Kilpatrick has pointed out that stories allow us temporarily to leave ourselves behind.[2] When I watch a good action movie, I usually do not think about myself during the movie. I enter the perspective of the protagonist, who in action movies is usually a handsome, muscular hero who defeats the forces of evil and wins the admiration of the beautiful leading lady. What a life! I walk out of the theater feeling a bold motivation to drop to the sidewalk and do a couple hundred pushups, eat wheat-germ by the bucket and run laps around the block. Usually by about pushup number three, I am transported back into my slightly less dangerous world.

Stories involve a plot with various characters taking on different roles. The plot gives the story meaning. Psychiatrist Viktor Frankl wrote the book *Man's Search for Meaning* about his survival in the Nazi prison camps of World War II. Frankl observed that the difference between those who died and those who survived was that the survivors had "a call of a potential meaning waiting to be fulfilled." Frankl observed that survival depended on the ability to envision a meaning-ful role in one's future story.[3]

The plot of our life story can take on various themes. Northrop Frye proposed that four great themes that guide the plot of stories.[4] Dan McAdams has applied Frye's narrative themes to the psychology of developing one's identity.[5]

The first narrative theme is comedy. Comedies are not humorous stories (although that is generally what we mean when we use the term nowadays). They are characterized by the hero or heroine successfully overcoming obstacles to reach the eventual union of people. The comedy theme could be summarized as "all's well that ends well." Comedy is the theme of spring.

The second narrative theme is romance. The plot of a romance is the adventure or successful quest. Indiana Jones is a romantic hero. Romance is the theme of summer.

The third narrative theme is tragedy. In a tragedy the hero or heroine is sadly destined for a fatal ending. Romeo and Juliet are a famous tragic couple. Tragedy is the theme of autumn.

The fourth narrative theme is irony. Ironic stories speak to the mysterious and chaotic forces of life. Life is seen as a puzzle with double meanings that cannot be completely solved. Irony is the theme of winter.

A person's identity can be thought of as a life story dominated by one, or perhaps two, of these themes. The plot of our story may swing toward tragedy or irony as we encounter pain and disappointments in life. Some people play the role of the tragic martyr who is destined to sacrifice his or her own happiness. The tragic martyr can at least take confidence in knowing ahead of time that the story will not end "happily ever after." Others view their life story as ironic and adopt the antihero role of the cynic. The cynic takes confidence in knowing that the story will never make sense, that life's ambiguities will never be resolved.

Development of life stories. Important life events, such as puberty or leaving home, can provide the backdrop for our story at a given point in time. Many developmental psychologists see life as a series of transitions with a new conflict to be resolved at each transition.[6] Perhaps the conflicts of development at these transitions work like acts in a play. Successful resolution of a conflict gives one the confidence to move on to the next act in the story. Unsuccessful resolution may keep one stuck in a certain part of the life story.

Let's consider an example of the influence of development on a plot. Erik Erikson theorized how identity develops across the life span. He suggested that each stage of life involves a developmental conflict. For example, between the ages of six and twelve a child typically wrestles with self-confidence as he or she deals with the demand of learning new skills at school. Success at performing new skills leads to self-confidence. Difficulties at this stage can lead to feelings of inferiority.[7]

When I (Steve) was at this stage of development, one of the major tasks I had to perform was the physical fitness test in gym class. I was pudgy and uncoordinated at that age. One of the tests was the fifty-yard dash. Pudgy kids are not usually very good at the fifty-yard dash, so I had adopted an indifferent attitude toward these tests. Then one of the popular girls in my class drew public attention to my performance: "Eight seconds! Why, you're slower than all the girls!" she exclaimed. I wanted to crawl under a rock. For a sixth-grade boy in 1978, being labeled slower than all the other girls was a social "kiss of death" and a strong blow to my sense of competence.

About eight years later I was talking with a wise friend who was trying to help me understand some insecurity I felt in relating to women. Suddenly this scene rushed into my mind with the fresh sting of shame and humiliation. I also felt a powerful resentment toward that girl as I related the story, though I had not seen her for years. My friend led me in my first exercise of forgiveness, which offered me a feeling of release from the power of that story to haunt me.

Do you have specific memories of painful actions by others in your past? Are any of those stories tied to important developmental issues, like the awkwardness of puberty or the push for independence at late adolescence? It could be that unforgiveness is related to the developmental importance of those stories to your identity.

Stuck in life stories. Time usually does not heal all wounds, despite popular opinion to the contrary. Wounds either are healed as we incorporate the events into our ongoing life story, or they are rubbed raw as we cling to unforgiveness. When we fail to forgive, the plot of our life story swings toward tragedy or irony in light of the hurts caused by others. Some of our greatest hopes and dreams end in crushing disappointment. Our pain and disappointment seem to move us in one of two directions: anger or denial. Sometimes our bitterness grows deep and strong. We become firmly entrenched on a course of proving someone wrong or getting even. In other cases, we cope with pain by denying our true feelings. We put on a smiling face and view our life story with superficial optimism, or we plod through life with sluggish boredom, afraid to feel anything because of the hurt and rage lying beneath the surface.

In either case, we can become "stuck" in a life story that provides little meaning. Unforgiveness in the form of brazen or veiled hostility freezes a person into one frame of a life story. For the person stuck in unforgiveness, every act of the drama looks about the same. His or her identity is predictable, like an actor who has been typecast. The business executive could be driven to prove her skeptical father wrong by achieving more than was expected of her. Her anger motivates her toward success, but at the cost of marital discord and constant stress. We can also guess at the life story of the friendly but aimless young man who quits everything he starts. He denies feeling any need to forgive his distant and rejecting parents, but he is also confused by his compulsive fascination with gratuitously violent movies. Denial covers his hidden anger but prevents him from making confident decisions in life.

Have you experienced friends or relatives who tell the same story over and over again? Maybe the story is about the coach who cut him from the high school team, the teacher who just did not like her or the mother who did not love him. Maybe the story is about a boss who would not let him go back to school part time or the mother who was never satisfied with anything she did. We all tell such stories at times, but when I hear the same painful story from a person three or four times, I begin to wonder how that story fits into his or her life story.

Stories and hope. People remember stories about the past and envision stories about the future. Each of us has a direction in life, however vague, that involves our future story. *Where is my life going? What are my goals and ambitions? What are my hopes and dreams?* Psychologist Paul Vitz suggests that the themes of comedy and romance contribute to the most healthy life story because both comedy and romance offer *hope* to your future story.[8]

Viewing your life as a comedy involves the hope that one can eventually find positive relationships or communion with others. This may require overcoming obstacles, but the lure of relationship with others provides the motivation to press on in the comic story. Viewing one's life as a romance requires the hope that the meaningful quest can be achieved. The romantic quest or pilgrimage involves taking risks to fulfill a calling, such as pursuing one's ambitions.

How does hope sustain positive stories about the future? Hope is the belief that desires in the present will be satisfied in one's future. Gabriel Marcel called hope a "memory of the future," and there is an important connection between hope and memory.[9] Hope is sustained by memories of promises kept in past relationships. A person who has few positive memories of trustworthy relationships will find it more challenging to look toward the future with hope.

Conflict with another person often engages our memories about past conflict in relationships. If I can remember past stories of forgiveness, I am more likely to be hopeful about the future resolution of my current conflict.

Some people find that despair, the opposite of hope, comes easier. These people feel like prisoners in a hopeless story. They cannot (or will not) remember hope-engendering stories from the past to give them strength to go on. When a client describes a person who has repeatedly hurt him or her, I (Steve) will sometimes ask, "What would you like for your relationship with him (or her) to be like?" Clients frequently say nervously, "Oh, he'll never change." It is easier to slam the door on one's hope that the other person could change than it is to imagine what that change would be like. Forgiveness does not require that the other person change, but forgiveness does awaken the hope that the other person could change. So forgiveness feels dangerous to those who prefer tragic stories.

Our future story engages our goals, desires and hopes. Each of us has some goals, whether conscious or unconscious. Most people hope to find satisfying relationships and meaningful work. More basically, most of us want to avoid pain and suffering.

University of Kansas psychologist C. R. Snyder says that hope depends on two factors—our *willpower* and our *waypower*. Willpower is the driving force of hopeful thinking. It is the determination, commitment and energy we have for achieving our goal. Waypower involves the plans or road map we have for accomplishing our goals. Willpower and waypower are both necessary to experience hope.[10]

Our goals in life are often blocked. Consider the example of Susan, a twenty-seven-year-old graduate student. Susan had been distant from her father for most of her teenage years after he and her mother divorced. Susan's father had not shown much interest in her, and on her occasional visits he usually got drunk. In the last three years, however, Susan's father has been in successful recovery from his alcoholism and has repeatedly initiated contact with her. Susan desired a good relationship with her father (her goal), and she was committed to this goal (willpower).

At the same time Susan could not deny hurtful memories about the past. Those memories intruded whenever she got together with her father. She could not make sense out of the story of her relationship with her father, and her capacity to hope was dampened by a lack of waypower. She did not know of a way to change the story and thus reach her goal.

Painful stories about our past can stifle our hope about the future. We need a way of viewing our past story that does not deny the facts but that does transform what the story means for our future. Forgiveness is the key twist in the plot.

Susan desperately wanted a way for the story of her relationship with her father to be changed, to be transformed into a story with a hopeful future. Other people want a way of interpreting the story of their past relationships that frees them from bondage to a tragic story. Forgiveness restores Susan's personal power by allowing her to change the meaning of a story. She can view herself as an ambassador of healing by forgiving her father for his past actions. She may find it difficult to trust her father for awhile and may fear that the past story will be repeated. But forgiveness offers her a way of viewing the past so that she is not paralyzed by it.

Exercise 10-1

The Funeral

Management expert Stephen Covey suggests a goal-setting exercise that entails looking at "the view from the end" of relationships. Covey recommends that we imagine our own funeral. At the funeral are all the significant people currently in our life—a spouse or romantic partner, siblings, friends, coworkers, children and so on. We are then asked to imagine the story we would like these people to tell about our impact on their life. This exercise may seem too morbid for some, but it is a good way to think about the larger story of our lives and relationships.[11]

Do you currently feel unforgiveness toward someone? If so, imagine the "view from the end" of your life. What would you hope to have her gain from having known you? What stories would you want him to tell about you?

Forgiveness requires a hopeful forgiver, but forgiveness can also inspire hope in the offender. That story is portrayed in Victor Hugo's novel Les Miserables. Jean Valjean spends nineteen oppressive years in a French prison for stealing a loaf of bread. After serving his term, he is released a hardened man and an outcast. Valjean cannot even get a room at the inn, so he walks the streets for four days and nights. Finally a kind bishop takes Valjean in and offers him food and lodging.

That night Valjean steals the Bishop's silver and flees into the darkness while all in the house are asleep. The next morning he is returned to the Bishop's house by the local police, who caught him with the stolen silver. The Bishop surprises both the police and Valjean with a larger story of forgiveness: " 'So here you are!' cried the Bishop. 'I'm delighted to see you. Have you forgotten that I gave you the candlesticks as well? They're silver like the rest, and worth a good 200 francs. Did you forget to take them?' "[12]

Jean Valjean's eyes widen. He is now staring at the old man with an expression no words can convey. The Bishop assures the police that the silver was a gift to Valjean. After the police leave, the Bishop says to Valjean, "Do not forget, do not ever forget, that you have promised to use the money to make yourself an honest man." Through this act of forgiveness, the Bishop is able to construct a future story that inspires Valjean's hope.[13]

Valjean's life story is transformed by his encounter with the Bishop. He keeps the candlesticks as a symbolic reminder of forgiveness and commits to a life of helping others. Valjean is stalked, however, by a merciless police inspector, Javert. Javert knows only the story of law and punishment, and he harasses Valjean for twenty years in the hope of returning him to prison. Finally Valjean extends forgiveness when Javert is in a vulnerable situation. Javert is unnerved by this act of grace and mercy and commits suicide. Hugo's novel is a parable in which the power of forgiveness is the key twist in the plot. Forgiveness can change the story of individuals and relationships.

Exercise 10-2

Hope for the Future

Pick one of the people you would like to forgive. Can you imagine how your relationship with that person might be different if you could completely forgive the person? Write some notes to yourself about how you would act and how the other person would act.

Suppose you forgave the person and began to act differently. What would the other person see you do? Might that affect the other person's behavior even if you did not tell the person that you forgave him or her?

Write a happy "ending"—or new beginning—to your story. By imagining a positive future for the relationship, you show yourself that there are positive goals that could be achieved if you forgave the person.

Relationships Are Stories

When I (Steve) started counseling couples, I found that relationships are really stories. One couple who had been married for thirty years came for counseling with serious, long-standing problems. Neither person had much hope that the problems could be worked out, for they had deeply hurt each other over recent years. I tried to understand their problems and asked them to describe their feelings about the marriage. Big mistake. Whenever the husband started talking about his feelings, the wife would bitterly disagree. When she expressed her feelings, he would look at the ceiling and scoff. Every session they were at each other's throats. I felt like the referee of a boxing match. I was surprised that they kept coming back.

After a couple months of watching this couple fight, I was ready to throw in the towel and declare it a double default. Then one session I asked, trying to hide my exasperation, "What attracted you to each other in the first place?" A strange silence came over the battlefield. Each paused to reflect. It had obviously been a long time since anyone asked them to think about anything positive in their marriage. The wife's voice took a softer tone as she began to recount how they first met back in high school. She told how they started dating and reminisced about the fun times. The husband described their first apartment after getting married. They laughed as he suggested that the apartment was no bigger than our consulting room. They told me about the borrowed furniture and the tight budget. We had moved to a different chapter in their story—one in which they had felt hope.

Experienced marital therapists know that it is important to get couples who are discouraged to tell the story of their early attraction. Relationships have a history. But the history is not just an accumulation of assorted facts. The history of a relationship is a story with a plot of romantic adventure, comic union or tragic despair. Relationships will always encounter obstacles to intimacy, and it is usually at the point of such obstacles that we must determine the plot of the story.

The stories of relationships can feel puzzling at times. Most of us would probably say that our important relationships are a mixture of joy and intimacy on the one hand and disappointment and pain on the other. But ultimately every relationship moves toward either a story of bitterness or a story of love.

In 1992 Joshua Sauñe sat on a plane headed from the United States back to his native Peru.[14] Joshua had seethed with hate since receiving word a few days earlier that two of his brothers and several relatives had been executed by terrorists along an Andes mountain roadside. The Sauñe family was heavily involved in Christian ministry to their own people—the Quechuas. So the Sauñes' leadership was seen as a threat by the Shining Path, a group of guerrillas trying to force a communist agenda on the Quechuas. Joshua's grandfather, a village pastor, had been brutally murdered in a public display by the Shining Path three years previously. Now they had struck the Sauñes again. Joshua describes his lust for revenge as he traveled home for the funeral of his brothers and relatives:

> I had decided that if I found the one who did it, I was going not only to kill him, but I was going to kill his grandparents if they were still alive, his brothers, his sisters, mother, father and children. Last I would kill him. That's how bitter I was.[15]

Joshua's mother met him at the airport and read the bitterness on his face. She told Joshua that revenge was "not worth it" and "that God had taken his brothers home." Still Joshua thirsted for revenge. He intended to invite those at the funeral to join his plan of revenge. But as Joshua stood to speak, he looked into the sad eyes of family and friends, and his story changed as he recalled a religious narrative about forgiveness: "In that moment I remembered how Jesus Christ was crucified, and it attracted people to him. And here were my brothers laying dead in front of thousands of Quechuas."

Joshua felt forgiveness growing in his heart. He saw that his brothers' death could be a story of hope only if he forgave. Joshua surrendered his own story of revenge and embraced a story of love and forgiveness that would give meaning to the tragedy. He spoke a message of hope and peace to the gathering and resolved to pick up the work his brothers had started.

Few of us will ever experience the brutal tragedies encountered by Joshua Sauñe, but eventually we all face suffering and loss. In our times of suffering, we must decide if the stories of our relationships will be about bitterness or love.

I was struck by the differences between stories of bitterness and stories of love when I worked with older adults in a nursing home a few years back. If you have been around the elderly, you know that many people in their later years like to tell stories about their life. I spent a lot of my time simply listening to people tell their stories.

This nursing home was what I would call "low budget." In fact, the conditions were deplorable. The rooms were in need of a fresh coat of paint to cover the dreary green walls. The hallways were often filthy. Most of the staff seemed apathetic at best, and residents complained of occasionally being bullied by the staff. How does one write the last chapter of his or her life story in such a place? I found that people do so in quite different ways.

Elaine was outspoken with a feisty sense of humor. She was eager to join all the social activities at the nursing home, which were limited in number. Elaine would sing loudly at the religious services and joke with the other residents. She was fun to be with.

But if you spent more than a few minutes with Elaine, you were going to hear about her son. He lived in a nearby affluent suburb and did not visit very often. Elaine's jovial personality would drop toward despair if we talked about her son. She would ask why he didn't visit more often, not expecting us to offer an answer. What haunted me the most was the tragic bitterness in Elaine's heart as she almost cursed her son. Her bitterness meant that the story of their relationship would not have a happy ending.

Anne, like Elaine, also had a wry wit. I met Anne because I was told that she needed someone to get her glasses repaired. She had fallen six weeks prior and broken them, and she could hardly see without them. I was surprised to find that she had a son who lived fifteen minutes away, but I didn't ask any questions. I had learned my lesson with Elaine.

Anne wasn't quick to tell her story. In fact, she was more interested in my story and the current events of my life. Eventually I drew out a tale of how Anne emigrated from Eastern Europe by herself to escape an abusive family when she was only sixteen years old. She told delightful and fascinating stories of her eighty-one years that would have captivated any audience.

Anne had suffered a hard life, and, as with Elaine, her children were not providing much support in return for all her sacrifices as a mother. But Anne was not one to complain. She was not afraid to express her disappointment that her children were not more involved in her life, but she could also show pictures of her children and grandchildren with joy. Anne could acknowledge both the good and the bad about her children. She had as much reason as Elaine to read the story of her life with bitter tears, but Anne chose to view her story as one of love. Why?

I'm not sure why people choose stories of forgiveness over stories of bitterness. Bitterness often makes sense, especially in cases like those of Elaine and Anne. But a story of bitterness offers no hope for the future. Anne was a woman who was looking ahead, whereas Elaine was looking behind.

During the time I knew Anne, she suffered from several serious illnesses, including heart disease. After her heart surgery, I visited her in the hospital. She asked mostly about my upcoming marriage in her usual manner of focusing on others. The surgery had been successful and Anne was feeling good. As I got ready to leave Anne beamed up at me with bright eyes and with spunky gusto exclaimed, "I'm gonna dance at your wedding!" It was the last time I ever saw Anne, for she took a turn for the worse that week and passed on. But her story of hope and forgiveness is an important chapter in my own story.

Authentic relationships usually tell a story with ups and downs, good and bad episodes. It is impossible for people to live together without occasionally hurting each other. Forgiveness is the balm that mends the tears in our commitments to each other. Forgiveness is the key difference between stories of bitterness and stories of love.

Stories Influence Relationships

When we reflect on our relationships, we can see that each relationship tells a story. We also build our relationships by telling each other stories or accounts.[16] For example, two people are standing on a street corner and witness a car accident. The police ask the two witnesses to give their personal accounts of the accident. The accounts may differ based on the personality and angle of the two people. One person knows a lot about cars, so she gives a detailed account of the mechanics of the accident. The other person has recently been in an accident, so his account is laced with emotional description. The same event leads to different accounts.

We also use accounts when we explain our actions to others. When a husband arrives at a restaurant to meet his wife an hour late, he needs to give an account, or a story, explaining why he is late. How does he know that he needs to give an account? The tense silence when he sits down at the table could be one clue.

The invitation to give an account or to explain oneself is called a "reproach." A reproach can come in various forms. Glaring eyes that demand an explanation offer a reproach that says "This story better be good!" A more directly hostile reproach would be "You're so late that I'm starving! I guess I wasted my effort getting here on time. Why are you late?" A calm and concerned reproach would be "I've been concerned. What happened?" Each reproach has a different influence on the account the man gives.

Some couples get into a pattern of serving up hostile reproaches to each other. This can lead to escalated conflict and potential violence or to secrets and lying. Conflict gets old after a while. Eventually the couple may find it is easier to avoid each other so they do not have to keep justifying their actions. Or one partner may discover that he or she had not been getting the real story about "late nights at the office." Hostile reproaches do not explain all conflicts in relationships, but the way we invite people to tell their stories will influence the stories they tell.

The accounts we offer in the midst of conflict with others can lead to avoiding or escalating the conflict. But we can also offer accounts that promote intimacy even in the midst of conflict.

Exercise 10-3
Reproaches and Rapprochement
Can you remember a misunderstanding that you had with a loved one? Perhaps you did something that offended your mate, your date, your parent, your child. Perhaps your loved one responded with a challenging reproach, one that made you angry. What did your loved one say or do that upset you? Has your loved one acted similarly before?

The temptation is to respond to a loved one's challenge in the same way every time. When we offend a loved one, we can often anticipate his or her response. Even before we face the loved one's reproach, we can prepare to avoid conflict by thinking through our response to the other person's reproach. How can you respond in love, even if the loved one might not act very lovingly? Write several alternatives you could employ.

One technique for helping couples deal with conflict is the couples' communication wheel developed by psychologist Sherod Miller. The "wheel" is a mat that goes on the floor. The mat has a circle on it that is divided into five sections like a pie. Each section contains a phrase representing an aspect of communication such as "I think" or "I feel." One partner stands on the mat and moves back and forth across the circle to communicate about an issue in their relationship. The other partner simply listens. The major goal is to help partners cover aspects of communication that they normally miss. For example, when I communicate with my wife I often tell her how I am thinking about a conflict, but I may leave out discussing my feelings.[17]

With the communication wheel, people will often work their way around the circle, describing thoughts, feelings and experiences to their partner. The last section, which reads "I want _____ for our relationship," usually slows people down. This is where stuttering often occurs. It is easy for most people to tell their side of the story of a conflict. But when asked what they want for their relationship, they are forced to imagine a story beyond the immediate conflict. They are reminded that relationships are more than just settling differences.

Some couples entrenched in conflict actually become embarrassed at this section of the wheel because it implies hope for an intimacy that has been buried and forgotten. The couple is asked to imagine an account of hope, not just an account of conflict.

Summing Up

Forgiveness is the key twist in the plot that turns stories of bitterness and despair into stories of love and hope. We have told many stories in this chapter because stories are one of the most proven methods of education. Find novels, plays or movies that tell stories of forgiveness. Save stories from newspapers or magazines about people who have been able to forgive. Meditate on religious narratives of forgiveness. As you identify with stories of forgiveness, you are likely to discover the power to change your own life story.

Eleven

Forgiveness &
Self-Condemnation

WHEN APRIL WAS TWENTY-FIVE YEARS OLD, SHE ABAN-
doned her husband and two small children. Now she
is forty-six years old. Her children have moved to the
other side of the country, and they do not want to be
in contact with her. She has no idea where her ex-husband is. She
regrets the things she has done and at least several times each day
wishes that she could undo the past.

April condemns herself for abandoning her family. Although she
has tried many techniques to help resolve her guilt (including several
years of psychological counseling), she still feels guilty. The self-condemnation is like a backache that won't go away. Even when the pain
is not acute, it is still there, just outside her awareness. Despite the
guilt, she has not contacted her family to make amends. It seems too
difficult, too painful, and requires too much contact with her past.

Do You Condemn Yourself?
All of us, at some point, regret things we have done that have had

terrible consequences for ourselves or for others:

"I should have checked the stove."

"The biopsy came back positive. Why did I smoke so long?

"I'll never forgive myself for abusing my kids."

"I cannot believe I actually said that to her. I wish there were some way to take it back."

Psychologist Paul Mauger and his colleagues devised a test for measuring the degree to which people forgive themselves.[1] Answer the questions in exercise 11-1 "true" or "false," and calculate your score using the instructions at the bottom of the scale.

Exercise 11-1

Forgiveness-of-Self Test

Answer each of the following items either true or false:

1. I don't think of myself as an evil person. T / F

2. I feel guilty because I don't do what I should for my loved ones. T / F

3. I often feel that no matter what I do now I will never make up for the mistakes I have made in the past. T / F

4. I regret things I do more often than other people seem to regret things they do. T / F

5. A lot of times I have feelings of guilt or regret for the things I have done. T / F

6. I often feel like I have failed to live the right kind of life. T / F

7. I rarely feel as though I have done something wrong or sinful. T / F

8. I often get in trouble for not being careful to follow the rules. T / F

9. I frequently put myself down for failing to work as hard as I should. T / F

10. It is easy for me to admit that I am wrong. T / F

11. I find it hard to forgive myself for some things that I have done. T / F

12. I frequently apologize for myself. T / F

13. I am often angry at myself for the stupid things I do. T / F

14. When I hear a sermon, I usually think about things that I have done wrong. T / F

15. I brood or think a lot about all the troubles I have. T / F

Directions for scoring:

1. Give yourself one point for every "true" response for items 2, 3, 4, 5, 6, 8, 9, 11, 12, 13, 14 and 15.

2. Give yourself one point for every "false" response for items 1, 7 and 10.

3. Add up your total points.

Scores on the forgiveness-of-self scale range from 0 to 15. How high is your score? According to Mauger's research, the higher your score, the more likely you are to suffer from depression, intense anger, anxious thoughts, feeling alienated from yourself and others, feeling persecuted and misunderstood.

In a study of people who "found forgiveness" through psychotherapy, psychologist Anthony Rooney interviewed five people who said they learned to forgive themselves through psychotherapy. For Rooney's participants, self-condemnation involved several negative aspects:

Feeling no longer fully acceptable or worthy of membership among the human race and feeling worthy of punishment

Experiencing a "split" inside themselves—part of them was perceived as a judge or accuser and another part as an inherently bad, though weak, victim of the accuser

Bearing within them a toxic secret that they longed to expel. This toxic secret involved the knowledge of their offenses and the fact that their offenses pointed to their inherent badness

Desiring to reveal their offenses and themselves to others but dreading the possible rejection or judgment that such a confession might elicit

Experiencing physical sensations such as pressure, weight and constriction that might interfere with the ability to breathe freely[2]

Mauger's and Rooney's research underscores the agony of self-condemnation. Is there any way to get out of this self-constructed prison? We believe that there is. But the solution is complex.

Complex problems often require complex solutions, and self-condemnation is no different. In this chapter we will explore the forces that contribute to self-condemnation. We will also suggest how to determine which of the forces may be influencing your capacity to forgive yourself. Finally, we will examine some strategies you can use to reduce your self-condemnation.

Cultural Factors in Self-Condemnation

At least three forces control our self-condemnation: culture, other people and our lack of empathy for our own humanness.[3] Who (or what) is this "self" that we often find ourselves condemning? Psychologist Philip Cushman suggests that each culture determines how it will understand the notion of *self*. The self is our culture's implicit definition of what it means to be a human being. According to Cushman, the culture of twentieth-century America, particularly post-World War II, has constructed a self that deemphasizes finding meaning in relation to relationships and institutions that we hold in common: family, community, religion and tradition.[4]

In traditional or communal-self cultures, people described who they were by saying "I'm John's son," "I'm a member of the Cherokee tribe," "I'm a Jew" or "I'm Irish." Instead of a self that is understood only in relation to others (one's family, community, religion or tradition), the twentieth-century American self is understood as an ungrounded entity that finds meaning only by indulging impulses to spend, consume and seek fulfillment. Rather than being imbedded in relationships, the modern self is empty and needs to be filled.

We still value relationships with others, but more frequently those relationships tend to be valued to the extent that they help to "fill" us. We don't depend on relationships for our identities; rather, we enter into relationships voluntarily and temporarily. The rise of the *empty self* in modern American culture can account partly for the prevalence of self-condemnation.

The empty self and guilt. In communal-self cultures, group membership forms identity. More accurately your group *is* your identity. If you lose your membership in the group, you literally lose your identity. In the time prior to the empty self, social and religious standards defined acceptable and unacceptable behavior. There was also consensus regarding what was expected of people. As a result, conformity to the norms of the group was considered crucial. If you broke the groups' norms by hurting another person, you ran the risk of losing your identity as a community member in good standing.

One way people regulated their behavior to insure that they would continue to maintain their good standing in their groups was the feeling of guilt. Guilt appears to be an inborn emotion.[5] Regardless of culture or background, we all have the capacity to feel guilt. However, our culture shapes how we will express and experience guilt.

Communal cultures make use of guilt feelings in order to maintain community harmony. They teach that guilt is an internal alarm to alert us that our behavior is not up to the standards of our community or relationships. The *feeling* of guilt is triggered by the fact that a person is *actually* guilty of breaking community standards. When people feel guilt, they soon try to figure out where they had hurt or neglected another person, how they could apologize and confess and how they could make amends for their transgressions so that they could maintain their identities as members of the community.

Because our culture widely (though not completely) embraces an empty self today, few of us belong to communities that have clear, consistent norms for right and wrong behavior. When we experience guilt, most of us don't look for visible community standards that we might have violated. We don't undergo a judgment by a community (unless our hurtful behavior also breaks a law). No community prescribes a course of action that we should take to clean up the mess we make. Afterward, no community receives us back as members in good standing.

People who are heavily influenced by the ideology of the empty self still feel guilt, but they don't look to a community to figure out what to do with it. Instead they figure out what to do with their guilt on their own. They may try to repair the relationship with the person that they hurt, they may avoid the person that they hurt or they may try to "forgive themselves."[6]

Self-forgiveness as a remedy for guilty feelings. Before modern society produced empty selves, traditions and rituals indicated how actions that hurt other people were to be treated. Each culture had rituals, whether they were forms of confession and penance, temporary (or enduring) isolation from the community, ritual ceremonies or (sometimes harsh) physical punishment. Rituals had psychological effects. They underscored the seriousness of hurtful interpersonal actions. They affirmed the objective reality of the community's ethical system, symbolized guilt, cleansed the offender of blame and then invited the offender back into the community, unburdened of guilt.

Such rituals still exist, although they are often treated with scorn or amazement by the culture of the empty self. Two examples are the Roman Catholic tradition and Alcoholics Anonymous (and other twelve-step programs).

The United States Catholic Conference specifies four aspects to the Rite of Penance, which directs Roman Catholics on how to react to their hurtful interpersonal behavior. People should first express contrition for their hurtful actions and then confess to a priest, who can speak for God regarding forgiveness. Then the person completes an act of penance. Penance should direct a person to repair some of the damage that his or her actions caused, although frequently penance involves religious behaviors (prayers or fasts) as well. Finally, the priest expresses absolution (that is, he declares that the penitent person has been freed from the penalties of sin). Absolution is celebrated through the Communion, which is a ritual for welcoming penitent people back into God's family and the community.[7]

Alcoholics Anonymous also values rituals for confessing moral and ethical failures, for receiving absolution and for being accepted back into a community of fellow strugglers. One of the Twelve Steps that form the basis of Alcoholics Anonymous encourages participants to conduct a moral inventory as a means of identifying their ethical failures and the ways that their behavior has hurt others in the past.

Employment of rituals like those used by the Roman Catholic church and Alcoholics Anonymous are the exception rather than the rule in the culture of the empty self. In a culture where the very notion of self is grounded in attempts to relieve emptiness, rather than being grounded in relationship to common values, people do not look for relief from the pain of guilt in relationships. Rather, the empty self seeks "self-forgiveness," which can dissipate guilt.

Your response to the empty self. You constantly bathe in a culture whose attitude toward seeking and granting forgiveness is, at best, lukewarm. The very notion of the empty self that you carry around handicaps you in your search to feel forgiven for your moral and ethical failures. If you want to feel forgiven, find a community of virtue that can nurture positive standards. Such a community can help you to see your moral failures and avoid self-condemnation when you have addressed your moral failures appropriately.

Interpersonal Roadblocks to Forgiving Yourself

Along with the ways that the empty self locks people into self-condemnation, aspects of our relationships with others can also limit our capacity to be freed from self-condemnation. In our culture, problems with guilt and self-condemnation are usually thought to be primarily *problems inside the person.* These are some of those problems that therapists might tell us need to be corrected when we feel guilty or self-condemning:

☐ Shaming thoughts

☐ Our perfectionism

☐ Our memories of how our parents taught us to be ashamed

☐ False beliefs that we must be perfect and never hurt other people

☐ Negative beliefs about ourselves

Whereas seeking freedom from self-condemnation by looking inward is probably important in many cases, the majority of problems with self-condemnation result because people are *relational*. Remember that one of the important themes of this book is that *forgiveness is relational*. Problems with self-forgiveness are also primarily relational problems. Thus we encourage you to look first to your relationships when you feel self-condemning.

April (described at the beginning of this chapter) was too ashamed and paralyzed by fear to reach out and risk the vulnerability of a sincere confession and apology for the past. Many people exhorted her that a sincere expression of her remorse, regardless of the response of her children and ex-husband, would help her to forgive herself. Nevertheless she couldn't, she wouldn't, apologize. She feared a hostile response from her abandoned family, and she might have been right.

Confession leaves us open to being rejected and hurt. Confession also has the potential to be the small change that can transform a relationship. It can be like seeding a cloud to stimulate a rainstorm—a small change that can bring life-giving rain to parched, dead ground. But it is a risk. April was not willing to take the risk. Are you?

What If There Is No One from Whom to Seek Forgiveness?
What about the occasions when we would seek forgiveness, confess and offer restitution or repayment to the people we have hurt, if only the person had not died or otherwise become unavailable? Many cannot forgive themselves because they are unable to use remorse, confession, apology and restitution to deal with the offenses they have committed in the past. Perhaps the person they have hurt has moved far away and cannot be contacted. Perhaps it is impractical to dredge up memories that are twenty years old. Perhaps the person they hurt has died.

Cases where it is physically or geographically impossible to receive forgiveness from another person are probably the exception rather than the rule. For most, freedom from self-condemnation remains a distant and unreachable goal because people refuse to seek forgiveness from the individuals they have hurt.

Empathize with our own humanness. In situations where we really cannot seek forgiveness, it may be best to seek freedom from self-condemnation by developing empathy for ourselves and by doing good to others. When we cannot seek forgiveness from someone and we have no one to empathize with us for our weaknesses and tendencies to hurt others, we sit in judgment of ourselves as criminals. We lose empathy with our human side—the side with the potential for redemption—and concentrate only on the side with the potential for hurting others. We treat ourselves as unforgivable.

To free ourselves from self-condemnation (if no one else is around to offer us forgiveness), we need to attempt to empathize with our whole self, seeing the evil that we do but also seeing the potential we have to love and to contribute to family, friends and society. Having viewed yourself as someone who can love and contribute to others, can you really condemn that person who has so much to offer? Chuck Colson, convicted and imprisoned for crimes during the Watergate scandal, changed and became a leader of a great ministry to criminals. If he can change, so can we. But we must hope that change is possible.

One final way that we may unburden ourselves of guilt and self-condemnation (even if we cannot contact the actual person we hurt) is to help other people in concrete, specific ways. Roy Baumeister and his colleagues reviewed extensive research on what people do when they feel guilty. They propose that guilt is caused by recognizing that our behavior has hurt others and damaged our social attachments; that is, we feel guilty when our behavior weakens our ties to others. Baumeister and his colleagues suggest that we might find relief from guilt by building our social attachments through *helping others, even if the person we help is not the person we hurt.* Helping others builds positive relations and may help us "cancel out" the guilt that we carry around from the social attachments that our hurtful actions damaged in the past.[8]

Summing Up

April has had a fierce battle trying to forgive herself for abandoning her children. It has required her to look at her relationship to the culture at large, especially her links with the great institutions of family, community and religion. She found much comfort in exploring religious roots that had long been dormant. In the context of her church, she found the hope that she had value and was worth forgiving. In our therapy together, we worked on her capacity to empathize with her humanness. She has become a volunteer with Special Olympics, which gives her an opportunity to help children all day long.

April is now considering the possibility of contacting her children to express her feelings of remorse for the past. April's gains were hard won, but she is beginning to feel free. Greater freedom will come after she seeks forgiveness directly from the people she hurt.

Exercise 11-2

Actions for Reducing Self-Condemnation

1. Evaluate your personal investment in the culture of the empty self. Do you live as if the self has the resources to solve its own problems with guilt, shame and self-condemnation?

2. Seek involvement in an institution (such as a community or church) that can help you to find standards for right and wrong you can believe in. The institution should give you hope that, even when you hurt others or act against those community standards, you can be forgiven and accepted back into right relationship with the people of the community.

3. Explore whether you can seek forgiveness from the person you have harmed. Read on to chapter twelve for more ideas about seeking the forgiveness of others.

4. After you seek the forgiveness of the people you have hurt, or if there seems to be no one to forgive you, work on your capacity to empathize with yourself. Evaluate your potential to love, and help your friends, family, community and world.

5. Build caring, positive relationships by finding concrete, specific ways to help others. By improving your positive attachments to others, you may be able to "cancel out" some of your self-condemnation.

Twelve

Forgiveness &
Your Own
Hurtful Actions

I(STEVE) WAS READING A NEWSPAPER AND MINDING MY OWN
business as I waited for my graduate psychology class to start. I
hardly noticed the professor walk into the room until he announced, "Please pass your papers to the front." My head
snapped to attention. *Papers? What papers?* When I caught a glimpse
of a classmate's paper, my heart began to race with panic, and the
internal dialogue started: *Oh no! You mean that paper is due today?*

The panic quickly turned to nausea as I realized what had happened. The professor had previously decided to allow us to turn in a
certain project late but had said nothing about an extension on this
particular paper. At my previous school, relaxed deadlines had been
commonplace, and students often turned in most of the semester's
work during finals week. This was my first semester at a new graduate
school, and I had presumed the same flexibility. But it was clear from
the papers passing by me that my classmates had taken this deadline
seriously.

Imagine that you are a new graduate student, eager to make a good impression. What would you do in this situation? Rather than immediately acknowledge that I had blown it in front of my peers, I decided to stall for time. The professor wouldn't know until after class that my paper was not in the stack. I sat through that entire lecture on a roller-coaster ride of emotions. *What will the professor think of me? What will my classmates say about me?* And though I wasn't conscious of it at the time, I later realized that a single commitment motivated me: "I must get out of this still looking good!" I had to save face.

Saving Face

"Face" is the social worth or esteem we feel from others. Sociologist Erving Goffman suggested that painful emotions, such as embarrassment or shame, come from a "loss of face" in front of others.[1] Most of us work to maintain social interactions that allow us to save face and feel social worth from others.

Losing face can be caused by accidents, negligence or intentional transgressions.[2] In general, accidents such as spilling coffee do not cause a serious loss of face because the offender is not worthy of blame. Negligence can cause a greater loss of face for the offender, but intentional transgressions bring about the greatest blameworthiness and loss of face. Intentional transgressions also threaten the victim's need for esteem. When someone intentionally wrongs another, it is an assault on the victim's social worth.

Strategies for saving face. My academic negligence was on the verge of earning me a major loss of face. I knew that by the end of the class period, I needed to produce some kind of explanation. Social psychologists who study the ways people manage their face needs have described four strategies: confessions, excuses, justifications and refusals.[3]

Confessions involve acknowledging one's offense, accepting full responsibility and expressing regret. Confession is the pathway to seeking forgiveness and surrenders the effort to protect one's own face. *Excuses* also involve acknowledging the offense, but only partial blame is accepted due to extenuating circumstances. *Justifications* involve accepting responsibility for the offense but then redefining the offense so that it is less objectionable. *Refusals* involve a blatant denial of responsibility for the offense or denying anyone the legitimacy to question you about the offense.

What options were open to me? Refusal was not an option if I intended to stay at that graduate school. Most professors do not take well to a first-semester graduate student saying "How dare you demand homework by the deadlines you set? I refuse to knuckle under to such authoritarianism!"

Instead I went to my instructor's office after class, hoping to explain my negligence as a case of unfortunate miscommunication based on my prior experience at a different school. I now recognize this strategy as a justification. My story sounded reasonable to me. I thought I would try to catch him alone. No such luck, as he had already noticed that my paper was missing and was headed down the hall to find me.

I met him and spontaneously started babbling my story of how I had misunderstood him about the other assignment, about how things were at my other school, about—my voice gradually descended in speed and volume. His disappointed face and sad eyes punctured my puffed-up story. Without saying a word, he turned and went back into his office. My justification was silenced by shame.

For several days I tried to fight off the nagging shame—to no avail. I then began to ask *why* I felt so ashamed. It became clear that my commitment to avoid a loss of face had led me to deny full responsibility for my negligence and, thereby, imply that my professor should have communicated more clearly. I could have simply offered him an honest confession without excuse and apologized. I could have even offered the excuse that I had fallen behind due to my work load and apologized. Instead I had chosen to share the blame with him to save face. Upon further reflection, I realized that I had put my professor in the awkward position of grading a late paper. I had been too absorbed in trying to save my own face to consider the inconvenience of my actions to anyone else.

Shame and saving face. Shame is a feeling of painful scrutiny or negative evaluation by oneself or by others. Psychologist June Price Tangney, a leading researcher of shame and guilt, suggests that shame involves feeling bad about oneself as a person, whereas guilt involves feeling bad about specific behaviors. Shame can arise when a person feels the threat of a significant loss of face. Tangney says that people prone to shame tend to become concerned primarily about themselves. People prone to guilt, however, are more capable of empathizing with others.[4]

In my misadventure with my professor, I initially felt shame about my negligence, but my shame intensified when I saw how hollow my justification really was. Later I felt guilty about the consequences of my actions on my professor. Seeking forgiveness and saving face represent the two paths we can choose when we come to a fork in the road. The path we choose has a lot to do with whether or not we feel shame.

Exercise 12-1

Your Response to Letting Someone Down

Recall a time when you disappointed someone. Perhaps you hurt the person. Perhaps you acted unwisely or did something that violated a parent's or employer's expectations. Analyze your response:

☐ What were your feelings? Did you feel embarrassed? Ashamed? Sad? Disappointed in yourself? Angry with the other person or with yourself or both?

☐ What kinds of thoughts went through your mind? Did you try to justify your actions in your own mind? Did you talk negatively and condemningly to yourself? Did you think about shifting the blame?

☐ What did you do? Did you attempt to cover up? Did you say anything to justify yourself? Did you put the blame on circumstances? On someone else? On your accuser? Did you try to undo the mistake you made? Did you try to make up for the mistake in some way?

When you feel shame, you tend to blame yourself as a defective person for making mistakes. When you feel guilt, you may be hard on yourself, but you see the problem as more tied to a specific situation. Which would you say characterizes your response in this case?

Seeking Forgiveness

Seeking forgiveness involves an awareness of one's moral and relational guilt for an offense. It is an expression of genuine contrition for a blameworthy offense. True accidents do not necessitate seeking forgiveness, though we should still express regret for the inconvenience and suffering that our actions caused the victim. Negligent offenses are a gray area because the degree of blame may vary. My offense in graduate school was not completely intentional, but I was worthy of blame.

Second, seeking forgiveness, at least for adults, involves empathy and a concern for the relationship. Obligatory apologies may be important for children, but adults should move toward seeking forgiveness out of a desire to repair a relationship. Offenses threaten the face needs of victims,[5] but they also challenge the trust in a relationship. By seeking forgiveness I honor three essential facets of a relationship: (1) I acknowledge the validity of certain moral guidelines in our relationship, despite having broken them; (2) I empathize with the other person; (3) I demonstrate that I care about the consequences of my actions for the victim and for our relationship.

Seeking forgiveness entails a willingness to lose face. Obviously expressions of seeking forgiveness will vary. We want to distinguish seeking forgiveness from superficial promises to "do better," manipulative efforts to "kiss and make up" and compulsive attempts to "pay back" one's victim. *Repentance* is the sincere promise to change one's behavior. *Reconciliation* comes from a mutual desire to restore trust in a relationship. *Restitution* is paying for the damage one has caused. Repentance, reconciliation and restitution can all be valid parts of seeking forgiveness, but none constitutes the entire process.

Alternatives to Seeking Forgiveness

Would you say your response to committing an offense in a relationship is more similar to that of Gomer Pyle or Barney Fife? If you remember *The Andy Griffith Show*, you probably don't like either of the alternatives.

Gomer was the clumsy gas station attendant who smothered people when he did something wrong. He would try so hard to make up for his wrongdoing that he would become more of an annoyance than was his original offense. Barney, on the other hand, was the defensive deputy who was perpetually making excuses or shifting the blame. He had to learn over and over the lesson that efforts to save face usually result in an even greater loss of face. If the town of Mayberry had a psychologist, he or she would have diagnosed both Gomer and Barney as highly sensitive to shame and loss of face.

Seeking forgiveness is awkward and often emotionally painful. I am placed in a vulnerable position when I humble myself before another person and accept the shame and loss of face that comes with admitting a wrongdoing. In the face of shame, a number of alternatives to seeking forgiveness often seem much easier. These alternatives include hiding, blaming, acting and atoning.

Hiding. One of the most common descriptions of shame experiences that people offer is the desire to hide. The book of Genesis tells the first story of shame and hiding as Adam and Eve try to evade God in the garden. Shame can induce avoiding the gaze of others in an attempt to avoid the loss of face. Theologian Dietrich Bonhoeffer noted that "sin always draws the culprit away from community," and this is due to the influence of shame.[6]

Hiding can take the passive form of simply avoiding contact with someone you have wronged in some way. Perhaps you can think of a person you have been avoiding lately for no reason other than an awareness that you have neglected an obligation or committed an offense.

Hiding can also take the active form of refusal. Refusal is a tough indifference to one's effect on others. Some people hide behind a refusal to acknowledge responsibility for their actions at all, much less seek forgiveness. For such people the feelings of shame are too overwhelming to be experienced.

Blaming. We can blame circumstances and make excuses to get ourselves off the hook, or we can blame others. In either case, blaming avoids shame and saves one's own face. Many times there are valid excuses or explanations, at least in part, for the things we do. But people who are extremely sensitive to shame tend to blame others more often.

June Price Tangney and her colleagues at George Mason University have done numerous studies revealing that people who are prone to shame are more likely to blame factors outside themselves for their wrongdoing. People who are prone to guilt, on the other hand, are more likely to accept responsibility for their actions and empathize with the offended party.[7]

I initially attempted to fend off shame about forgetting my graduate school deadline by directing some of the blame toward my professor for not being more clear about the deadline. This was so subtle I was not even consciously aware of what I was doing. But I felt too threatened by the shame to accept all the blame myself. Shame was a hot potato that I had to get rid of.

Tangney has also found that people who are prone to shame tend to be higher in interpersonal hostility and anger. For some people, the least suggestion of shame or loss of face brings on the defensive attack of a cornered animal. Most people do not like to be made aware of their need to repent or seek forgiveness.[8] Seeking forgiveness requires that we stop making excuses, quit blaming others and admit our shame to ourselves and the ones we have wronged.

Acting. Some individuals are adept at impression management. Like chameleons, these people can change colors depending on what will allow them to save face in various social situations. Talented actors can play a number of roles convincingly. A person can avoid acknowledging shame or a loss of face by pretending that everything is fine.

I (Steve) did a study of seeking forgiveness and impression management among college students. I asked students to think of a recent time when they offended another person. I gave them a test on seeking forgiveness from that person and a test of impression management. People who score high on the test of impression management are very conscious of the opinions of others and often act to try to maintain a positive impression. One question on the test even asked students if they had considered becoming an actor. I found that students higher in impression management tended to be lower in seeking forgiveness from others. It seems that actors attempt many forms of impression management instead of seeking forgiveness.[9]

Atoning. Atonement is paying the penalty for one's debt. Atoning is closer to seeking forgiveness than hiding, blaming or acting because it involves taking responsibility for one's offense. Penance is the ancient religious practice of working out one's atonement. In the movie *The Mission* Robert De Niro portrays a mercenary imprisoned for murder who accepts the challenge of atoning for his sins through the Catholic rite of penance. In a vivid scene, De Niro's character strains to climb a muddy mountain with a suit of armor and weaponry strapped to his back in an effort to work out his atonement.

Atonement in the form of taking responsibility for damage caused can be healthy. If I ruin a friend's coffeemaker, I ought to replace it. Tangney and her colleagues found that people who are prone to guilt tend to be more empathic and more willing to take responsibility for offenses. Attempts at atoning are unhealthy, though, when atoning precludes empathizing with the offended person.[10] Gomer Pyle was so frantic trying to atone for his wrongs that Andy (or whomever else he bothered) became burdened with the need to try to get Gomer to calm down. Gomer could not see that his atonement had become a nuisance.

Some people use atonement to avoid the more difficult and humbling realization that atonement is actually impossible. We cannot take back the hurtful names used in the heat of an argument. We cannot take back gossip about someone with whom we are angry. Seeking forgiveness comes from a humble willingness to admit and take responsibility for our moral failures.

Good Reasons to Seek Forgiveness

Several benefits can come from seeking forgiveness: benefits for oneself, the victim and the relationship.

Personal benefits: Authenticity. Seeking forgiveness allows us to be morally honest with others and with ourselves. It can be personally draining to deny our transgressions. Many people find it freeing to admit their failures because their deceit can stop and authenticity can be restored. Just ask anyone at the Virginia Department of Transportation (VDOT).

In 1994 the VDOT received in the mail an unsigned note and a money order in the amount of $150. The note explained, "Over 25 years ago I stole between 5 and 10 of those yellow flashing lights from various work sites in the Richmond area. This should more than pay for them. . . . I'm sorry. . . . Please forgive me."[11] Evidently a clear conscience was worth $150 to this former "road-light bandit."

Twelve-step groups practice corporate confession. Many people find that secrets lose their shaming power when they are confessed in front of others. One of the healing factors of therapeutic groups involves becoming aware of what Irvin Yalom calls "the universality" of our struggles. Yalom means that people who have been isolated in shame may believe that they are "unique in their wretchedness."[12] Those persons can find freedom in the experience of being accepted by others in spite of personal failures. Seeking forgiveness opens the possibility of more authentic living.

After I had wrestled with shame and guilt with regard to my professor for about a week, I went to him, apologized for shifting the blame and asked for forgiveness. The relief of a clear conscience was worth the loss of face. That did not turn out to be my only failure in working with the professor, yet he graciously invited me to work with him on this book.

Personal benefits: Acceptance. Several social psychologists have studied the effect of offering confessions, excuses, justifications and refusals on attitudes toward the offender. Some will remember that Richard Nixon never officially asked the American people for forgiveness in the Watergate scandal. Nixon claimed that he had suffered (atoned) enough. But do confessions and efforts to seek forgiveness successfully achieve acceptance from victims?

Psychologist Bernard Weiner and his colleagues reviewed numerous studies on confession and concluded that people who confess their wrongdoing are usually viewed more positively than are people who offer excuses or denials, particularly when confession is offered without prior accusation.[13]

Psychologist Marti Hope Gonzales has done several studies of victims' evaluations of offenders' explanations. In general Gonzales has found that as offenders' explanations express less personal responsibility for the offense, victims become less forgiving and more negative and sarcastic. Gonzales says that this is because offenders who do not accept blame are failing to acknowledge the face needs of their victims.[14]

Other studies have found that excuses can be effective with some people. Such people prefer less interpersonal conflict and would rather hear an excuse than a confession. Overall, though, the research suggests that cases of clear wrongdoing, confession and seeking forgiveness offer the best chance of receiving acceptance from others. Seeking forgiveness can also benefit victims by restoring the dignity needed to save face and by rebalancing power in the relationship.

Victim's benefits: Restoration of dignity. Offenders are not the only ones who can lose face through hurtful behaviors. Victims of hurtful actions can feel a loss of dignity or worth as a person. In other words, victims can lose face. An offender begins to restore face or dignity to his or her victim by confessing wrongdoing and seeking forgiveness.

By denying responsibility an offender threatens and disregards the face needs of the person who has been hurt. We believe that seeking forgiveness is a way of affirming the dignity of a victim. When I confess wrongdoing and seek forgiveness, I am in effect saying to another person, "You deserved to be treated better, as a person of worth."

The victim may or may not be an *innocent* victim. Long-term relationships usually include wrongs committed by both parties, so no one is completely innocent. But gridlock will persist as long as both people remain entrenched in a strategy of justifying their own hurtful behavior. So how does seeking forgiveness restore dignity to a person who has been hurt?

Tim was busy planning his upcoming wedding and sending out invitations, but he kept struggling with nagging guilt about a former girlfriend. This woman was not his most recent nor his most serious girlfriend prior to his fiancée. In fact, he had not talked to her for a couple of years. But he was troubled by the sense that he had led her on several times in order to take advantage of her. He tried to argue with his own conscience: *This is silly! What I did was no different from what happened all the time among our friends. Why should I apologize when other guys treated her even worse? Besides, it was so long ago she probably doesn't even remember.*

Eventually Tim decided to call the woman to apologize for the way he had treated her. He later admitted that his biggest fear was that she would think he was neurotic. Her actual response on the phone was "I can't believe you think enough of me to call and apologize after two years! That really makes me feel good."

Tim learned that empathizing with a person he had hurt felt awkward. But his empathy led to seeking forgiveness. Seeking forgiveness restores face and dignity to one who has been tarnished by shame and leads to healing for each person in the relationship.

Victim's benefits: Rebalance of power. To listen to and care about another person is to give that person some power in the relationship. Healthy relationships are characterized by a balance of the power to influence one another. Hurtful actions can work against the balance of power if the offender does not acknowledge his or her wrongdoing. Seeking forgiveness restores a measure of power or influence to the victim of an interpersonal offense. An offender who confesses and seeks forgiveness is saying to the other person, "You have the power to influence me. You have a moral voice in our relationship."

Since some people will use guilt manipulatively to gain power in a relationship, seeking forgiveness should not be understood as naively overlooking abuse against myself or assuming all the blame in a relationship. In fact, after I have sincerely confessed my wrongdoing and sought forgiveness, I may have earned the opportunity to talk about some ways I have been hurt in the same relationship (though doing so in the same conversation as admitting my guilt might be perceived as an excuse or justification). The paradox of seeking forgiveness is that we often gain the power of influence by giving it away. Intimacy will be blocked as long as I remain committed to holding all the power in a relationship.

Relational benefits: Restoration of moral guidelines. Seeking forgiveness acknowledges the legitimacy of moral guidelines in relationships. Moral guidelines are often assumed and unspoken. For example, at one time a coworker of mine (Steve's) had a tendency to snap at people when she was under stress. Occasionally she became quite disrespectful toward her coworkers, even denigrating them in front of customers. After being on the receiving end of her humiliating jabs a couple of times, I became resentful. I had assumed the moral guideline that coworkers should treat one another with respect, and she was violating that. One stressful day at work I used a sarcastic and abrasive tone of voice with her. I felt guilty immediately, but I kept reminding myself that she had done the same thing to everyone in the office.

It didn't help. If I expected the moral guideline of respect for coworkers to be followed, I needed to affirm that moral guideline to her. I went to her and apologized for my angry tone of voice. This simple apology initiated a subtle change in our relationship. The woman seemed to become more conscious of how she communicated with me. In addition, by seeking forgiveness I had interrupted my own pattern of getting even, and this in itself was beneficial to our relationship.

In some instances affirming a moral guideline may be crucial to restoring trust. When one partner violates the marital covenant by having an affair, a moral guideline has been broken. The faithful spouse will feel a betrayal of trust. Trust can be restored only after moral guidelines are reaffirmed. A repentant spouse who genuinely seeks forgiveness at the very least affirms a commitment to the moral principle of sexual fidelity in marriage. In the case of an affair, however, the mere confession of a repentant spouse will not immediately restore trust. Trust must be reearned over a time of fidelity. But without the confession of wrongdoing and the restoration of moral guidelines, trust is unlikely ever to be rebuilt.

Trust is at the heart of relational intimacy. Moral guidelines in a relationship allow trust to develop and thrive. By seeking forgiveness I communicate that I am committed to the moral guidelines that sustain trust.

Relational benefits: Shared suffering. Sharing the emotional suffering of another person may improve the quality of the relationship.[15] Psychologists Kenneth Locke and Leonard Horowitz were interested in studying how the similarity of emotional states between two people would affect their interactions. They found that two people experiencing similar emotional states (for example, both feeling sad) were more likely to have a positive interaction than were two people in mismatched emotional states. Seeking forgiveness can be a way of sharing the hurt of another person and redistributing the emotional pain in a relationship.[16]

I had just closed the door behind my friend after an enjoyable evening of dinner and conversation. A smile of satisfaction was still on my face as I turned around and saw the dejected look on my wife's face. "What's wrong?" I demanded with defensive impatience.

"Oh, just the usual," she replied in a sad tone of voice.

"What do you mean, 'the usual'?" My irritation was growing. My mind flashed an anxious reminder of the report I had to finish for the next morning, and I glanced intentionally at my watch.

"Well, when one of your friends comes for dinner you usually let me do the cooking, and you take care of the conversation for the evening. I've told you before that I feel left out when all you talk about is silly philosophical issues."

"Free will versus determinism is not a 'silly' issue!"

Danielle looked at me with pain and disbelief and then retreated to the bedroom.

By immediately defending myself, I expressed my feelings of annoyance and defended the nobility of philosophy. I also communicated to her that I did not care about her emotional pain. I was telling her, "Hey, this is your problem. Deal with it alone." And Danielle was too smart to enter a debate with someone who loves to spend evenings debating fine philosophical points. I won the battle but lost the war.

Somehow the hurt in Danielle's eyes penetrated the heart of this crusty armchair philosopher. She had made the same complaint before, and I was becoming suspicious of myself. I followed her to the bedroom and said, "I'm sorry I hurt your feelings. Tell me how I make you feel left out."

Listening to her hurt and frustration was emotionally costly. I shared her suffering for the first time on this issue and felt the consequences of my selfish insensitivity. I had dominated conversations to keep myself entertained and in control. Denying her feelings and downplaying their importance would only erode the intimacy of our relationship.

Seeking forgiveness means the person we offended will no longer have to bear all the hurt alone.

Steps Toward Seeking Forgiveness

Humble listening. The first step toward seeking forgiveness involves the humility of listening. University of Montana psychologist John Means and his colleagues believe that humility involves four factors.[17]

First, humility is a willingness to listen to one's conscience and admit one's faults. We have already described research that suggests that people who are prone to shame tend to respond defensively to losses of face. The insecurity that motivates this defensive pride is very different from the strength of humility. The humble person does not feel as though his or her entire identity is threatened by admitting specific faults.

Second, humility involves the recognition that one cannot control all interactions with others. Tangney and her colleagues found that people prone to shame also try to manipulate social interactions. This may reflect a desire to control others' opinions. Listening to the hurts of others involves surrendering an excessive desire to control.[18]

Third, humility requires an attitude of patience and gentleness with others. Listening to others requires patience and gentleness rather than defensive or self-justifying maneuvering. Humble listening involves sensitivity to the unspoken ways people tell us we have hurt them. We may notice the quiet withdrawal of our spouse or the nervous laughter of a friend after we make an insensitive joke. The humble person can even ask close friends dangerous questions such as "What is it like relating to me?"

Fourth, humility is the platform to empathy. This makes humility important, since empathy is also the springboard to forgiving others. The humble person is willing to consider the perspective of others and to enter into that person's situation. If I were in a conflict, humility would (hopefully) allow me to entertain the possibility that I am wrong (at least in part). I might then be motivated to empathize with the other person by considering his or her perspective as a way of better understanding the conflict.

Empathic guilt. Through humble listening I try to discern whether I have committed an interpersonal offense. If I determine that I have wronged someone, the next step involves the attitude of empathic guilt, which is a sense of sorrow or remorse for the impact of my actions on the person I have wronged and on our relationship. The concern is primarily for the other person. In contrast, the shame-prone person tends to regret his or her own loss of face and remains self-absorbed.

Tangney and her colleagues found that people who are prone to guilt (rather than shame) tend to be higher in interpersonal empathy, take more responsibility for wrong behavior and attempt more reparative strategies, such as seeking forgiveness. The research of Tangney and a number of other psychologists suggests that the guilt associated with empathic concern for others has positive consequences for relationships.[19]

Repentant confession. Seeking forgiveness also entails repentant confession. By "repentant" we mean that a person desires to do better. It may be possible for a person to feel contrite about his or her hurtful actions and the damage caused, to say a sincere "I'm sorry," but still know that the behavior is likely to recur. Repentance expresses an honest promise to try not to repeat the offense.

But what if I can't promise not to repeat the offense? That is a crucial question to wrestle with before seeking forgiveness. Am I willing to change my behavior? What measures are necessary to guard against repeating the hurtful action?

Confession to the one who was hurt should involve an honest acceptance of responsibility for the offense. The confession should also communicate an awareness of hurt or damage one has caused, as well as an awareness of how one should have acted.

Confessions may be met with hostile reactions, which open the door to defensiveness. The hardest part about confession and seeking forgiveness is that some people may want to tell us more than we care to know about how we have hurt or disappointed them. It is difficult to sit and absorb the pain of others.

Inviting reconciliation. By seeking forgiveness, we are ambassadors of reconciliation.[20] Good diplomacy suggests that ambassadors should invite, not demand, reconciliation between nations in conflict. At times I have sought forgiveness from people I have hurt and been surprised, even irritated, when the person did not skip into my arms for reconciliation. When seeking forgiveness, we must be sensitive and patient for the healing of broken trust and for reconciliation.

Seeking forgiveness should be an invitation to reconciliation and a restored relationship rather than simply "getting something off our chest." In seeking forgiveness we should communicate that we value our relationship with the one we have hurt and that we desire to improve the relationship.

Exercise 12-2
Steps Toward Seeking Forgiveness

Think of a specific time when you hurt someone. Did you hurt a romantic partner or spouse? A child? Your own parent? Someone you work with or a close friend? Was the hurt a one-time occurrence, or did it occur over a long period of time? Apply the steps in this chapter to analyze whether you need and want to seek forgiveness from the person you hurt.

1. *Humble listening.* Listen to your conscience. Without justifying yourself, examine your behavior to see whether you have harmed the person. Try not to justify that you hurt the person because he or she hurt you first. Identify an important specific instance to reflect on (even though you might have hurt the other person many times).

2. *Empathic guilt.* Can you determine whether you offended or hurt the other person? How do you think the other person felt? Angry? Disappointed? Sad?

3. *Repentant confession.* Do you feel sorry for having hurt the other person? Do you sincerely hope not to repeat such offenses? You might think that it is not humanly possible to avoid ever hurting the person again, but you should sincerely try. Would you like to confess to the other person? Before you do, play the scene in your imagination. Rehearse what you might say. The other person may have difficulty accepting your confession. Remember that you are not responsible for his or her response—only for your actions. Expect the person to retort angrily. Can you avoid becoming defensive and creating more conflict? Can you confess with humility and empathically understand the person's reaction to your confession?

4. *Inviting reconciliation.* Reconciliation is not always possible, but it often is. Analyze whether you think it would be wise to invite reconciliation. If so, invite the person to a restored relationship. Remember, if the other person was hurt, you cannot demand instant forgiveness. It may take the other person a while before he or she feels safe enough to accept your invitation to forgive and be reconciled. The fact that you have humbly repented, confessed and sought reconciliation does not obligate the other person to respond immediately. Often trust has been damaged, and it takes time to rebuild that trust. Understand the other person's point of view and be patient.

Summing Up

When our actions have hurt another person, we can choose either to seek forgiveness or to save face. There are many ways to save face, and most are far less costly in the short run than seeking forgiveness. Seeking forgiveness involves a surrender of our own desire to save face in order to affirm the face needs of the person who has been hurt. We affirm the person we have hurt through humble listening, empathic guilt, repentant confession and inviting reconciliation. Seeking forgiveness is beneficial not just for us but for the person we hurt and for the relationship between us.

Thirteen

Forgiveness & Its Consequences for You

AN ABUSE SURVIVOR STOPS FANTASIZING ABOUT REVENGE, and her stomachaches cease. A college student finds dignity and peace regarding her relationship with her parents. A businessman learns to accept himself and others after living a hostile, competitive lifestyle that led to a heart attack two years earlier. A husband and wife are reconciled after years of conflict. A retired woman becomes less depressed and fearful after forgiving her adult children for placing her in a retirement community.

Having read this far into the book, you have a better understanding of what forgiveness is and how it works. We hope you now can see that forgiveness is complex and involves changing how you think, feel and act. It involves empathy with the person who hurt you. It involves humility and a willingness to admit that you, too, have done wrong. Beyond empathy and humility, forgiveness involves the motivation to act.

Now we ask another question: What good can come from forgiving? Forgiveness is valued because it is the right thing to do. But many writers have also suggested that forgiveness yields good things—peace, happiness, health, reconciliation. Almost every aspect of forgiveness—confessing, asking for forgiveness, forgiving someone and receiving forgiveness—is hypothesized to promote health and wholeness. Forgiveness is also supposed to help us have better relationships with other people—our friends, family members and community.

But do we have any evidence that forgiveness really produces these good things? According to many psychologists (not just us), forgiveness is supposed to produce benefits such as better mental health, physical health, the restoration of personal control and spiritual benefits. In the next chapter we will examine the potential benefits of forgiveness for marriages and families. In the final chapter we will examine the potential of forgiveness for mending relationships in our communities and in the world around us. In this chapter we explore the potential benefits of forgiveness to our personal health and well-being.

Two kinds of studies can address the relationship between forgiveness and health. In the first kind, called a *correlational study,* a researcher evaluates people in terms of both their health and their forgiveness of another person. After gathering these data, the researcher can determine statistically whether increases in forgiveness are related to improvements in health.

In the second kind of study, called an *experiment,* the researcher randomly assigns participants to some form of treatment that is expected to improve forgiveness or that is not expected to improve forgiveness. Following the treatments, the researcher evaluates the participants' physical or mental health to determine whether the participants who completed a treatment that encouraged forgiveness experienced improvements in health that were greater than the health improvements of people who did not participate in the forgiveness treatment. The benefit of the experiment is that, because participants were randomly assigned to complete an intervention to improve their forgiveness, we can conclude that any change in their health was due to their participation in the treatment.

Mental Health and Forgiving

The hope that forgiving other people leads to better mental health has been the lure that has attracted the interest of pastors and psychologists. Forgiveness is hoped to be a magic bullet that makes people more mentally healthy. Letting go of resentment, hatred, mistrust and desire for revenge through forgiveness is often why people are encouraged to forgive.

Psychologist Elizabeth Gassin reviewed many empirical studies that have investigated the relationship between forgiving and psychological experiences such as anxiety and depression. Gassin found that across a wide variety of studies and groups of participants, forgiving appeared to be related to slightly better mental health.[1] We reviewed other research and also found more evidence that forgiveness might actually be good for us.[2]

Most of the research we reviewed was correlational. From that research we could not conclude that forgiving *caused* changes in mental health. Correlational studies showed only that people who forgave also tended to have fewer mental problems. It is possible that better mental health actually made people better at forgiving, instead of the other way around, or that a third variable could be responsible for making people both more mentally healthy and better at forgiving. For example, perhaps holding certain religious beliefs or coming from certain family backgrounds made people more healthy and more forgiving. To determine the real causes, what was needed was some good experimental research.

John Hebl and Robert Enright studied twenty-four older women to determine whether forgiveness could be promoted in group therapy. These women participated in either a group to give them skills that would help them forgive other people or in a discussion group that was not supposed to help them do anything except discuss their lives. This discussion group served as a *control group*. It was used to compare the effectiveness of the forgiveness group.[3]

Hebl and Enright found that their forgiveness group really did help the women to forgive better than did the discussion group. But both the forgiveness group and the discussion group helped reduce depression and anxiety, so the improvements in mental health could not be attributed clearly to learning how to forgive.

Perhaps Enright's study involved too few people, we thought. Perhaps we could detect the healthy effects of learning to forgive if we conducted a study with more people. In 1993 the three of us conducted such a study.[4] We described other aspects of this study in detail in chapter nine. We worked with college students who indicated that they wanted to forgive someone who had hurt them in the past, though they had not been able to forgive. Participants took part in one of three groups:

1. a group to help them forgive by generating empathy for their offender

2. a group to help them forgive by convincing them that revenge and withholding forgiveness were bad for them

3. a control group (these people did not participate in a treatment until after the study was conducted)

With eighty-one participants, we believed we would get some good information that would help us learn how forgiveness and mental health are related.

We assessed each of our participants' forgiveness, their psychological symptoms and two variables called *empathy* and *perspective-taking,* which measured the degree to which participants were able to identify with their offenders on both an emotional and a mental level. We assessed these attributes before they participated in the groups, directly after they participated and six weeks after the completion of the groups.

We found that our empathy-based forgiveness group was much more effective at encouraging forgiveness and encouraging empathy for the offender than either of the other groups. The two forgiveness groups appeared to be about equally effective at reducing psychological symptoms and increasing perspective-taking: people were less bothered by psychological symptoms six weeks after completing our groups and also had a greater ability to adopt the perspective of their offenders.

However, we wanted to determine whether the changes in forgiveness were *responsible* for reductions in our participants' psychological symptoms. We used a statistical technique called causal modeling to interpret our findings. Based on this technique, we could not explain the reductions in symptoms solely in terms of changes in forgiveness. We were, however, able to explain them as the result of changes in participants' capacity to feel with and take the cognitive perspective of the offender—that is, in participants' empathy for the offender.

Empathy, as we discussed in chapter eleven, is an emotional response to the problems and frailties of the offender. Empathy requires perspective-taking, which is the ability to stand in the shoes of other people and see life the way they do. Empathy appeared to be responsible for our participants' capacity to forgive their offenders.

At the writing of this book, our findings are the best that psychological science has to offer about how forgiving others might improve mental health. Better science may find different results later. At this time, though, it appears that if you do the hard work of developing empathy for your offender, not only do you end up being more likely to forgive, you may also improve your mental health.

Mental Health and Accepting Forgiveness

In chapters eleven and twelve we discussed the possibilities for seeking and finding forgiveness for yourself. Do the data show that receiving forgiveness from others leads to better mental health?

In a thirty-year-old study (the oldest scientific study of forgiveness with which we are familiar), J. G. Emerson looked at the relationship between feeling forgiven and one's self-image.[5] Emerson hypothesized that people who feel forgiven as a result of counseling, worship services or participation in groups should also be more accepting of who they are. Self-acceptance has long been considered a good measure of mental health: the smaller the disparity between how we perceive ourselves and who we would like to be, the reasoning goes, the more adjusted and happy we are.

Emerson's participants completed measures of feeling forgiven and the disparity between their real and ideal self-image both before and after participating in (1) counseling, (2) a worship service or (3) a one-hour class on marriage and family. Emerson's study used 153 participants. For 150 of them, the disparity between their ideal and actual self-images varied in the same direction as their change in feeling forgiven. That is, if they became happier with themselves through their participation in counseling, worship or the class, then their sense of being forgiven increased. Similarly, if they became less happy with themselves, then their sense of being forgiven also dropped. *How forgiven people feel, then, is related to their self-acceptance.*

As a kid, my (Mike's) brother liked to build things. But he also liked to take them apart. Occasionally he did not get all the pieces back into place. But he always ended up with a better understanding of how things worked. The science of psychology is similarly motivated. Psychologists want to know how things work, how forgiveness works. Why should it be that forgiving other people is followed by reductions in psychological symptoms? How might we explain that feeling forgiven is related to greater correspondence between who one is and who one would like to be?

Here's our guess: When we have been hurt by another person, our thoughts, attitudes, expectations and ways of seeing the world shift. We become more aware of our surroundings and our relationships, guarding against future hurts. If this situation is troubling enough, it is a psychological symptom called hypervigilance. However, it is more likely that most of us become only *slightly* more aware and tentative about being hurt again. We begin to believe that the world is a more threatening place, not a very safe place. We begin to think that we are less able to cope with life or to keep ourselves safe. Life seems more out of our control after we have been hurt by others.

When we feel guilty for hurting another person (or just guilty in general), similar changes in our thinking occur. We evaluate ourselves more negatively. We see ourselves as bad people. We feel less worthy of living. These beliefs spread through our understandings of ourselves and our surroundings, and the world becomes a more dreary place to live.

A field called cognitive psychology has taught us that such negative beliefs, attitudes and expectations are partially responsible for psychological disorders such as anxiety and depression. Cognitive therapies reduce anxiety and depression by directly modifying negative thinking. Being hurt by others, or being guilty of hurting others, distorts our thinking. Forgiveness, perhaps, heals these distortions.

Forgiving others might be a natural cognitive therapy. When we forgive others by developing empathy—feeling with them and seeing things from their perspective—we dispute the negative beliefs that we hold about other people, the world and our ability to cope. Forgiveness restores our belief that there are good people in the world. Even though we have been hurt, that hurt does not generalize to all people. Not all people will hurt us all of the time. Often other people *are* trustworthy. We also learn that we can cope with the cards we were dealt. We see ourselves as strong enough to survive and flourish, even though life is difficult and painful at times.

Being forgiven may also be a natural form of cognitive therapy. When we accept forgiveness from others or from God, we dispute the idea that we are worthless or that we do not count. We reduce our expectations that life will be a dreary jail term for the wrongs we have committed and the mistakes we have made. Life has new possibilities. We feel renewed and hopeful.

Physical Health and Forgiving

Could a forgiving attitude improve your physical well-being, reduce your risk of heart disease, reduce pain or unnecessary illness? Some researchers are beginning to answer yes. For example, G. A. Pettitt conducted workshops on forgiveness for patients with some severe medical problems. He reported that some of his patients recovered from a variety of illnesses and problems. They attributed their recoveries to forgiving people who had hurt them.

The mind, body and spirit may be more closely linked than we think. When we forgive, not only our thoughts change, our bodies respond as well. Perhaps our spirits are also healed. We want to describe three areas of recent research that suggest the power of forgiveness to heal the mind, body and spirit.

All three studies involve people with cardiovascular problems. Most were high achievers, successful in business, hyperefficient. So efficient, in fact, that any waste of time felt like a setback. Feeling as though they were in competition with others, they had a free-floating hostility, mistrust and resentment toward the people with whom they lived and worked. They were "Type A." They had heart attacks.

In 1972 a complex and courageous study was planned to determine whether the Type A behavior pattern could be reduced in men and women who had had heart attacks, and whether the reductions would lead to decreased recurrences of heart attacks. Almost six hundred people were assigned to meet in small groups to discuss their experiences with heart attack, how to care for their heart and how to deal with the free-floating hostility, sense of time urgency and other characteristics of the Type A behavior pattern. Another 270 people participated in small groups to discuss coronary care without discussing the Type A behavior pattern. The groups met for four and a half years.

Physicians followed these patients to study the recurrence of their Type A traits and heart attacks over time. By the end of the third year 7.2 percent of the patients in the Type A counseling had had fatal or nonfatal heart attacks. In the cardiac counseling groups 13 percent of the patients had recurrent heart attacks. The patients who continued with their Type A behavior were more likely to have recurrent heart attacks. Reducing the hostility, time urgency and impatience that characterize the Type A behavior pattern reduced the risk of recurrent heart attacks.[6]

Although reductions in the Type A behavior pattern reduced recurrent heart attacks, what *new behaviors* did the participants learn that also helped them in their avoidance of recurrent heart attacks? Berton Kaplan, one of the researchers who has been heavily involved in research on the Type A behavior pattern, observed that the participants learned to be themselves rather than what others expected, to develop and value relationships, to live a philosophically wiser life and to forgive.[7]

Redford Williams is a physician at Duke University who has also intensively studied the Type A behavior pattern for many years. Like most researchers who study Type A behavior, Williams believes that we must find ways to reduce our anger and hostility to avoid the harmful and potentially fatal effects of the Type A behavior pattern. Anger and hostility seem more related to cardiovascular problems than do a sense of time urgency and impatience. Williams suggests that forgiveness is one way to relieve anger and hostility.[8]

He also suggests three steps that can be implemented to become more forgiving:

1. Learn to recognize that anger will not help to change or undo the injustices done to us.

2. Institute a "policy decision" to forgive the injustice as a way of reducing our anger and hostility and moving on with life, beginning with the relatively minor hurts.

3. Repeat this process to forgive others for more painful injustices that we have suffered.

According to Williams, by practicing forgiveness in this way we can reduce the free-floating anger and hostility of the Type A behavior pattern. Correlational studies suggest that adopting a forgiving lifestyle is indeed related to reductions in anger.[9]

Psychologists Joseph Neumann and David Chi actually found that people who tended to forgive others who hurt them had lower levels of anger and hostility than did people who tended not to forgive. In a follow-up study, researcher Chris Rachal and I (Mike) found that people who forgave others, especially when the hurtful event was *severe* (for example, a lover's unfaithfulness or a parent's abuse), had lower levels of overall anger. These studies suggest that when we forgive we may be able to minimize our hostility. As the Type A research shows, when we reduce our anger and hostility we give our hearts a break.

Exercise 13-1

Forgiving When You Are Stressed Out, Angry and Feeling Hostile

When we get stressed out because we face too many demands for too little time, we can become frustrated, angry and hostile—especially if things start to go wrong. That anger, hostility and time pressure can be bad for our hearts and for our relationships. There may be several roots to the problem.

1. Examine your life and see whether you must do everything with such urgency as you now feel. If some tasks don't really need to be done right away, set them aside.

2. Most people put 80 percent of their effort into 20 percent of the tasks. That usually means that lots of tasks won't get done each day. If you pick the five most important tasks each morning and work systematically down the list, you'll probably finish the day with undone tasks on your list, but you'll have the satisfaction of knowing that you did the most important things. You'll feel better about your day.

3. Your stress may come from your lifestyle rather than from your time-management strategies. Examine yourself to see whether you push yourself in an unhealthy way, setting up situations in which interpersonal conflict is inevitable. Examine yourself to see whether you feel hurried and then justify abrasiveness as being time-efficient. If you carefully examine yourself, you might find some personality characteristics that you want to change (see exercise 13-2).

Forgiveness and Physical Health in Older Adults

In light of research on forgiveness, anger and the Type A behavior pattern, we might expect that forgiveness would be related to better physical health. Judith Strasser found that forgiveness actually was related to better health in fifty-nine older adults. The participants in Strasser's study described a painful interpersonal hurt that they had suffered. Although some of the hurts were relatively recent, many of the respondents described hurts that had occurred many years earlier. Most participants had been hurt by siblings, spouses and friends. About a third of the participants indicated that the hurts had not been completely resolved.[10]

Strasser's participants completed a battery of questionnaires that were designed to measure their mental health, physical health, satisfaction with life and forgiveness for the person who had hurt them earlier in life. Strasser found that forgiveness did not appear to be related to mental health or life satisfaction, but the more Strasser's participants had forgiven the people who had hurt them, the better their physical health in older adulthood.

Participants' motivations for forgiving were also important in understanding how forgiving was related to health. Forgiving for the sake of the offender, their relationship or for the intrinsic value placed on forgiveness (what we called *intrinsic forgiveness* in chapter nine) was related to better health. Forgiving as a way of seeking personal benefits or in order to live up to the expectations of other people (what we called *role-expected forgiveness* and *expedient forgiveness* in chapter nine) were *not* related to better health.

We draw two lessons from Strasser's research:

☐ If we forgive now, we may feel better physically as we age.

☐ We need to forgive for the right reasons in order for the forgiveness to help us feel better physically (we are better off if we forgive from the heart).

Physical Health and Confession

Confession is good for the soul. Perhaps it is also good for your health. At least that is the finding suggested by the work of James Pennebaker and his colleagues.[11]

To disclose something painful feels stressful. When you describe a traumatic or painful event to someone, several things may occur physiologically. Your blood pressure temporarily increases and then decreases again. You feel stressed out. Your voice quivers, and it is hard to say what is on your mind.

However, as you discuss this event, your skin conductance (which measures how stressed you feel in a given situation—it's used in lie detector tests) decreases. Moreover, the less you have talked about the event in the past, the greater reduction in skin conductance you experience. Somehow it seems to be relaxing to confess. You drop your guard as you share your feelings.

In several studies, Pennebaker has found that students and university employees who share their emotions and impressions of traumatic events actually reported fewer visits to the student health center over the six-month period following the confession. They also felt healthier and reported fewer days of restricted activity due to illness.

Does disclosing painful memories to someone have any application to what happens when we confess after we have offended someone else? Is it possible that confessing the ways we have hurt others is physically healing? When we hurt others and feel shame or guilt, we invest mental and emotional energy in storing and containing that memory. Shame and guilt, in terms of emotional energy, are costly. Hiding takes its toll.

Although confessing our offenses temporarily increases our stress level (as does disclosing our feelings about a traumatic event), we think psychological science will eventually confirm that confession promotes health. When we confess and receive forgiveness, it is as though a weight has been lifted off our shoulders. We feel free. This sense of freedom may indeed translate into concrete benefits—better health, less absenteeism and greater life satisfaction.

Exercise 13-2
Learning to Confess

Confess to yourself for the times you have hurt others. Then seek a safe person to confess to. That might be the person you offended. It might also be a group that you trust—friends or church members—or a counselor, a pastor, a sibling or a parent. It might be confession to God. Confession to a safe person who loves you is good for the soul.

Forgiveness and Personal Control

Forgiveness brings freedom. It restores our sense that our efforts and our lives make a difference. We feel a renewed freedom to exercise our free will, less inhibited by the anger, bitterness and bad memories that accompany unforgiveness.

When we have been hurt by others, we desire revenge. We think over and over about the offense and the offender. We experience inner turmoil about how to respond to our offender. We are frustrated because our plans for life have been altered by the actions of another person. When we are hurt by others, we lose control over several aspects of our lives: our integrity as human beings, our security, our relationships. Feeling out of control can, over the long haul, make us feel helpless and depressed.

Paradoxically, through forgiving we regain control by giving up our desire for control. We relinquish our determination for life to happen as we initially planned. We surrender our implicit demand that life meet all our needs for security and happiness. We give up our quest to undo the past.

Giving up control over things that are out of our control changes our perception of ourselves. Gradually we feel more in control of our lives, more capable of directing our future and more convinced that our actions in this world do, in fact, make a difference. Consequently we feel better about who we are. *Research with college students, churchgoers and older adults all show the same finding: If you want to regain the sense that your actions make a difference, forgive those who have, through hurting you, told you that you do not make a difference.*

Mary Trainer interviewed seventy-three persons who had been hurt during a divorce. She asked those people to describe how they felt about themselves and their ex-spouses at the worst point during the marital break-up and then "after the turning point," when they started to experience that the hurt of the divorce was subsiding.

Trainer found that, for those people who forgave from the heart, their sense of personal power increased over time. They felt more in control of their personal decisions, finances, feelings and responses to the offender. Those who did not forgive, or who forgave out of fear or out of a desire for personal gain, found that their sense of power *decreased* over time.[12]

Based on current research, we are left with a puzzle: Does forgiveness increase our sense of personal power, or does an increase in our sense of personal power increase our ability to forgive? Or both? At present the research is unclear. However, we think that research will confirm what philosophers and theologians have been telling us all along: To remove ourselves from the consequences of the hurts we have suffered, we must release our demands for control. When we forgive, we regain control by giving up the search for control.

Forgiveness and Spiritual Benefits

Forgiveness can improve mental health, reduce psychological and physical symptoms, lead to a greater sense of personal power and lead to greater life satisfaction. Morever, forgiveness can also help us reap spiritual benefits. Spiritual benefits include added meaning and value to our lives, and transcendence from the concerns of everyday life.[13]

After the usual postoperative care, the surgeon went to visit her patient on a monthly basis. It is most unusual for surgeons to provide postoperative care if their surgery was unsuccessful. But as a participant in research by Lane Gerber, this surgeon agreed to maintain a relationship with a cancer patient for whom surgery had been unsuccessful.

She was one of twenty surgeons in the study, each maintaining a doctor-patient relationship with a patient for whom treatment was not successful. Gerber asked the surgeons to tape record their reactions to interacting with the patient with whom they would continue to have a relationship and their reactions to a patient with whom they would not continue a relationship. Thus the study also involved forty patients.[14]

The surgeons felt differently regarding the patients that they continued to see than they did regarding those that they did not continue to see—they did not feel the customary isolation, shame, meaninglessness and sense of failure that they felt regarding the patients that they did not continue to see. Continuing the relationships gave the patients an opportunity to communicate their forgiveness to their surgeons. *Out of feeling forgiven,* Gerber concluded, *the surgeons were able to feel a new self-acceptance, a sense of renewal and the feeling that their future had both hope and meaning.*

When we have failed or hurt others, we often hide. Hiding may seem like a good way to avoid shame, but often hiding only leads to greater shame and may keep us from feeling connected with ourselves and the world. Hiding robs our lives of meaning and value. Lane Gerber's research suggests that entering into relationships when we have made mistakes or hurt others may help us to alleviate our shame and guilt and protect and restore our spiritual well-being.

Finding meaning in the midst of suffering is one of the spiritual benefits of receiving and granting forgiveness.[15] It also has the effect, often, of dispelling our sense of isolation: we feel more at one with others. We can feel more at peace in our religious faith. We realize that life has hope that extends beyond the pain of our present suffering.

Summing Up

Forgiveness leads to good things. We can expect that as we forgive others our beliefs, attitudes and expectations about other people, the world and how we cope with the world will change. As we accept forgiveness from others or from God, we will see ourselves more positively and realistically and view the world as more joyous and full of possibilities than before. Mental, physical and spiritual health will follow as well.

Though forgiveness appears to produce many benefits for the forgiver personally, forgiveness also brings the healing of relationships between people. We discuss the promise of forgiveness for mending families and communities in the next two chapters.

F o u r t e e n

Forgiveness &
the Family

T HIS CHAPTER AND THE NEXT ARE ABOUT THE POWER OF FOR-
giveness to heal wounds that are left after one person has
seriously hurt another (or after two have hurt each other).
First we will focus on the promise of forgiveness for healthy
and happy families; then we will talk about the promise forgiveness
holds for healing wounds in communities and ethnic groups.

A Family Without Forgiveness

It is a summer morning in 1912, somewhere on the New England
coast. We spend a day with the Tyrone family in Eugene O'Neill's play
Long Day's Journey into Night.[1] This is a family full of resentment and
bitterness, apparently incapable of forgiveness. The father, James
Tyrone, is a shabbily dressed man who is obsessed with saving money.
Everyone in the family suffers because of his stinginess. He is also
terribly disappointed about how little his sons have made of their lives.

Tyrone's older son, Jamie, is a cynical and irresponsible alcoholic—

"a lazy lunk," his father calls him.[2] Jamie spends his money on whiskey and prostitutes. He confronts his father early in the morning when Edmund, the younger son, becomes ill: "It might never have happened if you'd sent him to a real doctor when he first got sick!"[3]

In turn, Tyrone accuses his wife's bad genes for Edmund's illness: "It doesn't come from my side of the family. There wasn't one of us that didn't have lungs as strong as an ox."[4]

Jamie also exclaims that his father's stinginess is to blame for their mother's addiction to morphine. Tyrone retorts, "That's a lie! So I'm to blame! That's what you're driving at, is it? You evil-minded loafer."[5] Mary also blames Tyrone for her addiction:

Oh, I'm so sick and tired of pretending this is a home! You won't help me! You won't put yourself out the least bit! You don't know how to act in a home! You don't really want one! You never have wanted one—never since the day we were married! You should have remained a bachelor and lived in second-rate hotels and entertained your friends in barrooms! Then nothing would have ever happened.[6]

The Tyrone family is full of accusation, blame, insult, resentment and hostility. Each family member has hurt the others. It's a family without forgiveness.

Forgiveness Is Indispensable for Marriages and Families

The Tyrone family, and all families, must forgive in order to survive. Spouses and family members must give and receive forgiveness from each other regularly. Sometimes forgiveness will occur spontaneously, unconsciously and without fanfare. At other times it may be a bigger deal. But for families to succeed, they must be built on the capacity to forgive:

☐ Spouses must forgive each other so that bitterness does not build up. What would happen to two spouses who could not get over their anger at each other?

☐ Parents must forgive their children so that the children can grow up feeling loved and important, despite their flaws, weaknesses or propensity to hurt others. What would happen to children who thought that their flaws or transgressions were unforgivable?

☐ Children must forgive their parents so that they do not become bitter and distant from them. What would happen to children who could not forgive their parents, especially when, as adults, they became responsible for the care of their aging parents?

Families that value forgiveness are more likely to avoid negative outcomes. In this chapter we will describe research studies that examined the role of forgiveness in marriages, discuss how to build forgiveness into marriages and families and look at the complications that occur in the case of serious hurts, such as violence, abuse and destructive patterns of substance use.

Exercise 14-1

Making Forgiveness Real in Your Family Relationships

When we live with people, we will sometimes hurt them. At times we hurt each other intentionally. At other times we unintentionally hurt each other. Here are some guidelines for building forgiveness into your family relationships:

1. Examine your relationship with each member of your family. Are there strains in your relationship?

☐ with your spouse

☐ with your children

☐ with your parents

☐ with your brothers or sisters

2. Identify whether you need to do anything to repair the damage from those strains. Examine your conscience and learn to confess first. Don't make backhanded apologies—simply identify what you have done wrong and acknowledge that you would like to behave differently in the future.

3. Teach your children to examine their consciences. Remember that you can start to teach children about seeking and granting forgiveness while they are still very young.

4. Remember that very severe family offenses (such as addictions,

infidelity and violence) are not easily cured. Seek community help from churches, law enforcement and friends. Remember that in such cases forgiveness is meaningful only after the offender has demonstrated genuine repentance and has been rehabilitated. Forgiveness is the last step in healing.

Forgiving Relationships Are Good Relationships
Working independently, two researchers investigated whether forgiving relationships between spouses or romantic partners really are better and stronger than relationships that involve less forgiving. The couples they investigated were quite diverse. Psychologist Michelle Nelson examined college students in dating or marriage relationships.[7] Psychologist Tamela Woodman worked with adult married couples. Some of Woodman's couples reported that their relationships were doing well; others reported that they were having trouble. Some were in counseling for their difficulties.[8]

Each of these researchers asked their participants to describe the extent to which they felt they had forgiven their spouse or partner for any ways they might have hurt them in the past. Participants also completed questionnaires on the quality of their relationships. Some of the dimensions measured were commitment to each other, trust for each other, liking and loving each other, agreeing with each other on important matters, amount of positive emotions in their relationship and overall satisfaction with their relationship.

Nelson and Woodman both found that forgiving relationships were good relationships. *Forgiving partners had more commitment, trust, liking and loving for each other, agreement, positive emotions and satisfaction with the relationship.* These studies were based on *correlational,* rather than *experimental,* research. Since the researchers did not actually do anything to encourage forgiveness in these couples, it is impossible to tell whether forgiveness made the relationships better, whether better relationships made forgiveness possible or whether a third variable (such as family upbringing) made marriages more forgiving and improved their quality. Nevertheless, these studies do support the idea that *forgiving relationships are good relationships.*

Techniques for Forgiving in Marriages and Families

Throughout the book we have suggested that empathy is a gateway to forgiveness. Empathy is a critical factor in motivating family members both to seek and to grant forgiveness. Therefore we will analyze the techniques below in terms of how much they encourage people to empathize with each other's condition.

Tell your story. Despite the bitterness we witness in *Long Day's Journey into Night,* we also see brief flashes of compassion, sympathy and forgiveness. These moments are fueled by empathy, as Mary demonstrates by understanding her husband's story. "Your father is a strange man, Edmund," Mary elaborates.

"It took many years before I understood him. You must try to understand and forgive him too, and not feel contempt because he's close-fisted. His father deserted his mother and their six children a year or so after they came to America. He told them he had a premonition he would die soon, and he was homesick for Ireland, and wanted to go back there to die. So he went and he did die. He must have been a peculiar man, too. Your father had to go to work in a machine shop when he was only ten years old."

"Oh, for Pete's sake, Mama. I've heard Papa tell that machine shop story ten thousand times."

"Yes, dear, you've had to listen, but I don't think you've ever tried to understand."[9]

When children are put in touch with the stories of their parents, the children often realize that some of the pain and hurt their parents cause is partially a function of the hurts the parents themselves received in their families of origin. A painful past is not a license or an excuse for hurting people, but talking about one's painful past can sometimes put the hurtful behavior in context. *When we recognize that hurtful actions are sometimes motivated by our loved one's own painful past, we can empathize and then forgive.*

The same principle applies to families in general, not just marriages.[10] Telling your story puts others in touch with your predicament, promotes empathy and motivates forgiveness.

Examine your conscience regularly. The Jewish holy day called the Day of Atonement is a time for people to examine their conscience and determine how they have hurt God or other people during the previous year. On this day the devout are expected to confess to others and ask forgiveness for specific ways they hurt each other. It is a good idea, regardless of one's religious faith, to observe "days of atonement." Examining your conscience is an important part of encouraging forgiveness in families.

One helpful strategy for examining your conscience is to switch roles in your imagination with the people you have interacted with during the day. Try to determine how your actions may have affected them, positively or negatively. Taking time to imagine the impact of your actions on your spouse, children or parents will help you to get in touch with the areas of your life for which you might want to confess and ask forgiveness. Putting yourself in the shoes of the people with whom you interact and with whom you have conflicts or disagreements helps you generate empathy, forgive and seek forgiveness for the ways you have wronged them.

Confess first. When you have been locked in conflict with another family member, you sometimes begin to feel that your spouse or children owe you an apology. To fight that tendency to get an apology before being willing to apologize, you should be willing to confess to the person you have hurt. Asking for forgiveness breaks the ice in relationships that have grown cold or distant because of long-standing patterns of mutual hurt. Asking for forgiveness, rather than expecting that others will ask you for forgiveness, can warm the heart. That warmth will encourage your spouse, child or parent to forgive you. The reflected warmth may also encourage them to examine their conscience and ask for forgiveness in return.

Don't make backhanded confessions. When you confess your wrongdoings, it is sometimes easy to use your confession as a time to drop hints about the things that your spouse, child or parent should be confessing to you:

☐ "I'm sorry for yelling at you after you called me lazy and ignorant."

☐ "Forgive me for embarrassing you in public (even though that's what you really deserved)."

☐ "Sorry for what I said yesterday, but you gotta admit, you really had it coming."

Backhanded confessions are stock-in-trade for the Tyrone family. Mary starts with a sincere confession about her hurtful accusations against Tyrone:

I'm sorry if I sounded bitter, James. I'm not. It's all so far away. But I did feel a little hurt when you wished you hadn't come home. I was so relieved and happy when you came, and grateful to you. It's very dreary and sad to be here alone in the fog with night falling.

So far so good. The confession warms Tyrone's heart: "I'm glad I came, Mary, when you act like your real self."

Mary continues, "I was so lonesome I kept Cathleen with me just to have someone to talk to. You know what I was telling her, dear? About the night my father took me to your dressing room and I first fell in love with you. Do you remember?"

"Can you think I'd ever forget, Mary?"

"No. I know you still love me, James, in spite of everything."

"Yes! As God is my judge! Always and forever, Mary!"

At this point the Tyrones have some of the ingredients for a reconciliation. But just as we begin to think that they may be successful, Mary twists these ingredients into an accusation:

And I love you, dear, in spite of everything. But I must confess, James, although I couldn't help loving you, I would never have married you if I'd known you drank so much. I remember the first night your barroom friends had to help you up to the door of our hotel room, and knocked and then ran away before I came to the door. We were still on our honeymoon, do you remember?[11]

Mary's "confession," and other backhanded confessions like them, has the emotional impact of wet spaghetti. Moreover, as Ev and his colleague Fred DiBlasio point out in an article on marital counseling, such confessions make forgiveness harder, not easier.[12] Backhanded confessions are accusations that will, in turn, need forgiveness.

Stick to describing what you did wrong and communicating that you feel bad about it. Let your partner figure out what he or she did wrong.

Accept sincere confessions from others (no matter how imperfect). If you are on the receiving end of a backhanded confession, accept the sincere part of the confession (if it truly does seem sincere) and ignore the backhanded accusation. We are all prone to use backhanded confessions, but you can still use the "good" part of a confession to generate positive change in your relationship.

Further, don't make your partner confess twice, and don't critique the confession. Don't correct grammar. Don't criticize your partner's mumbling. Just accept the sincere part of the confession with gratitude and also with empathy, because you know how hard confession is! Hearing sincere confessions should promote empathy. Use these opportunities to listen to someone who has hurt you. Imagine yourself in his or her shoes and recognize the strength and courage that a sincere apology and confession require. Putting yourself in the shoes of the confessor may motivate you to forgive and restore your relationship with the family member who offended you.

Encourage children to examine their consciences. Children can join in the family's practice of forgiveness. From as young as two or three, children have the "psychological equipment" to detect when they have hurt others, even if they do not have the language with which to express their contrition. As they mature, they will be more able to examine their consciences independently and express their feelings using language.

As children develop language, they will become able to examine their consciences. However, don't coerce; help them to search their consciences on their own. Then help them articulate what they find.

For example, imagine this interaction between a father and his three-year-old son:

Father: "When you hit Sally, she feels sad because you *hurt* her."
The child blushes and appears ashamed.
Father: "It feels bad when you hurt someone, doesn't it?"
Child nods and begins to cry.
Child: "I'm sorry."
Father: "That looked like it was hard. Saying 'I'm sorry' was a very grown up thing to do! I'm very proud of you."

If children learn to examine their consciences of their own volition, they will avoid making mental associations between forgiveness and punishment or shame that will cloud their conscience later in life.

In early childhood, link empathy to bodily sensations or distress that children can perceive in their siblings or caregivers. When young children lash out at each other or act selfishly, help them to link the hurts they cause each other with familiar physical distress. Emphasize that when they hurt each other emotionally, the effects are similar to when a child might be hurt physically.

For example, when a young child calls another child a name, use the gestures and facial expressions that one might use to express physical pain. Very young children are sensitive to winces, grimaces and other faces that show that someone is in pain. Some experts say, in fact, that young children will associate these expressions of pain with their personal experiences of pain and perhaps experience emotional (not physical) distress as if the pain were their own.

Children may learn to experience empathy for people they hurt emotionally by linking the hurts with cues that they already link with their own physical injuries. The ability to pick up these cues is the root of empathy, says New York University psychologist Martin Hoffman.[13] And with these roots of empathy firmly planted, children will begin to examine their consciences.

When children are two to three years old, begin encouraging them to step into the shoes of the person they hurt (or who hurt them) and consider how the other person must be feeling. As children mature, they become attuned to the feelings of other people, not simply their facial or verbal expressions of distress. Direct children older than three to consider other people's feelings. If they are informed about how their actions made another child or parent feel "sad" or "hurt" or "bad," such prompting will often produce empathy, which may motivate them to confess or ask for forgiveness from others they have hurt. As children age, continue encouraging them to think of others. By five or six they will begin to consider others spontaneously.

By late childhood, children can be encouraged to empathize with a person's history, identity and circumstances. By age eight most children can empathize without even getting information about how their actions made another person feel. They can usually guess from their own experiences the impact that their actions have on others. Beyond age eight, children can be prompted to consider the effects of their actions on others. That prompt will likely produce empathy, which may motivate them to confess and ask forgiveness.

There are many ways to make confession and forgiveness palatable. Forgiveness does not need to be relegated to a "family meeting," to a disciplinary event or to a single tactic. Each family can discover and develop the techniques that will work best for them.

Forgiving During Times of Crisis

In *Long Day's Journey into Night* Mary, the mother, is addicted to morphine. She has recently been released from a hospital where she went to recover from her addiction. Everyone thought Mary had kicked the habit, but she continues to use morphine in the middle of the night. The family can't forgive her for the broken promises about ending her morphine use and for the damage her addiction has caused. Yet she continues to cover up her addiction and its damage.

When Edmund pleads with his mother to take care of herself so that she does not return to her morphine use, she replies, "There's absolutely no reason to talk as if you expected something dreadful! Of course, I promise you. I give you my sacred word of honor! But I suppose you're remembering I've promised before on my word of honor."[14]

Everyone hoped in Mary. They wanted her to get better. But again and again she returned to morphine to soothe the pain of life. When we enter the Tyrone home, we discover that Mary has broken her promise again. Tyrone summarizes the situation bitterly: "We've lived with this before and now we must again. There's no help for it. Only I wish she hadn't led me to hope this time. By God, I never will again!"[15]

Although all of us probably hurt each other more frequently than we care to imagine, some offenses are more grave, more rebellious and more damaging to people and relationships than are others. This list of critical offenses might include addiction and substance abuse; spouse, child or elder abuse; extramarital affairs; sexual, physical or emotional violence; and neglect.

When families experience crises such as these, forgiveness will not smooth over problems and make them go away. In such situations, the person who has been hurt often hopes that forgiveness might bring an end to the abuse, neglect or hurt. He or she also hopes, perhaps, for a restored relationship with the offender. Love and concern for the offender give the person a capacity to empathize that can make the desire to forgive overwhelming:

☐ "Perhaps if I forgave, he'd feel the freedom to end his abuse."

☐ "I just have to forgive and forget. That will help me to cope."

☐ "I still want her in my life. How could I not forgive her?"

Often the offender desires to be immediately relieved of guilt for the abuse or neglect. He or she may even approach a spouse, child or parent and express heartfelt and sincere contrition for what he or she has done wrong. Because family members often have empathy for those whom they have hurt, the guilt and desire to have that guilt lifted can also be overwhelming:

☐ "I have learned my lesson and have decided to stop drinking."

☐ "I will never hit our kids again."

☐ "I am so ashamed for how I have hurt you and the children."

The problem is, though, that patterns of behavior such as abuse and violence cannot be fixed with contrition and forgiveness alone. They are usually too ingrained, habitual and complex to be dealt with *exclusively* by means of forgiveness. Justice must be served. The offender must be rehabilitated and demonstrate a sincere and time-tested desire to change. Forgiveness must be, as Marie Fortune writes, "the last step," not the only step.[16]

Before forgiveness can have its desired effect in restoring relationships following such severe abuses of trust, Fortune suggests that two tasks need to be accomplished. First, the offender must be called to accountability by an authority (whether a family member, district attorney, clergy or therapist) and encouraged to take responsibility for the harm he or she has done. Second, the offender needs to show a change of heart (the kind of repentance we described in chapter six). Repentance, as Fortune points out, is much deeper than simple contrition or "feeling sorry" for one's actions and their consequences. A good demonstration of repentance might be, for example, getting psychological treatment, with no excuses about missing sessions, feeling too sick to go or "not agreeing with the therapist's methods."

The community can also help the victim of severe family violence to begin healing and may also be helpful in eventually restoring the relationship. Concerned friends and church or community members can mobilize around families that have been torn by serious offenses by (1) expressing concern to the victim and being willing to listen to the entire story of the violence, (2) encouraging the victim to seek help from authorities and (3) insuring that family members who are at risk are adequately protected from future harm.

When Ellen finally figured out that Terry's husband had been hitting her, she listened deeply as Terry told her story. She held Terry's hand as she wept. She encouraged Terry to show her the bruises and welts on her arms. She did not attempt to minimize the pain Terry was feeling or encourage her to "forgive and forget." She took Terry's pain seriously and also made sure that Terry knew, without a doubt, that her life was in danger if she stayed in her abusive family situation.

Family violence and abuse, like Mary's addiction to morphine, is often difficult to stop. Sometimes the empathy we feel for an offender tempts us to forgive prematurely, before justice can be served and the offender can receive adequate treatment and demonstrate a willingness to change. However, a combination of justice, accountability and rehabilitation will sometimes prompt offenders to sincerely repent. Then genuine forgiveness can be offered and received, and families can begin to rebuild themselves.[17] But it won't happen easily or quickly.

Summing Up

Forgiveness is vital to building healthy and happy marriages and families. Because we regularly hurt each other even when we don't intend to, we must be ready to seek and grant forgiveness to keep those hurts from building up and causing deep divisions in our relationships. The Tyrone family illustrates the tragic fate that awaits families who cannot forgive. Without forgiveness there is no end to the long night of blame, guilt, hostility and mistrust.

Techniques to encourage people to empathize with the effects of their behavior on others or to empathize with the historical events that are partially responsible for an offender's transgression are helpful in developing the empathy that motivates forgiveness. Forgiveness can be actively promoted in marriages and families and even with young children. When a family experiences abuse and neglect, though, forgiveness should be considered the final step in restoring the health of the family. By using forgiveness in these ways, we can help our marriages and families to have long, bright futures.

Fifteen

Forgiveness & the Healing of Communities

*I*N PREVIOUS CHAPTERS WE EXAMINED HOW FORGIVENESS might benefit the forgiver, the person who is forgiven and marriage and family relationships. In this final chapter we examine the promise of forgiveness for healing wounds that divide communities of people or ethnic groups.

The Dilemma of Forgiveness in Ethnic Conflict

The Sunflower. Simon Wiesenthal is a Polish Jew who spent World War II in a concentration camp. He is most famous for establishing a center for gathering information that helps to bring Nazi war criminals to justice. His book *The Sunflower* tells of the moral dilemma that arose while prisoner Wiesenthal worked in a German army hospital. He was called by a German nurse to the bedside of a dying soldier bandaged from head to toe. This young German soldier, Karl, was dying before his eyes. He shared with Wiesenthal the story of how he became enamored of the Nazi Party, joined the SS in his enthusiasm, abandoned his religious and family ties and soon became indoctrinated.

One afternoon booby traps had killed thirty soldiers in Karl's unit. Out of vengeance, SS men—including Karl—rounded up three hundred Jews, gathered them like sheep into an empty house and poured gasoline over the house. Then they ignited it with grenades and watched it burn. The SS soldiers surrounded the house and shot all who tried to escape the inferno.

After telling his story, Karl concludes with an awful request:

I am left here with my guilt. . . . I know what I have told you is terrible. In the long nights while I have been waiting for death, time and time again I have longed to talk about it with a Jew and beg forgiveness from him. Only I didn't know whether there were any Jews left. . . . I know what I am asking is almost too much for you, but without your answer I cannot die in peace.

Wiesenthal was anguished about the decision that lay before him: to forgive or not to forgive the soldier. "At last I made up my mind," Wiesenthal writes, "and without a word I left the room."

Wiesenthal spends the rest of the story second-guessing himself about whether he should have forgiven Karl. He consults the wisest and most virtuous men he knows. Many offer quick solutions to help Wiesenthal's aching conscience. But no response seems satisfactory. Years later, after being released from the prison camp, Wiesenthal asked thirty-two men and women in the realms of law, literature, religion and diplomacy to respond to his dilemma, which continued to haunt him. Thirty-two different responses were given. Whether he should have forgiven Karl remained a great mystery that even the greatest thinkers in the world did not seem able to solve.[1]

Reading *The Sunflower* cautions us to avoid glib, easy answers about the value of forgiveness in healing deep wounds between groups of people. When we discuss forgiveness between groups that are locked in conflict, forgiveness becomes more complicated than forgiving a specific person for one or more transgressions—a situation we call *simple forgiveness.*

Old wounds. Wounds that divide groups are often old wounds. They have to do with the pain that one's loved ones have encountered. The pain of these wounds produces anger at groups rather than at specific persons, and the initial acts of aggression are usually forgotten in a meaningless cycle of retaliation.

On the way to a conference in St. Petersburg, Russia, I sat next to a man who was also headed to the former Soviet Union. Our conversation eventually turned to our respective business there.

"I am going to speak at a conference," he told me.

"Oh? What is the subject of your conference?"

"The history of Crimea. Do you know where Crimea is?"

Searching my memory, I responded tentatively, "Is Crimea the same thing as the Crimean Peninsula?"

"Yes. This summer marks the fiftieth anniversary since the Crimean Tartars were moved en masse from the Crimean Peninsula during World War II by the Russians."

"What do you mean when you say they were moved en masse?"

"I mean that every Tartar who could be rounded up—every man, woman and child—was deported, almost overnight. Remember that this deportation occurred during World War II, when Russia was locked in conflict with Germany. Russia claimed that they suspected the Crimean Tartars were colluding with the Germans against Russia. So the entire population of Crimean Tartars was loaded into freight cars and transported to a land where they would not threaten the Russian cause. The people took with them only what they could carry on their backs. They were never allowed to return home and have not been given back the peninsula to this day."

I inquired about his work for a few more minutes; then he asked me, "So why are you going to St. Petersburg?"

"I am going to speak at a conference as well."

"Oh, really?" he responded. "What is the topic of your presentation?"

"Forgiveness as a means for resolving ethnic conflict."

Representatives of groups such as the Crimean Tartars continue to fight for recognition from the Russian government, but their cause goes largely unsupported. For many, the wounds of these ethnic conflicts are old but still painful.

Fifty years is a long time to be separated from one's homeland. Many Crimean Tartars have died without ever seeing their homeland again. Many still will die without returning. If forgiveness is to help in such situations, the people involved in encouraging forgiveness must recognize that the wounds of ethnic conflict are deep.

Wounds against loved ones are felt personally. The wounds created in group or ethnic conflict are not only against oneself, they are also against people who are important to us. Conflict between black and white Americans has been costly. Violence and discrimination have probably touched every family of black Americans—ethnic conflict has hurt their children, parents, grandparents and other friends and loved ones. Each African-American carries wounds that were suffered vicariously through the wounding of loved ones. These wounds are cumulative and can create as much pain and bitterness as do wounds received directly.

Although the wounds are felt personally, often aggressors are not remembered as individuals but only as groups of people. Years and years of aggression between the Japanese and the Koreans came to a boiling point earlier in this century when the Japanese attacked and brutally killed and maimed thousands of Korean citizens. These atrocities are remembered by some Koreans as being committed by "Japan" or by "the Japanese," not by individual persons.

The inability to identify one aggressor or wrongdoer makes forgiving more difficult in old ethnic conflict. There is no one person to forgive. There are only hordes of nameless aggressors. Further, those aggressors brought violence and destruction to many, not just to a single victim.

Initial acts of aggression get lost in the cycle of retaliation. Another factor that makes situations of ethnic conflict more complicated than forgiving a clearly identifiable transgressor is that the initial acts that started the conflict are usually forgotten and remembered only as an endless cycle of retaliation and revenge.

Can you recall the history of the relationships among the ethnic groups that occupy the former Yugoslavia? How did the conflicts between the Serbs, Bosnians and Croats get started? If you are like us, you probably don't remember. The roots are centuries old. No one, it seems, recalls who fired the first shot. In real life individual Bosnians, Serbs and Croats are responding to aggression from the other groups. They are not returning fire for events that occurred centuries ago. Instead they are avenging the children who were torn from them, the wives who were raped, or the hospital, full of people, that was bombed. Whereas the roots of these conflicts are centuries old, the gunfire and slaughter on Tuesday are often motivated in the hearts and minds of individual aggressors by the desire to even the score for the atrocities that the enemy committed on Monday.

Is it even possible to forgive someone other than the person who directly hurt you? Can a black South African forgive the white minority that helped perpetuate a racist society? Can Koreans forgive the Japanese? Many philosophers would say no. When we talk about forgiving groups of people, we are really talking about trying to reestablish some kind of right relating with that group, rather than actually dispensing forgiveness to the group as a whole.

When I try to think of what it might mean to actually forgive Nazis, white South Africans, communists or any other group, my head spins. The rules of simple forgiveness simply do not apply. Perhaps the actual wrongdoers—the people who hurt me or my family—are long gone. I cannot forgive them. They cannot express regret, cannot vow not to repeat the hurt, cannot beg for forgiveness.

Promoting Secondary Forgiveness

In such situations forgiveness, strictly speaking, is not the solution. Whom are we to forgive on behalf of the dead, or our ancestors, or anyone else for that matter? We can forgive only for the ways we have been directly hurt, and we can forgive only the persons who directly hurt us. Forgiveness has to occur between people, not between a person and an institution or between "the Nazis" and "the Jews."

Maybe, though, there is a sort of forgiveness we can offer in these situations. Perhaps by virtue of being part of a community—like the Jewish community, the African-American community or any other group whose identity transcends the here and now—we inherit those old wounds that our ancestors experienced directly. As people who indirectly experience the wounds, maybe we can indirectly forgive. Maybe, as ancestors of the people who did the hurting, we can ask for forgiveness on behalf of our community.

This alternative form of forgiveness, which Elliott Dorff, a philosopher at the University of Judaism in Los Angeles, has called *secondary forgiveness,* is an alternative that has power to heal old wounds. It capitalizes on some of the central components of forgiveness we have discussed in previous chapters. The secondary forgiveness method encourages people to confess and repent for the transgressions of their group.[2]

Our vision is that one day representatives of different ethnic groups that are locked in old conflicts might be able to come together prepared to mutually confess and repent for the transgressions that they or other members of their group experienced. By tapping the roots of forgiveness that we have discussed throughout the book—empathy and confession—groups of people might reconcile even after severe conflicts and strife.

A success story in Liberia. Liberia has been torn apart by brutal tribal conflict since 1980, when a military leader assumed power during a violent coup. The brutality and humiliation has been unprecedented. Duane Elmer tells how he was sent to Liberia to facilitate a conference among the representatives of the various Liberian factions. About five hundred representatives of the various tribal groups and governmental bodies were invited to attend. They had only two things in common: they all wanted to live in Liberia, and they all wanted the war to stop.[3]

The discussion could have easily ended in a stalemate, with nothing accomplished. It could have also ended with even more conflict than before the discussion began. Elmer writes that a turning point for the conference occurred when he asked the participants to break into groups of three and share the greatest trauma they had experienced during the prior year.

The stories they exchanged were grotesque, brutal and tragic. Children had watched as their parents were executed. Mothers had seen their sons taken away. Women had been raped. Not one person had been spared tragedy during the previous year. As they exchanged stories, many wept. After each person told his or her story, the other group members prayed that God would heal the storytellers of the pain they described.

As the conference participants heard stories of the pain and heartache of other participants, they developed empathy for each other. Men and women from different tribes and factions empathized with their enemies. *They realized that their differences were not as important as their shared experiences of suffering.* Empathy, we suspect, gave participants the insight that their enemies were human and that those enemies suffered the same kinds of grief and loss they suffered themselves.

Empathy is the plow that breaks up the hard ground of our hearts. The tenderness and compassion that follow empathy are seeds that sprout and grow until sworn enemies can sometimes surrender their hatred. Exchanging stories of the pain one has suffered as a result of ethnic conflict is a first step in healing those wounds. When an aggressor understands and has empathy for the pain that his or her enemy has endured, that empathy promotes two important qualities. The first is regret; the second is restitution.

Regret. Confession humanizes an offender. Just as we are moved to hear how our enemies suffer pain and heartache as a result of conflict, we are moved to hear that our aggressors feel sorrow and regret for the violence they or other members of their group have done to us. Therefore, though I might not *be* guilty for the situations that led to the institution of slavery in America, as a white person I can *feel regret* for what members of my group—European Americans—did to African slaves and their children. My regret would be an appropriate moral response. If I did not feel at least some regret, most people would say that something was wrong with my moral equipment. Martin Golding has suggested three kinds of regret, all of which are important.[4]

First, there is *intellectual regret,* the recognition that we misjudged the facts. We second-guess our actions. We realize that our actions have backfired. By itself, intellectual regret is nothing special. We might regret the past for many reasons, some of which are not very moral. Do we regret the actions that harmed our enemies *because they did not bring about the results we desired,* or do we genuinely regret that our actions brought harm to them in the first place?

Were Nazi officers who expressed regret for their actions regretful because of the evil of their actions or because the Nazi cause was squelched? Would they have felt differently about their actions had they won? Would Liberian tribal leaders have regretted the brutalities they committed against other tribes if those acts of brutality had helped them defeat their enemies? Intellectual regret is a good beginning, but more is needed to promote healing.

We also need *moral regret,* or the recognition that an action not only was a bad idea but was also, at its core, immoral. Moral regret involves the recognition that one's actions have created a debt to other people that cannot be wiped away or ignored. Would Liberian tribal leaders be able to recognize that the aggression in Liberia had a moral element— that evils were committed? Can I—a white southerner—recognize not only that slavery was a bad idea but that it was also evil and wrong?

Third, regret must involve *other-oriented regret,* or the regret that comes from recognizing that one's actions have hurt particular persons. In Liberia aggressors did not commit crimes against other tribes but against individual persons: pregnant women, street vendors, sometimes even their own neighbors. Recognition that one's actions have hurt people with identities, not just a group or a cause, is the capstone of regret.

How would genuine regret look? Would it involve tears? Maybe. Does it involve saying something to the victim? Perhaps. Does it involve a resolution to restore relationships? It might. To express regret effectively for the actions of one's group, offending groups may offer some form of restitution. Restitution might take the form of medical aid, financial help, educational advantages or governmental policies that help the victimized group to rebuild. However regret is demonstrated, the victims can probably discern true regret when they see it.

Expressing one's regret communicates to one's former enemies, "I am a human being with the same moral sensitivities as you. Because we both agree that what has happened to you was not the way things should have been, was morally repugnant and was something that hurt you personally, I hope that we can build a bridge between us." Regret rehumanizes the offender, just as telling one's own painful story rehumanizes one's enemies.

What the victim must do. Expressing genuine regret and (probably) offering restitution are what the offender must do to heal the wounds of group conflict. The group that has been injured also must accomplish some tasks for the wounds to heal:

☐ *Perceive the regret.* The victimized group must eventually recognize that their offenders have humbled themselves, and that their contrition is honest. They must recognize sincere and heartfelt needs for forgiveness. Can they recognize intellectual, moral and other-oriented regret from their offenders?

☐ *Evaluate whether the offense is likely to recur.* This is the other side of perceiving the offender's regret. Is the regret deep and sincere? Does the regret stand the test of time?

☐ *Develop some standards for restitution.* What amends must be made? How much restitution is enough? When should the measures instituted to make restitution be discontinued? Should they ever be discontinued?

☐ *Cease to judge the offender.* At some point the offending group should cease to be considered an enemy (or even a former enemy) and instead should be considered a friend. This may take generations.

☐ *Develop plans for cooperative efforts that will continue to build trust.* How can the two groups continue to build trust and good relations, even after regret, restitution and forgiveness have occurred? Perhaps cooperative projects could be organized that would help goodwill and friendship to grow.

Applying These Principles in Real Conflicts

We think these principles could be used to bring together groups of people who have been locked in conflict for many years. The three of us have lived in Richmond, Virginia—a city with many wounds left over from the Civil War and slavery. Relationships between black and white Richmonders are not exactly hostile, but there is a divisive spirit in the city. Too many bad memories and, among some, a continuing subtle racism encourage blacks and whites to keep a cold distance from each other.

We can envision a weekend when leaders from various civic groups, churches and neighborhoods come together for a conference like the one Duane Elmer helped to orchestrate in Liberia. Perhaps in a context such as that (perhaps with the help of a conflict mediator such as Elmer), black and white people in Richmond could sit down and listen to each other's stories. For some it would probably be the first time they had ever heard a black person tell them about the pain of living as a black person in Richmond. For some it might be the first time they ever heard a white person express genuine regret for how racism has been perpetuated in the city. It might be the first time that a constructive plan for restitution and the cessation of judgment is given serious, reverent consideration.

Perhaps similar principles could be used to mediate conflicts between gangs who are at war with each other, between management and labor, between organizations in the midst of conflict or between groups of children in the school system who are polarized along racial lines. On the basis of the principles for healing communities that we have described, perhaps such groups could begin to rebuild.

Forgiveness in the Criminal Justice System

One of the great tragedies of our criminal justice system is the lack of closure between the convicted criminal and the victims. After a criminal has been convicted for a crime, there is usually no formal opportunity for the criminal to offer an expression of sorrow, contrition or remorse to the victim or to the victim's family. We don't know how many criminals experience contrition for their actions—maybe not many. In those cases where they do, though, they are offered no formal opportunity to speak about their crimes with their victims or the survivors of the victim. The way criminals are separated from the people they have hurt is a tragedy on at least two counts.

First, the victims of crime suffer a great deal after the novelty and adrenaline related to a trial are long forgotten. Much of their continued suffering is perpetuated by having no opportunity to understand why the offender committed the crime, how the offender felt about it and if the offender felt sorry about the crime.

Second, expressing genuine contrition and sorrow may be an important unmet need for criminals. Perhaps one reason violent crime has become so out of control is that offenders have such limited contact with the people they victimize or the survivors of the people they kill. Could it be that separating the criminal from the victim actually cuts the criminal off from one of the most powerful deterrents to committing similar crimes in the future?

Conversely, perhaps the recognition of being forgiven for one's crimes also serves as a deterrent to crime in the future. How many criminals could be deterred from future crimes by accepting the consequences of being forgiven for those crimes they have already committed? Maybe only a few. But maybe a significant number. Most never get the chance.

The criminal justice system is tragic—nobody wins. But it has not always been so impersonal. It used to be that those who committed crimes were confronted by the victim, the survivors of the victim and the members of their community. Committing a crime was more personal.

Confession and Forgiveness with Criminals?

Could it be that someday it is possible to orchestrate meetings in which

offenders and victims might come together and talk? Perhaps words
of confession and contrition would be exchanged. Perhaps words of
forgiveness would be expressed. Such meetings could be life-chang-
ing.[5]

Do you remember when, in chapter nine, we told about Pope John
Paul II and his visit with Mehmet Ali Agca, the man who tried to ass-
assinate him? That meeting proved to be fateful for Agca:

> Agca proclaimed that he was renouncing terrorism to become a
> man of peace. . . . He traced his transformation to a prison visit with
> the Pope last year. . . . After close reading of the Koran, Agca said,
> he had become a devout Muslim with "profound respect" for
> Christianity. And he promised that if he were freed, he would
> become "a preacher, going to all nations of the world preaching
> good and the truth to all people."[6]

Forgiveness can change the human heart.

Summing Up

In this book we have looked at what forgiveness is and how it fits into
morality and rational thought. We examined how people change to
become more forgiving. We looked at how forgiveness involves our
brain, mind and memory. We examined the importance of empathy,
intrinsic motivation and revised stories for helping us forgive. We have
thought about how to deal with unremitting self-condemnation. We
emphasized the importance of confession and seeking forgiveness as
a solution to guilt and shame. We looked at the potential benefits of
forgiveness for individual well-being, marriage and family stability and
for addressing ethnic conflict and the criminal justice system.

We've covered a lot of ground. Even so, the main themes of the
book can be boiled down into four lessons: (1) forgiveness involves
the entire person; (2) empathy is at the heart of forgiveness; (3)
forgiveness is relational; (4) forgiveness requires commitment.

Forgiveness involves the entire person. Forgiveness will involve every
dimension of who you are. It is not simply an emotional change or a
change in how you think about an offender; it involves your morality

and ethics, your memory, how you reason, your willingness to forgive, how you think about your own history with guilt and forgiveness, your fundamental attitude toward the offense and the offender and your understanding of relationships. *Forgiveness will change you.*

Forgiveness requires empathy. Although forgiveness may seem complex, one aspect of forgiveness—empathy—is quite simple. Empathy is a central component to living an other-oriented lifestyle. Developing greater empathy for your offender will help you grant forgiveness more readily. It will also help you to seek forgiveness when you have hurt others. *Forgiveness will make you feel the pain of others.*

Forgiveness is relational. We do not forgive only for ourselves. Whereas forgiveness appears to make people happier and perhaps even healthier, forgiveness operates best when we are motivated to forgive out of a desire for right relationships. We may never be able to restore relationships with some of the people who hurt us (or whom we have hurt), but forgiveness helps us set our hearts on the possibility that such reconciliation might one day be possible. *We yearn for forgiveness because we long for relationship.*

Forgiveness requires persistence and commitment. Forgiveness is complex, and it takes time. Therefore we sometimes look for easier ways to deal with interpersonal pain—we try to forget or overlook, we deny, we try to take revenge, we avoid the people who hurt us (or whom we hurt). Moreover, sometimes when we think that we have finally "accomplished" forgiveness, we slip back into old habits or find that the gains we made have disappeared. At such times we must take courage. With persistence and commitment we will slowly, almost imperceptibly, be transformed into people whose lives are characterized by forgiveness. *Take heart—you can forgive.*

Notes

Chapter 1: Forgiveness & You
[1]William Klassen, *The Forgiving Community* (Philadelphia: Westminster Press, 1966), p. 19-20.
[2]L. Gregory Jones, *Embodying Forgiveness: A Theological Analysis* (Grand Rapids, Mich.: Eerdmans, 1995).
[3]Gallup Organization, *Life Survey on Prayer* (Princeton, N.J.: Gallup Organization, 1993).
[4]Richard L. Gorsuch and Judith Y. Hao, "Forgiveness: An Exploratory Factor Analysis and Its Relationship to Religious Variables," *Review of Religious Research* 34 (1993): 333-47.
[5]Frederick A. DiBlasio, "Forgiveness in Psychotherapy: A Comparison of Younger and Older Therapists," *Journal of Psychology and Christianity* 11 (1990): 181-87.
[6]Michael E. McCullough and Everett L. Worthington Jr., "Promoting Forgiveness: A Comparison of Two Brief Psychoeducational Interventions with a Waiting-List Control," *Counseling and Values* 40 (1995): 55-68.

Chapter 2: Forgiveness & the Moral Sense
[1]James Q. Wilson, *The Moral Sense* (New York: Free Press, 1993), pp. 9-25.
[2]For an excellent discussion of moral universals, see C. S. Lewis, *The Abolition of Man* (New York: Macmillan, 1947).
[3]Margaret R. Holmgren, "Forgiveness and the Intrinsic Value of Persons," *American Philosophical Quarterly* 30 (1993): 341-52.
[4]J. Arthur Martin, "A Realistic Theory of Forgiveness," in *The Return to Reason: Essays in Realistic Philosophy*, ed. John D. Wild (Chicago: Regnery, 1953), pp. 313-32.
[5]J. Kellenberger, *Relationship Morality* (University Park, Penn.: Pennsylvania State University Press, 1995), pp. 407-27.
[6]William J. Bennett, *The Book of Virtues: A Treasury of Great Moral Stories* (New York: Simon & Schuster, 1993); Howard Fineman, "The Virtuecrats," *Newsweek,* June 16, 1994, pp. 30-36.
[7]Aristotle, *Nicomachean Ethics*, trans. T. Irwin (Indianapolis: Hackett, 1985).
[8]Works relevant to the connection between virtue, ethics and psychology include

the following: Augustus E. Jordan and Naomi M. Meara, "Ethics and the Professional Practice of Psychologists: The Role of Virtues and Principles," *Professional Psychology: Research and Practice* 21 (1990): 107-14; Alasdair MacIntyre, *After Virtue: A Study in Moral Theory*, 2nd ed. (Notre Dame, Ind.: University of Notre Dame Press, 1984); Robert C. Roberts, "Psychotherapeutic Virtues and the Grammar of Faith," *Journal of Psychology and Theology* 15 (1987): 191-204. For an excellent discussion of forgiveness as a virtue, see L. Gregory Jones, *Embodying Forgiveness: A Theological Analysis* (Grand Rapids, Mich.: Eerdmans, 1995).

[9]Karl Menninger, *Whatever Became of Sin?* (New York: Hawthorn, 1973).

[10]J. Sabini and M. Silver, "Dispositional vs. Situational Interpretations of Milgram's Obedience Experiments: 'The Fundamental Attribution Error,' " *Journal for the Theory of Social Behavior* 13 (1983): 147-54.

[11]Robert C. Roberts, *Taking the Word to Heart: Self and Other in an Age of Therapies* (Grand Rapids, Mich.: Eerdmans, 1993), pp. 189-204.

[12]Woody Allen, director, *Crimes and Misdemeanors* (Orion Pictures, 1989).

[13]Ivan Boszormenyi-Nagy and Barbara R. Krasner, *Between Give and Take: A Clinical Guide to Contextual Therapy* (New York: Brunner/Mazel, 1986). Also see Terry D. Hargrave, *Families and Forgiveness: Healing Wounds in the Intergenerational Family* (New York: Brunner/Mazel, 1994).

[14]Philip Yancey, "Holocaust and Ethnic Cleansing: Can Forgiveness Overcome the Horror?" *Christianity Today,* August 16, 1993, p. 28.

[15]This story is told in a biography about Joshua Chamberlain by Alice Rains Trulock, *In the Hands of Providence: Joshua L. Chamberlain and the American Civil War* (Chapel Hill, N. C.: University of North Carolina Press, 1992), pp. 304-5.

[16]Stanley Hauerwas, *Dispatches from the Front: Theological Engagements with the Secular* (Durham, N.C.: Duke University Press, 1994), pp. 31-57.

Chapter 3: Forgiveness & Rational Thought

[1]For an excellent review of psychological theories of moral development from a Christian perspective, see Bonnidell Clouse, *Teaching for Moral Growth: A Guide for the Christian Community, Parents and Pastors* (Wheaton, Ill.: Victor, 1993).

[2]Jean Piaget, *The Moral Judgment of the Child* (1932; reprint New York: Free Press, 1966).

[3]Robert D. Enright, Elizabeth A. Gassin and Ching-Ru Wu, "Forgiveness: A Developmental View," *Journal of Moral Education* 21 (1992): 99-114.

[4]This application is adapted from an exercise to teach children justice and mercy suggested by Linda and Richard Eyre, *Teaching Your Children Values* (New York: Simon & Schuster, 1993), p. 232.

[5]This approach to teaching values is also suggested by the Eyres in ibid., p. 34.

[6]Ibid., pp. 234-37.

[7]The following discussion about the views of Piaget and Enright on forgiveness is

drawn from Robert D. Enright and the Human Development Study Group, "Piaget on the Moral Development of Forgiveness: Identity or Reciprocity?" *Human Development* 37 (1994): 63-80.

[8]Robert D. Enright, Maria J. D. Santos and Radhi Al-Mabuk, "The Adolescent as Forgiver," *Journal of Adolescence* 12 (1989): 95-110.

[9]S. T. Tina Huang, "Cross-cultural and Real-Life Validations of the Theory of Forgiveness in Taiwan, the Republic of China," Ph.D. diss., University of Wisconsin-Madison, 1990.

[10]Younghee O. Park, Robert D. Enright and Elizabeth A. Gassin, "The Development of Forgiveness in the Context of Friendship Conflict in Korea," paper presented at the Annual Meeting of the Christian Association for Psychological Studies, Kansas City, Mo., April 1993.

[11]Huang, "Cross-cultural and Real-Life Validations."

[12]D. K. Lapsley, R. D. Enright and R. C. Serlin, "Moral and Social Education," in *The Adolescent as Decision-Maker: Applications to Development and Education,* ed. J. Worell and F. Danner (San Diego, Calif.: Academic Press, 1989).

[13]Kenneth A. Dodge, "Social-Cognitive Mechanisms in the Development of Conduct Disorder and Depression," *Annual Review of Psychology* 44 (1993): 559-84.

[14]T. Lickona, *Raising Good Children: Helping Your Child through the Stages of Moral Development* (New York: Bantam, 1983).

[15]This point about intentionality is discussed by Clouse, *Teaching for Moral Growth,* p. 271.

[16]Eyre and Eyre, *Teaching Your Children Values,* p. 236.

Chapter 4: Forgiveness & Rational Thought: *Limitations*

[1]Lawrence Martin Jenco, *Bound to Forgive: The Pilgrimage to Reconciliation of a Beirut Hostage* (Notre Dame, Ind.: Ave Maria, 1995).

[2]Ibid., p. 14.

[3]See Lawrence Kohlberg, *Essays on Moral Development: The Philosophy of Moral Development* (New York: Harper & Row, 1981), 1:140-41.

[4]Jenco, *Bound to Forgive, p. 30*

[5]Martin L. Hoffman, "Empathy, Social Cognition and Moral Education," in *Approaches to Moral Development: New Research and Emerging Themes,* ed. Andrew Garrod (New York: Teachers College Press, 1993), pp. 157-79.

[6]Carol Magai and Susan H. McFadden, *The Role of Emotions in Social and Personality Development: History, Theory and Research* (New York: Plenum, 1995).

[7]Carol Gilligan, *In a Different Voice: Psychological Theory and Women's Development* (Cambridge, Mass.: Harvard University Press, 1993).

[8]Blythe McVicker Clinchy, "Ways of Knowing and Ways of Being: Epistemological and Moral Development in Undergraduate Women," in *Approaches to Moral Development: New Research and Emerging Themes,* ed. Andrew Garrod (New York: Teachers

College Press, 1993), pp. 180-200.

[9]Roy F. Baumeister, Sara R. Wotman and Arlene Stillwell, "Unrequited Love: On Heartbreak, Anger, Guilt, Scriptlessness and Humiliation," *Journal of Personality and Social Psychology* 64 (1993): 377-94.

[10]P. Kutnick, "The Relationship of Moral Judgment and Moral Action: Kohlberg's Theory, Criticism and Revision," in *Lawrence Kohlberg: Consensus and Controversy*, ed. Sohan Modgil and Celia Modgil (Philadelphia: Falmer, 1986), pp. 125-48; and James Rest, *Moral Development: Advances in Research and Theory* (New York: Praeger, 1986).

[11]Robert Coles, *The Moral Life of Children* (New York: Atlantic Monthly Press, 1986), pp. 21-27. For a helpful discussion of the psychological issues raised by Coles, see Paul C. Vitz, "The Use of Stories in Moral Development: New Psychological Reasons for an Old Educational Method," *American Psychologist* 45 (1990): 709-20.

[12]For reviews of studies of religiously conservative ideology and moral reasoning, see I. R. Getz, "Moral Judgment and Religion: A Review of the Literature," *Counseling and Values* 28 (1984): 94-116, and P. Scott Richards, "The Relation Between Conservative Religious Ideology and Principled Moral Reasoning: A Review," *Review of Religious Research* 32 (1991): 359-68.

[13]Richards, "Relation Between Conservative Religious Ideology."

[14]Jenco, *Bound to Forgive*, p. 99.

[15]Ibid., p. 83.

Chapter 5: Forgiveness & Your Response to Hurts

[1]Sheldon Cashdan, *Object Relations Therapy: Using the Relationship* (New York: Norton, 1988), pp. 139-42.

[2]These beliefs are discussed in greater detail in Fritz Heider, *The Psychology of Interpersonal Relations* (New York: Wiley & Sons, 1958), pp. 252-76, and Albert Ellis, *Reason and Emotion in Psychotherapy* (Secaucus, N.J.: Citadel, 1962).

[3]Beverly Flanigan, "Forgiving," a workshop presented at the Mendota Mental Health Institute, Madison, Wis., September 1987.

[4]Timothy Boyd, "Bridge-Building: A Toolbox of Practical Forgiveness Strategies for the Christian Community," paper presented at the annual meeting of the Christian Associaton for Psychological Studies, Kansas City, Mo., April 1993.

Chapter 6: Forgiveness & Transformation

[1]Thomas S. Kuhn, *The Structure of Scientific Revolutions*, 2nd ed. (New York: New American Library, 1970).

[2]Kenneth L. Sell and W. Mack Goldsmith, "Concerns About Professional Counseling: An Exploration of Five Factors and the Role of Christian Orthodoxy," *Journal of Psychology and Christianity* 7 (1988): 5-21.

[3]V. I. Arnold, *Catastrophe Theory* (Berlin: Springer-Verlag, 1986). See also R. Fivaz, "Thermodynamics of Complexity," *Systems Research* 9 (1991): 19-32.

[4]John Mordechai Gottman, *What Predicts Divorce? The Relationship Between Marital Processes and Marital Outcomes* (Hillsdale, N.J.: Erlbaum, 1994).

[5]Robert Frost, "Mending Wall," in *A Pocket Book of Robert Frost's Poems*, ed. Louis Untermeyer (New York: Washington Square, 1967), pp. 94-95.

[6]Lewis Smedes, *Forgive and Forget* (New York: Pocket Books/Simon & Schuster, 1984), p. 48.

Chapter 7: Forgiveness, the Brain & the Mind

[1]James Kennedy and Jerry Newcomb, *What If Jesus Had Never Lived?* (Nashville, Tenn.: Nelson, 1994).

[2]*Robert Coles, Teacher*, videotape (New York: Social/Media Productions [First Run Features, 153 Waverly Place, New York, N.Y.]).

[3]Donald Meichenbaum, *Cognitive-Behavior Modification: An Integrative Approach* (New York: Plenum, 1977).

[4]Kennedy and Newcomb, *What If Jesus Had Never Lived?*

Chapter 8: Forgiveness & Your Memory

[1]James Kennedy and Jerry Newcomb, *What If Jesus Had Never Lived?* (Nashville, Tenn.: Nelson, 1994).

[2]Charles Dickens, *Great Expectations* (New York: Book League of America, n.d.), p. 40.

[3]Ibid., pp. 280-81.

[4]J. T. Wixted and E. B. Ebbesen, "On the Form of Forgetting," *Psychological Science* 2 (1991): 409-15.

[5]Daniel Wegner, *White Bears and Other Unwanted Thoughts: Suppression, Obsession and the Psychology of Mental Control* (New York: Guilford, 1994), pp. 77-98.

[6]L. R. Squire, ed., *Encyclopedia of Learning and Memory* (New York: Macmillan, 1992).

[7]For a review of her studies, see E. F. Loftus, "When a Lie Becomes Memory's Truth: Memory Distortion After Exposure to Misinformation," *Current Directions in Psychological Science* 1 (1992): 121-23.

[8]For a review of both Loftus's "overwriting hypothesis" and McCloskey and Zaragoza's "coexistence hypothesis," see D. Stephen Lindsay, "Eyewitness Suggestibility," *Current Directions in Psychological Science* 2 (1993): 86-89.

[9]Dickens, *Great Expectations*, p. 307.

[10]A. Paivio, *Mental Representations: A Dual Coding Approach* (New York: Oxford University Press, 1986).

[11]Lewis Smedes, *Forgive and Forget* (New York: Pocket Books/Simon & Schuster, 1984), p. 47.

Chapter 9: Forgiveness & Motivation

[1]Lance Morrow, "I Spoke . . . as a Brother," *Time*, January 9, 1984.

[2]Mary F. Trainer, "Forgiveness: Intrinsic, Role-Expected, Expedient, in the Context of Divorce," Ph.D. diss., Boston University, 1981.

[3]Emily F. Carter, Michael E. McCullough, Steven J. Sandage and Everett L. Worthington Jr., "What Happens When People Forgive? Theories, Speculations and Implications for Individual and Marital Therapy," paper presented at the annual meeting of the American Psychological Association, Los Angeles, Calif., August 1994; Bruce W. Darby and Barry R. Schlenker, "Children's Reactions to Apologies," *Journal of Peronality and Social Psychology* 43 (1982): 742-53; Bernard Weiner et al., "Public Confession and Forgiveness," *Journal of Personality* 59 (1991): 281-312.

[4]Lee Ross, "The Intuitive Scientist and His Shortcomings: Distortions in the Attribution Process," in *Advances in Experimental Social Psychology*, ed. L. Berkowitz (New York: Academic, 1977), 10:173-220.

[5]Allan Fenigstein and Charles S. Carver, "Self-Focusing Effects of Heartbeat Feedback," *Journal of Personality and Social Psychology* 36 (1978): 1241-50.

[6]Robert D. Enright and the Human Development Study Group, "Piaget on the Moral Development of Forgiveness: Identity or Reciprocity?" *Human Development* 37 (1994): 63-80.

[7]Lewis Smedes, *Forgive and Forget* (New York: Pocket Books/Simon & Schuster, 1984).

[8]Corrie ten Boom and Jamie Buckingham, *Tramp for the Lord* (New York: Jove, 1974), pp. 53-55.

[9]Michael E. McCullough and Everett L. Worthington Jr., "Encouraging Clients to Forgive People Who Have Hurt Them: Review, Critique and Research Prospectus," *Journal of Psychology and Theology* (1994): 3-20. See also Richard L. Gorsuch and Judith Y. Hao, "Forgiveness: An Exploratory Factor Analysis and Its Relationship to Religious Variables," *Review of Religious Research* 34 (1993): 333-47, and Kathryn Rhodes Meek, Jeanne S. Albright and Mark R. McMinn, "Religious Orientation, Guilt, Confession and Forgiveness," *Journal of Psychology and Theology* 23 (1995): 190-97.

[10]Kenneth C. Rachal and Michael E. McCullough, "Religiousness, Empathy and Forgiveness," unpublished data set, Louisiana Tech University, 1996.

[11]Michael E. McCullough, "Forgiveness as Altruism: Toward a Social-Psychological Theory of Forgiveness and Tests of Its Validity," Ph.D. diss., Virginia Commonwealth University, 1995.

[12]Sharman Stein, "Some Examples of Forgiveness Are to Die For," *Chicago Tribune*, October 22, 1995, sec. 2, p. 8.

Chapter 10: Forgiveness & Stories

[1]Theodore R. Sarbin, "The Narrative as a Root Metaphor for Psychology," in *Narrative Psychology: The Storied Nature of Human Conduct*, ed. T. R. Sarbin (New York: Praeger, 1986), pp. 3-21.

[2]W. Kirk Kilpatrick, "Moral Character, Story-Telling and Virtue," in *Psychological Foundations of Moral Education and Character Development*, ed. Richard T. Knowles and George F. McLean (New York: University Press of America, 1986), pp. 183-99.

[3]Viktor E. Frankl, *Man's Search for Meaning* (New York: Washington Square, 1959).

[4]Northrop Frye, *Anatomy of Criticism* (Princeton, N.J.: Princeton University Press, 1957).

[5]Dan P. McAdams, *Power, Intimacy and the Life Story* (New York: Guilford, 1988). McAdams's more recent work in narrative psychology is *The Stories We Live By: Personal Myths and the Making of the Self* (New York: William Morrow, 1993).

[6]Gregory S. Pettit, "Developmental Theories," in *Handbook of Social Development: A Lifespan Perspective*, ed. Vincent B. Van Hasselt and Michel Hersen (New York: Plenum, 1992), pp. 3-28.

[7]Erik H. Erickson, *Identity: Youth and Crisis* (New York: Norton, 1968).

[8]Paul C. Vitz, "Narratives and Counseling, Part 1: From Analysis of the Past to Stories About It," *Journal of Psychology and Theology* 20 (1992): 11-19.

[9]Gabriel Marcel, *Homo Viator*, trans. E. Crawford (New York: Harper, 1965), p. 53.

[10]C. R. Snyder, *The Psychology of Hope: You Can Get There from Here* (New York: Free Press, 1994).

[11]Stephen R. Covey, *The Seven Habits of Highly Effective People: Powerful Lessons in Personal Change* (New York: Simon & Schuster, 1989).

[12]Victor Hugo, *Les Miserables* (New York: Signet, 1987). For insightful application of *Les Miserables* to the topic of forgiveness, see Doris Donnelly, *Spiritual Fitness: Everyday Exercises for Body and Soul* (New York: HarperSanFrancisco, 1993), pp. 129-50, and Philip Yancey, "An Unnatural Act," *Christianity Today*, April 8, 1991, pp. 36-39.

[13]Hugo, *Les Miserables*, p. 106.

[14]The story of Joshua Saune is recounted by Andy Butcher in "Violent Mercy," *New Man* 2 (March-April 1995): 20-23, 78.

[15]Ibid., p. 22.

[16]P. Schonbach, *Account Episodes: The Management and Escalation of Conflict* (Cambridge, Mass.: Cambridge University Press, 1990).

[17]Sherod Miller et al., *Couple Communication Instructor Manual* (Littleton, Colo.: Interpersonal Communication Program, 1992).

Chapter 11: Forgiveness & Self-Condemnation

[1]Paul A. Mauger et al., "The Measurement of Forgiveness: Preliminary Research," *Journal of Psychology and Christianity* 11 (1992): 170-80.

[2]Anthony J. Rooney, "Finding Forgiveness Through Psychotherapy: An Empirical Phenomenonological Investigation," Ph.D. diss., Georgia State University (Atlanta), 1989, pp. 110-18.

[3]Lewis B. Smedes, *Forgive and Forget* (New York: Pocket Books/Simon & Schuster,

1984), pp. 96-105.

[4]Philip Cushman, "Why the Self Is Empty: Toward a Historically Situated Psychology," *American Psychologist* 45 (1990): 599-611. This cultural dilemma is also discussed in Michael E. McCullough, Steven J. Sandage and Everett L. Worthington Jr., "Forgiving the Empty Self," paper presented at the annual convention of the Christian Association for Psychological Studies, Virginia Beach, Va., April 1995.

[5]C. Zahn-Waxler and G. Kochanska, "The Origins of Guilt," in *The Nebraska Symposium on Motivation 1988: Socioemotional Development*, ed. R. A. Thompson (Lincoln, Nebr.: University of Nebraska Press, 1988), pp. 182-258.

[6]Roy F. Baumeister, Arlene M. Stillwell and Todd F. Heatherton, "Guilt: An Interpersonal Approach," *Journal of Personality and Social Psychology* 115 (1994): 243-67.

[7]United States Catholic Conference, *Rite of Penance* (Washington, D.C.: Author, 1975).

[8]Baumeister, Stillwell and Heatherton, "Guilt," pp. 243-67.

Chapter 12: Forgiveness & Your Own Hurtful Actions

[1]Erving Goffman, *Interaction Ritual: Essays on Face-to-Face Behavior* (New York: Aldine, 1967), pp. 8-31.

[2]Our discussion of the categories of accidents, negligence and intentional transgressions is drawn from F. Heider, *The Psychology of Interpersonal Relations* (New York: Wiley, 1958), and Marti Hope Gonzales, Debra J. Manning and Julie A. Haugen, "Explaining Our Sins: Factors Influencing Offender Accounts and Anticipated Victim Responses," *Journal of Personality and Social Psychology* 62 (1992): 958-71.

[3]For a more elaborate description of these four strategies, see P. Schonbach, *Account Episodes: The Management and Escalation of Conflict* (Cambridge, Mass.: Cambridge University Press, 1990), and Gonzales, Manning and Haugen, "Explaining Our Sins."

[4]June Price Tangney, "Shame and Guilt in Interpersonal Relationships," in *Self-Conscious Emotions: The Psychology of Shame, Guilt, Embarrassment and Pride*, ed. June Price Tangney and Kurt W. Fischer (New York: Guilford, 1995), pp. 114-39.

[5]Gonzales, Manning and Haugen, "Explaining Our Sins," pp. 958-71.

[6]Dietrich Bonhoeffer, *Life Together*, trans. J. W. Doberstein (New York: Harper & Row, 1954), p. 112.

[7]June Price Tangney et al., "Shamed into Anger? The Relation of Shame and Guilt to Anger and Self-Reported Aggression," *Journal of Personality and Social Psychology* 62 (1992): 669-75.

[8]Ibid.

[9]Steven J. Sandage, "Narcissism and Seeking Forgiveness," master's thesis, Virginia Commonwealth University, 1995.

[10]June Price Tangney, Susan A. Bruggraf and Patricia E. Wagner, "Shame-Proneness, Guilt-Proneness and Psychological Symptoms," in *Self-Conscious Emotions*, pp. 343-67.

[11]Charles Slack, "Remorseful Thief Pays Off," *Richmond Times-Dispatch*, January 26, 1995, p. A1.

[12]Irvin D. Yalom, *The Theory and Practice of Group Psychotherapy*, 3rd ed. (New York: BasicBooks, 1985), pp. 8-9.

[13]Bernard Weiner et al., "Public Confession and Forgiveness," *Journal of Personality* 59 (1991): 281-312.

[14]See Gonzales, Manning and Haugen, "Explaining Our Sins," and Marti Hope Gonzales, Julie A. Haugen and Debra J. Manning, "Victims as 'Narrative Critics': Factors Influencing Rejoinders and Evaluative Responses to Offenders' Accounts," *Personality and Social Psychology Bulletin* 20 (1994): 691-704.

[15]This idea is suggested by Roy F. Baumeister, Arlene M. Stillwell and Todd F. Heatherton in "Guilt: An Interpersonal Approach," *Psychological Bulletin* 115 (1994): 243-67.

[16]Kenneth D. Locke and Leonard M. Horowitz, "Satisfaction in Interpersonal Interactions as a Function of Similarity in Level of Dysphoria," *Journal of Personality and Social Psychology* 53 (1990): 823-31.

[17]John R. Means et al., "Humility as Psychotherapeutic Formulation," *Counseling Psychology Quarterly* 3 (1990): 211-15.

[18]Richard Gramzow and June Price Tangney, "Proneness to Shame and the Narcissistic Personality," *Personality and Social Psychology Bulletin* 18 (1992): 369-76. See also Dan B. Alexander and Tremper Longman III, *Bold Love* (Colorado Springs, Colo.: Navpress, 1992), pp. 255-84.

[19]See Martin Hoffman, "Development of Prosocial Motivation: Empathy and Guilt," in *The Development of Prosocial Behavior*, ed. Nancy Eisenberg (New York: Academic, 1982), pp. 281-313, and Carolyn Zahn-Waxler and Joann Robinson, "Empathy and Guilt: Early Origins of Feelings of Responsibility," in *Self-Conscious Emotions*, pp. 143-73.

[20]Tangney, "Shame and Guilt."

[21]The term and concept *ambassadors of reconciliation* is borrowed from Doris Donnelly, "Ambassadors of Reconciliation," *Weavings: A Journal of the Christian Spiritual Life* 5 (1990): 18-29. Donnelly's inspiration for the term is drawn from the apostle Paul's second letter to the Corinthians (2 Corinthians 5:18).

Chapter 13: Forgiveness & Its Consequences for You

[1]Elizabeth A. Gassin, "Forgiveness and Psychological Wholeness: A Review of the Empirical Literature," paper presented at the Annual Meeting of the Christian Association for Psychological Studies, San Antonio, Tex., March 1994.

[2]Michael E. McCullough and Everett L. Worthington Jr., "Encouraging Clients to Forgive People Who Have Hurt Them: Review, Critique, and Research Prospectus," *Journal of Psychology and Theology* 22 (1994): 3-20.

[3]John H. Hebl and Robert D. Enright, "Forgiveness as a Psychotherapeutic Goal

with Elderly Females," *Psychotherapy* 30 (1993): 658-67.

[4]Michael E. McCullough, "Forgiveness as Altruism: A Social-Psychological Theory of Forgiveness and Tests of Its Validity," Ph.D. diss., Virginia Commonwealth University, 1995.

[5]J. G. Emerson Jr., *The Dynamics of Forgiveness* (Philadelphia: Westminster Press, 1964).

[6]M. Freedman et al., "Alterations of Type A Behavior and its Effects on Cardiac Recurrence in Post-Myocardial Infarction Patients: Summary Results of the Coronary Prevention Recurrence Project," *American Heart Journal* 112 (1986): 653-65.

[7]Berton H. Kaplan, "Social Health and the Forgiving Heart: The Type B Story," *Journal of Behavioral Medicine* 15 (1992): 3-14.

[8]Redford Williams and Virginia Williams, *Anger Kills* (New York: Random House, 1993), and Redford Williams, *The Trusting Heart* (New York: Random House, 1989).

[9]Joseph K. Neumann and David S. Chi, "Total T-Cells and Forgiveness," paper presented at the annual meeting of the Christian Association for Psychological Studies, Kansas City, Mo., April 1993; and Kenneth C. Rachal and Michael E. McCullough, "Interpersonal Forgiveness as a Buffer Against Anger," typescript.

[10]Judith A Strasser, "The Relation of General Forgiveness and Forgiveness Type to Reported Health in the Elderly," Ph.D. diss., Catholic University of America, 1984.

[11]James W. Pennebaker, Cheryl F. Hughes and Robin C. O'Heeron, "The Psychophysiology of Confession: Linking Inhibitory and Psychosomatic Processes," *Journal of Personality and Social Psychology* 52 (1987): 781-93.

[12]Mary F. Trainer, "Forgiveness: Intrinsic, Role-Expected, Expedient, in the Context of Divorce," Ph.D. diss., Boston University, 1981.

[13]Elizabeth D. Dreelin, "The Relationship Between Christian Maturity and Forgiveness," paper presented at the Second International Congress on Christian Counseling, Atlanta, Ga., November 1992.

[14]Lane A. Gerber, "Transformations in Self-Understanding in Surgeons Whose Treatment Efforts Were Not Successful," *American Journal of Psychotherapy* 44 (1990): 75-84.

[15]Elizabeth A. Gassin and Robert D. Enright, "The Will to Meaning in the Process of Forgiveness," *Journal of Psychology and Christianity* 14 (1995): 38-49.

Chapter 14: Forgiveness & the Family

[1]Eugene O'Neill, *Long Day's Journey into Night*, in *Complete Plays* (New York: Literary Classics, 1988), pp. 713-828. For a fine academic treatment of the issue of forgiveness in O'Neill's plays, see Steen B. Halling, "Eugene O'Neill's Understanding of Forgiveness," in *Duquesne Studies in Phenomenological Psychology*, ed. A. Giorgi, R. Knowles and D. L. Smith (Pittsburgh, Penn.: Duquesne University Press), 3:193-208.

[2]O'Neill, *Long Day's Journey into Night*, p. 730.

[3]Ibid., p. 729.

[4]Ibid., p. 760.

[5]Ibid., p. 735.

[6]Ibid., p. 753.

[7]Michelle K. Nelson, "A New Theory of Forgiveness," Ph.D. diss., Purdue University, 1992.

[8]Tamela Woodman, "The Role of Forgiveness in Marital Adjustment," Ph.D. diss., Fuller Graduate School of Psychology, 1991.

[9]O'Neill, *Long Day's Journey into Night*, p. 786-87.

[10]John Byng-Hall, "Family Scripts: A Concept Which Can Bridge Child Psychotherapy and Family Therapy Thinking," *Journal of Child Psychotherapy* (1986): 3-13.

[11]O'Neill, *Long Day's Journey into Night*, pp. 782-83.

[12]Everett L. Worthington Jr. and Frederick A. DiBlasio, "Promoting Mutual Forgiveness Within the Fractured Relationship," *Psychotherapy* 27 (1990): 219-23.

[13]Martin Hoffman, "Empathy and Justice Motivation," *Motivation and Emotion* 14 (1990): 151-72.

[14]O'Neill, *Long Day's Journey into Night*, p. 741.

[15]Ibid., p. 759.

[16]Marie Fortune, "Forgiveness: The Last Step," in *Abuse and Religion: When Praying Isn't Enough,* ed. A. L. Horton and J. A. Williamson (Washington, D.C.: Heath, 1988), pp. 215-20.

[17]For more academic discussions of family techniques designed to promote forgiveness in situations of abuse, marital affairs or incest, see J. Lee Jagers, "Putting Humpty Together Again: Reconciling the Post-affair Marriage," *Journal of Psychology and Christianity* (1989): 63-72, and Cloe Madanes, "Strategic Family Therapy," in *Handbook of Family Therapy,* ed. A. S. Gurman and D. P. Kniskern (New York: Brunner/Mazel, 1991), 2:396-416.

Chapter 15: Forgiveness & the Healing of Communities

[1]Simon Wiesenthal, *The Sunflower* (New York: Schocken, 1976).

[2]Elliott N. Dorff, "Individual and Communal Forgiveness," in *Autonomy and Judaism,* ed. D. H. Frank. (Albany, N.Y.: State University of New York Press, 1992), pp. 193-218.

[3]Duane Elmer, "A Severe Forgiveness," *Christianity Today,* February 7, 1994, pp. 30-32.

[4]Martin P. Golding, "Forgiveness and Regret," *Philosophical Forum* 16 (1984-1985): 121-37.

[5]Mark Umbreit, *Crime and Reconciliation: Creative Options for Victims and Offenders* (Nashville, Tenn: Abingdon, 1985).

[6]Walter J. Burghardt, "A Brother Whom I Have Pardoned," *The Living Pulpit* 3 (April-June 1994): 10-11.

CPSIA information can be obtained at www.ICGtesting.com
Printed in the USA
266777BV00002B/33/P